In this book the Halletts have examined dramatic form in Shakespeare's plays and have found the overall pattern of pacing and action to be independent of the scene. They have identified within scenes and acts hidden units of articulation defined here as the beat, the sequence, and the frame, each unit type having a distinct but different purpose within the larger whole. For both scholar and practitioner, their observations offer new insights about how the building blocks of the plays are deployed. Detailed analysis of the unfolding action reveals that Shakespeare's scenes frequently consist of a series of sequences, each with its own individual climax, and these sequences are regularly built up of a succession of smaller units, or beats. Several sequences usually work together to create a still larger action, or frame. Study of these components yields valuable information about Shakespeare's playwriting techniques (information not readily available elsewhere in critical literature) and is of immense value in articulating the dramatic rhythms and structure of Shakespeare's action. This analytical method, while especially tuned to Shakespeare, can also be adapted to other dramatists in varying degrees. The book will be of interest to students and scholars of Shakespeare and theater studies as well as to actors and directors.

D1740137

Analyzing Shakespeare's Action

Analyzing
Shakespeare's Action

Scene versus Sequence

CHARLES A. HALLETT

and

ELAINE S. HALLETT

*The right of the
University of Cambridge
to print and sell
all manner of books
was granted by
Henry VIII in 1534.
The University has printed
and published continuously
since 1584.*

CAMBRIDGE UNIVERSITY PRESS

Cambridge

New York   Port Chester

Melbourne   Sydney

CAMBRIDGE UNIVERSITY PRESS
Cambridge, New York, Melbourne, Madrid, Cape Town, Singapore, São Paulo

Cambridge University Press
The Edinburgh Building, Cambridge CB2 2RU, UK

Published in the United States of America by Cambridge University Press, New York

www.cambridge.org
Information on this title: www.cambridge.org/9780521392037

First published 1991
This digitally printed first paperback version 2006

A catalogue record for this publication is available from the British Library

Library of Congress Cataloguing in Publication data
Hallett, Charles A.
Analyzing Shakespeare's Action / Charles A. Hallett and Elaine S.
Hallett.
p.   cm.
Includes bibliographical references.
ISBN 0 521 39203 9
1. Shakespeare, William, 1564–1616 – Technique. 2. Drama –
Technique. I. Hallett, Elaine S., 1935–   . II. Title.
PR2995.H26 1991
822.3'3–dc20   90–40404 CIP

ISBN-13 978-0-521-39203-7 hardback
ISBN-10 0-521-39203-9 hardback

ISBN-13 978-0-521-03037-3 paperback
ISBN-10 0-521-03037-4 paperback

To Cecy

and to all of the Jácome family
in whom the virtues Shakespeare admired
are resplendent

It becomes an author generally to divide a book,
as it does a butcher to joint his meat,
for such assistance is of great help to both the reader and the carver.

Henry Fielding

Contents

Acknowledgments

We are grateful to Fordham University, to the University of Warwick, and to The American Council of Learned Societies for their financial support of our work on Shakespeare's units of action and to the staff of Dartmouth's Baker Library, who provided office space for us at the college and who were lavish with their time and computer resources. In addition, we are deeply indebted to Ronnie Mulryne, our first and most fervent sponsor: this work was begun during a teaching stint at the University of Warwick and owes its existence not only to Ronnie's continued interest in our approach but also to his diligence in finding the manuscript a publisher. Ronnie's several readings of the book led to many improvements. James Morgan helped us immensely by commenting on our work from the perspective of the director and actor; the present form of the book is in no small part the result of James's labors. He was always ready to review yet another version and made himself available to argue out and refine the concepts as they were taking shape. We are happy to acknowledge here how invaluable his friendship and unfailing encouragement have been to us over the years. Many others gave generously of their time to improve the quality of various drafts. David Landman helped us to recognize some of the differences between Shakespeare's technique and Beaumont and Fletcher's, particularly with regard to the reversal; June Schlueter took time out of her Christmas holiday to provide useful comments on the entire book; and Alan Bloss came to our rescue when it was time to cut the manuscript to a reasonable size (the reader can be as grateful to him as we are). Sincere thanks are also due to Richard David, the consultant reader for Cambridge, who gave us a sensitive critical report that helped us to strengthen the arguments, and to Stanley Wells, who also made important comments on the manuscript at this stage. This book represents the combined efforts of all of these people, as well as of Sarah Stanton and Victoria Cooper, at Cambridge University Press, who shepherded it during the publication process. We also want to thank Alvin Sullivan for permission to reprint parts of "Analyzing Action in

Shakespeare's Plays: The Beat," from *Papers on Language and Literature* 19 (1983), 124–44. Citations in the text are to *The Riverside Shakespeare*, ed. G. B. Evans *et al.* (Boston: Houghton Mifflin Co., 1974), unless otherwise noted.

1

Scene versus sequence in Shakespeare's plays

In the lexicon of dramatic terms the word *scene* has great authority. Yet, like many terms used with reference to Shakespeare's plays (*tragedy*, for example, or *action*), the term *scene* has never been anchored to a single, easily definable entity. Because the clearing of the stage normally signals a change of setting, people usually define the scene as a temporal/spatial unit. For Mark Rose, the scene is any unit set apart from other units by "a cleared stage indicating change of place or lapse of time," wherein "the action is plainly continuous."[1] But we also use the word *scene* to describe a unit of action in which tensions build toward a significant moment and then taper off. Distinctions between these two radically opposed senses of the word are generally ignored, so that *scene* is often assumed to mean both things simultaneously. Since the entities described remain as unlike as they ever were, this seemingly reliable term may distort what it is meant to clarify. It seems imperative therefore to examine our assumptions about the unit we too confidently call Shakespeare's *scene*.

The purpose of this inquiry is not to mount a tedious attack against the use of scene designations in Shakespeare's texts. Most of the conventional scene designations in Shakespeare represent divisions made in his essentially undivided text by editors from John Heminge and Henry Condell on, for whom the cleared stage is the crucial factor in distinguishing one unit from another. Still, the scene is not merely a creation of Shakespeare's editors. We all acknowledge that even though the actual scene designations are later insertions, both Elizabethan playwrights and the companies who staged their work envisioned plays as a series of "scenes." Shakespeare created such units and marked them out silently by emptying the stage of all characters – even though he lacked Jonson's interest in numbering the scenes in his text. Further, the numerical designations assigned to Shakespeare's scenes have valid uses – they indicate the boundary lines between individual units of time and/ or place.

What this study does question is the widespread assumption that to analyze a *designated scene* is to analyze an *action*. Many people take it for granted that as long as they stay within the confines of this unit called the scene, they are dealing with a single dramatic action which invariably progresses through stages of exposition, complication, climax, and dénouement. Any attempt to distinguish between the scene as a unit of place and the scene as a unit of action in Shakespeare's plays might strike them as odd, if not futile. The tendency to venerate the designated scene becomes less pronounced the closer one moves to the theater and actual production, yet even in performance theory there is no really thorough grasp of the principles that distinguish Shakespeare's units of place and time from his units of action. Once detected, however, the difference cuts deep.

Is the designated scene in Shakespeare *ever* a unit of action? Certainly. At times. Think of the scene printed as *Macbeth* 1.7 where Lady Macbeth manipulates her husband until he agrees to "bend up / Each corporal agent to this terrible feat" of murdering Duncan. Think of the scene designated in most texts as *Coriolanus* 3.2, where Volumnia chastises her too-absolute son for his refusal to humble himself before the Roman voters, until he finally submits to her wishes. Or the scene known generally as *Hamlet* 3.4, where another too-absolute son forces his mother to see her hasty remarriage in its full reality, as "an act / That blurs the grace and blush of modesty," "plucks the very soul" out of the marriage contract, and makes a mockery of "sweet religion." Each of these units of place is also a unit of action. In them the scene and the action run concurrently. But how often does this happen? Are the designated scenes always units of action?

Take another important scene in *Hamlet* – the formal scene in 1.2 in which the new king displays his efficiency by successfully processing three contrasting affairs, each related to one of the play's plots. Shakespeare's strategy of approaching Claudius's interview with Hamlet through a series of formal audiences of ever-increasing significance gives that final encounter between the two antagonists an impact it might otherwise not have had. Yet this scene (unit of action) which climaxes with the introduction of Hamlet concludes well before the scene (unit of place) does. We cannot really call the action 1.2, for it occupies only 159 of the 257 lines in the total scene. Shakespeare does not empty his stage after *every* action. Before ending 1.2, he writes another 98 lines, and these lines, too, constitute a complete unit of action: Hamlet receives Horatio, hears him describe the mysterious visitations of the Ghost, and determines to investigate the phenomenon. In this scene, then, there are two separate sequences, 1.2.1–159 and 1.2.160–257 – each sequence a full action, with its own introduction, development, climax, and conclusion.

Or take the Ghost's dramatic appearance in act 1, scene 5. Surely this is a *complete* action, building as it does from Hamlet's insistence that the Ghost speak to him to the Ghost's revelation of a murder. Yet once more the action ends (the Ghost vanishes at line 112), while the scene goes on: before Shakespeare clears the stage, he treats us to the cellarage "scene" (1.5.113–90). Again the scene has *two* well-crafted actions. Take the scenes Shakespeare wrote for Ophelia. Invariably one finds the Ophelia action complete in itself, yet paired with another. For example, Ophelia's "scene" with Polonius, where she reports Hamlet's visit, occupies only half a scene (2.1.71–117); it follows an independent action between Polonius and Reynaldo (2.1.1–71). Her "mad scene" occupies only half of 4.5; the other half concerns itself with Laertes, who bursts in on Claudius after her exit. When we take unit analysis seriously, Shakespeare's scenes and his units of action seem to slip apart. Apparently the designated scenes are not *always* units of action.

This disparity between scene and action is not unique to the scenes just touched on. So consistently do Shakespeare's scenes contain more than one unit of action that Mark Rose can posit a whole category of two-part scenes structured as "diptychs," along with a category of three-part scenes constructed in a "framing" or ABA pattern. So obvious is this segmenting process that James Hirsh in *The Structure of Shakespearean Scenes* can title certain chapters "Two-Part Scenes" and "Multipartite Scenes."[2] Though neither Rose nor Hirsh makes the observation, the parts these writers isolate are frequently separate actions.

Evidently Shakespeare's scenes are not always units of action. We cannot say that the two-part scene *is* a unit of action but must rather say "Such a scene *contains* units of action." We could even wish for a term that would differentiate more clearly between these actions and the scene as a whole: *sequences*, for example. "A single scene may contain more than one sequence."

Think now of the scene in which Falstaff becomes the incomparable character he is. This is truly a scene, in the sense that all 550 lines of it unfold in the Boar's Head Tavern at Eastcheap. Editors call this scene 2.4. Here Falstaff struts onto the stage issuing a proclamation: "A plague of all cowards, I say, and a vengeance too! marry and amen!" Throughout the scene he will repeat this proclamation, obviously intended to incriminate Prince Hal, who is only waiting to expose the true coward, Falstaff himself. Tension mounts until at last the Prince springs his trap. Nimble Jack, of course, triumphantly evades the inevitable – on "instinct."

Perfectly crafted as it is, the coward "scene" occurs in the middle of a scene – its textual designation would be 2.4.113–283, hardly equivalent to the full scene's 2.4.1–550. Moreover, this sequence has a counterpart within the scene which has many admirers. For Derek Traversi, analyzing 2.4 in *An Approach to Shakespeare*, the scene has two key incidents, not one. First, "the Gadshill adventure, recently worked out in reality to Falstaff's discomfiture," and, second, "the incident to which the whole scene leads," in which both Hal and Falstaff "combine to enact in comic anticipation the crucial meeting between father and son" – the delightful play episode, 2.4.373–481.[3] Both incidents highlighted by Traversi qualify as sequences – complete actions nested within a longer scene.

Here again the scene breaks down into two major parts. However, Traversi's concentration on themes led him to focus only on the most obvious units. The two sequences described so far account for only 309 of the scene's 550 lines: what are we to make of the remaining 241 lines? In a more detailed analysis of this scene's structure than Traversi makes, Waldo McNeir noted that scene 4 resembles a miniature drama, in that it "has five 'acts' or movements, and an epilogue." For McNeir the scene breaks down as follows:

(1) The practical joke played by Hal and Poins on Francis, the drawer (1–106).

(2) The exposure of Falstaff's lies in his account of what happened at Gad's Hill (107–274).

(3) The first intrusion on the revelry when Sir John Bracy arrives with news from the court (275–364).

(4) The play-acting of Falstaff and Hal as they impersonate, in turn, the King and the Prince (365–464).

(5) The second intrusion on the revelry when the Sheriff and the watch arrive in pursuit of the Gad's Hill robbers (464–507).

(Epilogue) The inventory of Falstaff's pockets by Hal and Poins (508–31).[4]

There seems to us little reason to dispute this division. Any commentator (and presumably any director) who attempts to break the scene down into its component parts will propose almost identical unit boundaries. Both Mark Rose and Emrys Jones, for example, make observations that confirm McNeir's.

Rose analyzes the tavern scene to support his point in *Shakespearean Design* that "small individually designed units are combined like atoms in the formation of a molecule" and discovers the same five units. For him, "the contrasted Francis and Falstaff panels complete the first major movement" of the scene, a kind of "diptych," while the second half of the scene is designed on the ABA principle, "the two messengers framing the centerpiece," wherein Falstaff and Hal take the role of the King by turns. Shakespeare ends the scene with "a brief coda to sum up the position to which the preceding action has brought us" (pp. 49–59). In a chapter on Shakespeare as "scenic poet," Emrys Jones arrives at essentially the same conclusions. For him, the scene's "short dialogue-units" include Hal's teasing of Francis, Falstaff's boasting of his prowess at Gadshill and subsequent exposure, Falstaff's exit to meet the "nobleman of the court" and his return to announce the rebellions, Falstaff and Hal's rehearsal of the coming interview with the King, and Hal's final interview with the Sheriff.[5]

The obvious similarities between Jones's "dialogue-units," Rose's "panels," and McNeir's "movements" all point to one striking fact: though we still have only one scene, we now have *five* actions – or five *sequences*. The tavern scene is hardly unique in this regard. All three commentators consider it but one of many "multipartite" scenes.

As soon as the tavern scene is compared with the coward sequence, a radical difference in structure stands out. Whatever unity there is in this five-sequence scene is not achieved primarily through a rising action. The five individual sequences do not, taken together, progress toward a climax. Nothing at the end of the scene rivals in impact the force of the coward sequence, an impact Shakespeare placed as early in the scene as possible. As many critics have demonstrated, unity among these segments is achieved not through the unity of action but through patterns of design, through an elaborate system of thematic echoes, parallels, and inversions. Often in such long scenes there is no perceptible rising action but rather a series of seemingly independent actions or sequences. What is the action of the tavern scene? Hard to say. What is the action of the coward sequence? That is obvious.

If this crucial difference is acknowledged we can learn much about Shakespeare's action by identifying individual sequences. What can be said about these units nested within Shakespeare's extended scenes? What are the characteristics of the sequence? It will take the whole of this book to respond adequately to that question. But one thing can be made clear now. While the scene is not always a unit of action, the sequence is. The sequence is always an action, propelled in a discernible direction by the desires, goals, and objectives of its characters. That action, once introduced, advances toward a climax, then enters a stage of decrescence that brings it rapidly to a conclusion. Because the sequence is structured upon a single dramatic question, it almost invariably communicates a sense of completeness, despite the pulsing energies it shapes and organizes. This is a point that deserves emphasis: each sequence in these long scenes has a dramatic structure that is recognizably an action.

Let us study the relationship between the scene and the sequence from

5

another vantage point, that of the very short scene. Many of Shakespeare's scenes run for a scant fifteen to twenty lines. Such scenes are hardly complete actions, nor do they, like the multipartite scenes, contain an action. It often takes several of these short scenes to complete a sequence. The penultimate sequence of *Macbeth*, for example, embraces three scenes.

In this sequence, Shakespeare develops an action in which Macduff kills Macbeth. This climactic confrontation functions as an action, because it has the basic criterion for all sequences, a strongly focused dramatic question. Ever since the witches had predicted that no man born of woman could harm him, Macbeth has considered himself invulnerable. Yet Macduff has sworn to slay this bloody tyrant. Macbeth, as Malcolm predicts, is "ripe for shaking." Will he fall? Can Macduff kill him? Is this second of the witches' prophecies merely fiendish equivocation, or will it prove true? Some such question hovers in the air when in act 5, scene 6, the enemy army arrives at Dunsinane. The drama inherent in that question had better be played out on stage, for toward its resolution most of the play's final act has been driving.

But look at scene 6. We quote it in full:

> MALCOLM Now near enough; your leafy screens throw down,
> And show like those your are. You, worthy uncle,
> Shall with my cousin, your right noble son,
> Lead our first battle. Worthy Macduff and we
> Shall take upon's what else remains to do,
> According to our order.
> SIWARD   Fare you well.
> Do we but find the tyrant's power tonight,
> Let us be beaten, if we cannot fight.
> MACDUFF Make all our trumpets speak, give them all breath,
> Those clamorous harbingers of blood and death.
>
> *Exeunt, Alarums continued.*
>
> (5.6.1–10)

After ten lines Shakespeare clears the stage. Does this scene *contain* an action? Or is it *itself* an action? No. The scene tells us where we are. Its clamorous trumpets summon Macbeth to battle. But that in itself is not an action. The unit merely introduces an action.

What about scene 7? It seems to intensify – in three stages – the action begun in scene 6. First, Macbeth fights Young Siward, gaining from the victory a still greater faith in his invincibility. The stage empties. Then Macduff dashes on in search of Macbeth: here before us stands the primary threat to Macbeth's invincibility. But Shakespeare delays the meeting – Macduff goes off. Malcolm and Old Siward, entering "with Drum and Colors," now pass into the castle. These three segments of scene 7 increase the tension by bringing Macbeth and Macduff closer together while simultaneously delaying their encounter. However, scene 7 is not an action in itself. And when it ends, the action which began in scene 6 still has not climaxed.

Scenes 6 and 7 – two whole scenes – have merely prepared us for the main event of the sequence; the action reaches its apex in scene 8. Here Macduff and Macbeth finally meet and here Macbeth discovers the full perfidy of the witches' prophecies: Macduff was not born in the normal manner but was "from his mother's womb untimely ripped." Ultimately, the tyrant is slain. Only when scenes 6, 7 and 8 are combined do we have a complete action.[6]

Shakespeare has turned upside down the procedure he used to build the tavern scene. There the scene was constructed of sequences. Here he has constructed a sequence out of scenes. Each of these short scenes constitutes only a fragment of the sequential action. Obviously, when we turn from Shakespeare's extended scenes to his very brief ones, the rift between the scene and the unit of action widens still further.

There are many instances in the canon when an action embraces two or more scenes: *Othello* 2.2 and 2.3, where in 2.2 the Herald has a "scene" of his own to introduce the revels that in 2.3 will undo Cassio, for example, or *Coriolanus* 5.4 and 5.5, where Volumnia is expected back in Rome throughout 5.4 and arrives in climactic triumph in 5.5. Multi-scene sequences occur almost naturally if the action focuses on a battle, as in the *Macbeth* example cited above – for instance, both the battle of Actium in *Antony and Cleopatra* (sequence 3.7.1 to 3.10.36) and the skirmish near Alexandria in the same play (sequence 4.10.1 to 4.13.10) span four scenes. Any director staging these actions would ignore the scene breaks, knowing that Shakespeare felt no embarrassment about clearing the stage in the middle of an action.

Throughout this book, then, *sequence* will be our term for that unit of action in which Shakespeare raises a single dramatic question and answers it. Direction in the sequence comes from the thrust toward some climactic resolution of the pending question, and the action moves consecutively through stages of exposition and complication toward the climax, following which Shakespeare normally provides a brief summary or conclusion. Though the sequence is structured upon the conventional "dramatic curve," it may or may not run concurrently with a designated scene.

Three things should be apparent from this survey of the relationship between the scene and the sequence. First, though both scene and sequence exist as units, both must be discovered through careful observation of the characteristics of each unit type, for in many of Shakespeare's plays published prior to the First Folio, neither the scene nor the sequence was marked out. Second, the rules for finding each type are quite different. The scene is a unit of place, and its boundaries are determined primarily by the silence (or space) found at each end. Its beginnings and endings are punctuated by the clearing of the stage. The sequence, in contrast, is a unit of action, and its boundaries are determined by the rising and falling rhythms of that action: the sequence, not the scene, is the unit that contains the dramatic structure. Third, the relationship between scene and sequence is fairly complicated. Scenes come in a variety of sizes. Generally speaking, the shorter scene, containing only a few isolated lines, functions as a component of the sequence and thus must be linked to other scenes to form a dramatic action; the middle-sized scene, with its more fully developed action, often runs concurrently with the sequence; and the longer scene tends to act as a container holding several sequences together. Because of these complexities, any analysis of a "scene" must differentiate between units of time and place (the scene) and units of action (the sequence). Each unit type serves a different function within the drama.

Up to now directors and scholars alike have operated on intuition in discerning the boundaries of Shakespeare's units of action. The situation is clearer in the theater, where the exigencies of rehearsal and production require that plays be broken down into smaller segments and the actor's effectiveness depends upon his awareness not only of the play's rhythms but of the character's objectives. Since certain unit boundaries are determined by the fulfillment of some objective, the theatrical practice of dividing the play into "motivational units"[7] is bound to result in a deeper awareness of Shakespeare's habit of writing in sequences. Yet while most textbooks advise student directors "to divide the script into the smallest meaningful sections," the process is somewhat arbitrary,[8] and a clarifying discussion of specific unit types should prove helpful.

Scholars too depend on intuition in analyzing Shakespeare's action. The units are sensed and our commentaries reflect this – witness the widespread references to the "waves and troughs" of Shakespeare's action or the inevitable selectivity through which we focus on certain familiar segments. Intuitively we recognize Shakespeare's units. We even coin convenient tags for them – the cellarage scene, the nunnery scene, the recorder scene – as if they were of the same "kind" as the designated scene. Yet so unaware are we of their significance as actions that the very terminology that reveals the correctness of our intuitions can draw criticism. Scholars so wholeheartedly maintain that "Shakespeare's actual unit of construction was what we would call the scene" – and only the scene – that they can still deem it "a somewhat inappropriate mental 'set'" to approach the plays through such units as the "recorder scene" in *Hamlet* or the "porter scene" in *Macbeth*, because "none of these episodes is, properly speaking, a scene."[9] Nonetheless, there is a growing recognition of the importance of the unit we have called the sequence, as well as an obvious groping for terms that will enable us to discuss Shakespeare's action with a conscious understanding of how that action is constructed.

The immediate goal of this study is to define the nature of the sequence and its relationship to Shakespeare's other units, those units smaller and larger than the sequence. Our first step will be to offer a method for isolating sequences in the printed text. Sequence boundaries are not easily discernible because Shakespeare dovetails these units; one sequence normally flows into or overlaps the next and it is often difficult to say where the earlier sequence ends and the subsequent one begins, until one develops an eye for the playwright's mortises and tenons. Because the ability to delimit a sequence is a needed skill in this process of unit analysis, we shall begin with it. In our initial chapters we isolate the sequence by examining its parts. Later we look at sequences themselves and then at the way Shakespeare combines his sequences into larger units.

Ultimately, of course, understanding the sequence is only a means to an end, which is to experience the emotional rhythms of the play more fully. By giving the reader exacting insights into the playwriting techniques through which Shakespeare paces and weights, combines and orchestrates his sequences, unit analysis provides a solid basis for the many meticulous judgments required of performers who are attempting to translate these rhythms onto the stage. For the viewer, it creates an awareness of the differences between story and action, thereby increasing sensitivity to and aesthetic appreciation of the play's emotional peaks and valleys and opening the way to a deeper experience of the constantly alternating tensions. What is at stake here is the full realization of a play's dramatic rhythms in any given performance.

Speculating upon the approaches to Shakespeare that will dominate the next decade, Robert Hapgood writes that "already Shakespeare is regarded as more a 'man of the theater' than in the recent past, a trend which seems likely to continue," but that more is necessary. Hapgood "would also like to see our sense of his authorial presence redefined, neither as an Author (in the nineteenth-century sense) nor an Absence (whose creative function is dispersed in all directions) but as a playwright, working within a collaborative team with players and playgoers. This might lead to a larger and looser, less thematic, feeling for what is unifying in Shakespeare's art."[10] Perhaps this book will help to fill that need.

2

The beat defined

I

The sequence cannot be fully appreciated without an understanding of the unit from which it is constructed – the beat.[1] Distinct from the line (a unit of poetry), from the sentence (a unit of grammar), and from the speech (a unit of expression), the beat functions as a unit of action. But it differs from the sequence in that each beat completes only a *portion* of the action to which it contributes: the beat relates to a sequence as the stanza does to a canto. This chapter therefore approaches the sequence by analyzing its parts. Since beats perform many functions and each beat is unique, no single definition can explain every beat, but general guidelines can be set down which hold true in a significant number of cases.

The first point is that in constructing the action of a sequence Shakespeare tends to articulate each stage of that action as a beat; in other words, beats are highly specialized – some have introductory functions, others intensify the action, and still others summarize or conclude. We have kept these categories simple, and they may seem rather obvious, but the oversimplification will be corrected as we get deeper into the subject. Meanwhile, the point has to be made: to locate the boundaries of a beat one must be clear about its *function*, for when the function changes, so does the beat.

The change of function normally involves a change of subject. Thus, in any beat the characters will be concerned with only one subject. However, a stronger force than subject matter often governs beat structure: the subject is usually closely linked to some desire.

The beat is in essence a unit of motivation. That characters are supplied with motives is hardly a startling observation: some kind of motivation can be detected in almost any line an actor delivers. The more characters there are in the beat, the more motives to be found in it, and motives in drama tend to be conflicting motives. But critical distinctions must be made between dominant and subordinate motives. Generally speaking, where there are many motives, Shakespeare makes one of them the *propelling* motive of the beat. All of the other motives have been subordinated to that propelling motive. Through it, the beat is given direction.

To these structural elements that combine to distinguish a beat – the single dramaturgical function, the single subject, and the single propelling motive – Shakespeare might add rhetorical elements that will give the beat greater coherence. Devices such as word repetition or enclosing are employed in certain circumstances to make the lines of a beat cohere.

Again, while these factors work together toward beat unity, not all are found in every beat. There are no infallible rules for identifying Shakespeare's beats. Yet sequences do unfold in stages, and these stages are apparent enough to foster fairly widespread agreement about where they begin and end (skilled directors may even feel that to argue for their existence is to belabor the obvious). As the next few chapters will reveal, much can be learned about Shakespeare's sequences by focusing on these beats from which the sequences have been built.

In an early play like *Richard III* it is possible to look behind the action and watch Shakespeare laying the "building blocks" that form that action. The peacemaking sequence at King Edward's court, where Edward attempts to reconcile the opposing factions under his government (2.1.1–141), provides an almost schematic example of the use of beats as building blocks. To analyze this action properly, one must be aware of its goals. The climax Shakespeare builds toward is the shock that occurs in the middle of the sequence when Richard announces Clarence's death and thereby thwarts Edward's attempt to establish peace at court. This shock, almost comic in its devastation of the prosaic souls whose illusions it destroys, highlights a dramaturgical usurpation of power by Richard that prefigures the literal usurpation to come. One tends to move hurriedly over the lines leading up to Richard's outburst, finding little order and much sentimentality in the seemingly endless embracing. Sentimentality there is, but not disorder. Shakespeare generally prepares well for so dramatic a reversal. And that preparation comes in the form of beats.

But it is not enough to notice that the sequence is constructed of beats. The point is to see the beat functions clearly. Each beat has a specialized function in the sequence.

The peacemaking sequence opens with a six-line beat of introduction:

> EDWARD Why, so: now have I done a good day's work.
> You peers, continue this united league.
> I every day expect an embassage
> From my Redeemer to redeem me hence;

And more in peace my soul shall part to heaven,
Since I have made my friends at peace on earth.

(2.1.1–6)

Such *introductory beats* function much like topic sentences: they ensure that the audience has the proper orientation before the action moves forward. This one establishes a controlling figure – Edward – and makes apparent the figure's motive: to restore peace at court.[2] Shakespeare cleverly brings the characters on stage when the endeavor is nearly complete: Edward seems to have achieved his objective. But he has more yet to do. The dramatic question becomes in fact, *Can Edward truly reconcile the various competing factions of his kingdom?*

The playwright next provides four beats in which Edward's goal is illustrated and reinforced. These work as *intensifying beats*: they develop the action of the sequence. Because their effectiveness depends upon heightened contrasts, intensifying beats rarely appear singly. Shakespeare writes them in clusters of two or more, each successively increasing the degree of tension and building toward the moment of climax. If the sequence is powerfully dramatic, the build grows naturally out of the action. If not, Shakespeare imposes some external order on the action that results in a build.

The intensifying mechanism in the peacemaking beats derives from the hierarchical ordering of the alliance: the King progresses from the weaker personalities at court to the stronger. He begins by bringing Lord Hastings into the bosom of his family. In lines 7 to 17, he effects a reconciliation between Hastings and the Queen's brother, Earl Rivers:

> EDWARD Hastings and Rivers, take each other's hand,
> Dissemble not your hatred, swear your love.
> RIVERS By heaven, my soul is purg'd from grudging hate.
> And with my hand I seal my true heart's love.
> HASTINGS So thrive I, as I truly swear the like!
> EDWARD Take heed you dally not before your king,
> Lest He that is the supreme Kings of kings
> Confound your hidden falsehood and award
> Either of you to be the other's end.
> HASTINGS So prosper I, as I swear perfect love!
> RIVERS And I, as I love Hastings with my heart!

(2.1.7–17)

In the next beat, Edward requires Hastings to make peace with the Queen and her son Dorset. The beat structure is similar – command followed by compliance – but from Rivers (the Queen's brother), Hastings "ascends" to the Queen herself:

> EDWARD Madam, yourself is not exempt from this;
> Nor you, son Dorset; Buckingham, nor you;
> You have been factious one against the other.
> Wife, love Lord Hastings, let him kiss your hand,
> And what you do, do it unfeignedly.
>   ELIZABETH There, Hastings, I will never more remember
> Our former hatred, so thrive I and mine!
>   EDWARD Dorset, embrace him; Hastings, love Lord Marquess.
>   DORSET This interchange of love, I here protest,
> Upon my part shall be inviolable.
>   HASTINGS And so swear I.

$$(2.1.18-28)$$

The glance at Buckingham early in this beat supplies a bit of foreshadowing that points beyond the reconciliation of Hastings and Elizabeth (which is the concern of this beat) to even greater achievement. In beat 4, Edward goes still further. He brings the potent Duke of Buckingham into amity with the others:

> EDWARD Now, princely Buckingham, seal thou this league
> With thy embracements to my wife's allies,
> And make me happy in your unity.
>   BUCKINGHAM When ever Buckingham doth turn his hate
> Upon your Grace [*to the Queen*], but with all duteous love
> Doth cherish you and yours, God punish me
> With hate in those where I expect most love!
> When I have most need to employ a friend,
> And most assured that he is a friend,
> Deep, hollow, treacherous, and full of guile
> Be he unto me! This do I beg of God,
> When I am cold in love to you or yours.
>   EDWARD A pleasing cordial, princely Buckingham,
> Is this thy vow unto my sickly heart.

$$(2.1.29-42)$$

Finally, in a fifth beat, Edward turns his attention to the most powerful personality of the play. Richard, too, must join the accord; his submission will "make the blessed period of this peace."

Not only does the beat structure maintain order on stage, identifying each group and giving it its moment of attention from the audience; it also shows us the peace proceeding through higher and higher stages of the political pecking order. With Edward's wish to draw Richard into the accord, phase one of the build finds its completion. There is a resting-point at this plateau, while Richard of Gloucester is ushered into the room.

Despite the entrance of a new character, the action does not resume at ground level. What follows is the final stage of the intensification. Edward boasts joyfully to Richard of his success, having "made peace of enmity, fair love of hate, / Between these swelling wrong-incensed peers." Richard praises this "blessed labor," assures Edward that "Tis death to me to be at enmity; / I hate it, and desire all good men's love," and entreats each person there to dismiss "any grudge. . .lodg'd between us." At the end of this beat the King's goal has been achieved, so much so that his wife can say, "A holy day shall this be kept hereafter."

The intensification is complete. It has been accomplished through a carefully structured progression of beats, the effect of which is cumulative. Each character, from the least effectual to the most powerful at court, has been the focus of a beat. Each has been drawn into the "united league" Edward hopes to leave behind him at his death. This series of intensifying beats has put everything in readiness for the sequence climax, in which the expectations so far established will be shattered. A chance word uttered by Elizabeth, an innocent wish that the King's benevolence might extend further, even to his imprisoned brother, the Duke of Clarence (76–7), gives the diabolical Richard the opportunity to turn all that Edward has accomplished to chaos. In the *climactic beat*, Richard announces that Clarence is dead:

> RICHARD Why, madam, have I offer'd love for this,
> To be so flouted in this royal presence?
> Who knows not that the gentle Duke is dead?
> You do him injury to scorn his corpse.
>
> (2.1.78–81)

By deliberately shattering Edward's peace Richard effects a startling reversal of direction in the ongoing action. In this feigned outrage we find a climactic beat.

Having created an explosion, Shakespeare sustains its impact by allowing for a period of adjustment during which the people on stage absorb the shock Richard has thrust upon them. The adjustment comes in two stages – the initial response to Richard's announcement is total confusion (beat 82–6), the subsequent response a demand for clarification (beat 87–95). "*Is* Clarence dead?" These two beats extend the impact of the sequence climax for fourteen lines. They function in the sequence as *sustaining beats*.

Shakespeare now slows down the pace, beginning a new beat with the King's new motive, to contemplate the meaning of Clarence's death (96–134): the action passes into its decrescent stage. This beat serves a concluding function.

The motivational structure which shapes this *concluding beat* is worth noticing. With the entrance of Lord Stanley to beg for his servant's life, an entirely new subject is raised. Under other circumstances, the arrival of a new character with new goals would be material for an introductory beat. But the introduction of Stanley is nicely subordinated as Edward uses Stanley's request as his text for a meditation upon Clarence. The sequence is obviously drawing to a close. Its dramatic question, *Can Edward reconcile the various competing factions of his kingdom?*, has now been answered. Tensions have been released. The propelling character is ready to leave the stage. All of this gives that definite sense of aftermath to the action that makes this unit a pure example of falling action following a climax.

The decrescent pitch identifies this as a concluding beat, but so also does the retrospective analysis of the events of the sequence. From King Edward's commentary, we learn where Edward stands, psychologically, as a result of the blow dealt him by Richard. The fear that God's vengeance will be exacted upon all present expressed by Edward as he retires is neatly contrasted with his earlier expectations of universal harmony. This summing up by the character whose motives organize the sequence gives that sequence a satisfying conclusion.

The beat which follows, the last of the sequence, gives Richard's summary of the events. By providing for exits it too suggests finality. But it also glances toward the future, when Gloucester will attack Edward's widow in his attempt to gain the crown for himself:

> GLOUCESTER This is the fruits of rashness! Mark'd you not
> How that the guilty kindred of the Queen
> Look'd pale when they did hear of Clarence' death?
> O, they did urge it still unto the King!
> God will revenge it. Come, lords, will you go
> To comfort Edward with our company?
> BUCKINGHAM We wait upon your grace.

$$(2.1.135-41)$$

Functioning more as a coda, this beat simultaneously completes the sequence and points toward future developments.

Analysis of the beat functions reveals careful structuring, with Richard's power as a shatteringly divisive force made all the more evident by contrast with the cumulative build of the intensifying beats towards perfect harmony. This analysis also shows how the scene is best played. Success depends upon the scene's being perceived and acted as a single sequence. The director must not be confused by the several entrances that occur within the sequence, dividing it into French scenes and staging it as two or three contrasted units rather than in the sequential form described. Stanley's entrance has no introductory function; his petition supplies the context from which Edward's concluding meditation can spring. And though the build of the sequence occurs in two phases, phase one being completed with Edward's desire to draw Richard into the general amity and phase two underscoring Richard's inherent contentiousness, the second phase opens at a very high pitch, continuing the rising action. Any significant break at Richard's entrance will destroy all continuity. Nor should the director be embarrassed by King Edward's attempts at reviving Eden and speed through the preparatory beats, thus flattening out the build. Richard's bombshell will have its greatest impact only if the beats are recognized and built into a solid structure, so that there is an edifice on stage for him to explode.

The sequence just analyzed happens to run concurrently with a scene; however, the same kinds of beats will be characteristic of any sequence, whether it is part of a multi-sequence scene, like *Hamlet* 4.5.96–220, or whether, like *Macbeth* 5.6.1 to 5.8.34, it consists of a series of shorter scenes. All sequences are constructed of beats.

Well constructed as this sequence is, it does have flaws. The beats do propel the action. Yet the movement seems mechanical. The beat structure hardly renders an action that could have occurred in life; people rarely move from enmity to accord so easily. Instead, one senses in the beats a rhetorical patterning imposed upon the characters by the author. In later Shakespeare the armature on which the action hangs is less nakedly exposed, the movement more natural. But the very nakedness of that armature serves our purposes here: it allows us to study the various beat functions that shape a sequence.

By examining beats in context we have isolated one of the primary characteristics of Shakespeare's beat – the division of labor that occurs among beats in a sequence. Beats can be highly specialized. Some are designed as introductory, orienting the audience and preparing them for the direction the sequence will take. Others intensify; they build – step by step (each step a separate beat) – toward the climax. Still others draw loose strands together and sum up, rounding off the action with a conclusion. Less often Shakespeare writes climactic and/or sustaining beats. And entrance or exit beats to get characters on or off the stage are ubiquitous. Every beat serves at least one of these functions.

II

Function is central; the beat exists because it has a specific job to do, and anyone analyzing action will want to be aware of that function. But no description of Shakespeare's beat that takes function alone into consideration can stand scrutiny. Beats, even when their function is to introduce or conclude – and certainly when their function is to intensify – effect movement. If narrative is to become drama, some character must be given a desire, a motive, which will engage him with the other characters on the stage.

That two characters on stage simultaneously must influence one another in some way goes without saying. Rarely, however, are Character A and Character B exactly equal. At any given moment one or the other is in the ascendant. One is in a primary or "active" position, the other in a secondary or responding role. The motive of the active character is always the dominant motive in the beat and therefore becomes the force which gives direction to the action.

Emphasis falls heavily here on a single dominant motive, assigned to one character, who is *temporarily* controlling the action. That emphasis on the dominant motive is intended. Certainly conflicting motives do exist in any beat. There may be as many motives in a beat as there are characters on stage, sometimes more. It is impossible and undesirable that all other motives in the unit be eliminated. Indeed, drama requires resistance to the active character, and resistance often provides a strong opposing motive. But not all motives are given equal weight. Distinctions must be made between dominant and secondary motives.

The term *dominant* should be interpreted with care, for there is a difference between a dominant motive and a dominant character. At any given moment one character or the other has the dominant motive. But dominance is not a prerogative of the protagonist, who is often cast into a secondary position (think of Hamlet throughout his interview with the Ghost where his most important task is to listen). Nor is dominance synonymous with force. Strong resistance, rebelliousness, or opposition (for example, the bluster of Hotspur or Coriolanus) should not be automatically construed as dominance. The term becomes misleading if associated with either of these concepts. The character with the dominant motive is not in every way the play's dominant character. In some cases it will be safer to speak of him only as the *active* or *propelling* character.

In each of Shakespeare's beats, then, one motive supplies the governing force. That motive delimits, orients, and unifies the beat, and

18

all other motives in that beat will be subordinated to it. Let us apply this theory to some of the beats just examined. How do motives shape the beats in the peacemaking sequence?

Initially, Shakespeare uses Edward's motives to move the action forward. At the beginning of the beat he depicts Edward expressing a desire:

> EDWARD Hastings and Rivers, take each other's hand,
> Dissemble not your hatred, swear your love.

At its completion he depicts the fulfilling response:

> HASTINGS I swear perfect love!
> RIVERS And I, as I love Hastings with my heart!

So with Edward's subsequent objectives – first, to reconcile Lord Hastings to the Queen and her son Dorset; second, to make peace between the Queen and Buckingham; and third, to bring Richard of Gloucester into harmony with the others. The pattern, once detected, is obvious: desire/response, desire/response, desire/response. Each change of objective corresponds with a change of beat.

Edward's motives not only give direction; they also dominate. When Buckingham makes peace with the Queen, the motivation for his action comes first of all from Edward: "Now, princely Buckingham, seal thou this league / With thy embracements to my wife's allies . . ." Buckingham's action in this beat is a response; he accedes to the King's request. Richard, too (beat 47–75), appears totally submissive. But notice that Shakespeare highlights Edward's fall by placing him in a responding position later on. In the concluding beat, for example, he gives Lord Stanley the "dominant" or "propelling" motive.

It will help if we understand the playwright's problem. Edward has been happy in the illusion that the vows of amity elicited from various factions within his court will usher in a new era of peace. In shattering his illusion Richard has brought Edward face to face with reality. The question, *Can Edward enforce a permanent peace?*, has been answered with a resounding no. The action is ended. It remains now for the playwright to round it off with a conclusion. Shakespeare apparently wished, in that conclusion, to show us Edward at this new stage of comprehension. His problem was to find some action that would enable Edward to reveal his mind. In examining how Shakespeare used Stanley's motives to structure this beat, we obtain a glimpse of a craftsman at work.

In what sense does Lord Stanley control the action here? He does not have authority; that remains with Edward. Stanley must request a boon and Edward retains the power to grant or refuse it. Stanley is hardly a central character in this sequence, let alone in the play. He appears to arrive by chance: he has not enough rank to have been among those summoned to Edward's chambers. Nor has Stanley the potency of Richard, whose power, when he wields it, withers everything around him. Though his importance increases three acts later, here in this concluding beat Stanley seems less a character than a device used to evoke a response, for the news of Clarence's death has penetrated Edward to the center of his soul. The illusions that had absorbed him during the first portions of the scene have been shattered. Indeed, Edward has been shocked into silence, as we learn from his first response to Stanley, "I prithee peace, my soul is full of sorrow." But Stanley's persistence forces Edward to hear his request and then to respond. Stanley "causes" Edward to make a decision:

> EDWARD You straight are on your knees for pardon, pardon,
> And I (unjustly too) must grant it you.
>
> (2.1.125–6)

Since Edward hears Stanley's petition for his servant's life immediately after he has learned of his own brother's death, the two concerns combine in his psyche. Shakespeare's strategy of using Stanley to force a response from Edward – at a time when, left to himself, Edward might have retreated into silence – results in the concluding meditation, in which Edward rises above his usual mediocrity to glimpse reality. Stanley must be seen to have the dominant motive in this beat because he is the character whose desire determines the direction in which the beat unfolds. Edward has the longer part, but his monologue is delivered in response to the stimulus given him by Stanley.

To see Shakespeare organize a network of conflicting motives, one may study the unity in multiplicity that he constructed as the setting for the meeting of Romeo and Juliet – the Capulets' masquerade ball (1.5.1–144). In this one sequence, Shakespeare brings on stage at least twenty characters. Besides Capulet, Lady Capulet, Juliet, her Nurse, Tybalt, and a multitude of invited Guests and Gentlewomen, there are the intruders – Romeo, Mercutio, and Benvolio, with five or six other Maskers plus Torchbearers. Beyond these central figures, Shakespeare also reckons with a quantity of servants – Anthony, Potpan, Susan Grindstone, Nell, and two others never specifically named. Here, if anywhere, the reader might expect to find as many motives as there are characters. And so there are, yet throughout the sequence there is also a sensitive ordering of motives. The ballroom sequence not only provides firm proof that

The beat defined

Shakespeare is writing in beats – it also offers evidence of the value of the beat structure in bringing order out of potential chaos. Above all, it is an excellent place to observe how motivation becomes the shaping force behind the beat.

In line-by-line readings Shakespeare's methods for maintaining order among the welter of conflicting desires might not be noticed. The desires that propel the action will seem ordered by chance. Yet were several characters to assert themselves simultaneously, the stage would be filled with confusion. This in fact is exactly the technique used by Jacobean playwrights to create their madhouse scenes: every character demands attention at once; there is no foreground, no background, no subordination of characters to a dominant figure – just unmitigated clamor.[3] But Shakespeare eliminates any suggestion of chaos. By dividing the action of his crowd scenes into beats, each having its dominant and its secondary characters, he both suggests a multiplicity of overlapping events and at the same time gives each character the chance to display his own will.

Everyone from the noble Capulet to the lowly Potpan is caught up in the whirl of activity in the ballroom scene. The servants are sent out first to create a flurry of anticipation and excitement:

> 1 SERVANT Where's Potpan, that he helps not to take away?
> He shift a trencher? he scrape a trencher?
> 2 SERVANT When good manners shall lie all in one or two
> men's hands, and they unwash'd too, 'tis a foul thing.
> 1 SERVANT Away with the joint-stools, remove the court-
> cupboard, look to the plate. Good thou, save me a piece of
> marchpane, and, as thou lovest me, let the porter let in Susan
> Grindstone and Nell. [*Exit Second Servant.*] Anthony and Potpan!
> [*Enter,* ANTHONY *and* POTPAN]
> ANTHONY Ay, boy, ready.
> 1 SERVANT You are look'd for and call'd for, ask'd for and
> sought for, in the great chamber.
> POTPAN We cannot be here and there too. Cheerly, boys, be
> brisk a while, and the longer liver take all.
> > *Exeunt.*
> > (1.5.1–15)

This introductory beat provides a schematic illustration of the artistic process through which motivation structures the action. Shakespeare gives the First Servant the dominant role; as the man-in-charge, he presides over the beat, and the other servants respond in various ways to his desires. It appears initially as if the First Servant's desires are manifold. He gives a series of different orders. Yet running throughout

21

the beat and binding it into a coherent unit there is one primary motive: the First Servant is trying to locate Potpan. As soon as Potpan turns up, Shakespeare ends the beat, sweeping the servants off the stage.[4]

Capulet dominates the next section, which contains two separate beats. Shakespeare presents him in the role of host and all his activity gains coherence from that unifying factor. Capulet's desire to make his guests feel welcome provides the focus for beat 2 (1.5.16–28). When he settles down to give attention to his aged cousin, the beat changes (beat 3, 1.5.29–40).

Shakespeare lets Romeo initiate the fourth beat (1.5.41–53). Romeo wants to know "What lady's that?" All that has gone before has been introductory – scene-setting, as it were. Not until this fourth beat does Shakespeare introduce the primary action of the sequence. Reduced to its essence, that action appears deceptively simple: Romeo, smitten by Juliet's beauty, determines to meet her. Such a statement hardly does justice to Romeo's emotion; still, in reacting to that emotion, one should not lose sight of the dramatic structure that underlies it. Romeo, in this beat, makes the fatal decision to approach Juliet.

Unless one is conscious of the importance of this moment to the action of the play, the daring with which that action is abruptly halted may be missed. Shakespeare follows Romeo's declaration not with the lovers' meeting but with a quarrel in which the deadly feud between the warring families threatens to erupt again. Tybalt, given the chance to exercise his will, expresses a desire to strike Romeo dead. As a testament to craftsmanship the shift is superb, for the love, barely announced, is immediately set in the context of danger.

Again character motivation governs the beat structure. In a loose analysis of the action, lines 54–92 could be treated as a single beat with emphasis placed solely upon Tybalt's anger. But finer discrimination is necessary. This section contains a miniature drama that develops in two stages. Shakespeare gives Tybalt the lead in the first of these paired beats and then has Capulet dominate him. He first permits Tybalt to wrest attention away from Romeo when the former recognizes Romeo as a Montague and sends for his rapier with the intent of driving Romeo out (beat 5, 1.5.54–76). He then gives Capulet, a secondary character in beat 5, a passionate resolve to silence Tybalt that makes Capulet's motive the one that shapes beat 6 (1.5.76–92). The change in dominance denotes the change in beat.

These two beats mark out a contrast between two fits of temper – the young man's hostility toward threats from outside the family unit and the older man's fury in the face of youthful insubordination from within it. This contrast foreshadows the characters' future actions, which are precipitated by these very traits – Tybalt will angrily attack Romeo with the rapier, and Capulet will greet Juliet's insubordination with a similar burst of rage. By transferring power from one character to the other in the middle of the quarrel Shakespeare has revealed as much about Capulet as about Tybalt, even as he sets Tybalt up as the more immediate threat to the lovers.

Having removed Tybalt from the stage, Shakespeare gives control back to Romeo. Beat 7 (1.5.93–110) treats Romeo's desire to kiss Juliet; beat 8 (1.5.111–18) his attempt to discover her identity. Though in this eighth beat the Nurse has more lines, Romeo's question, "What is her mother?," contains the motivation that governs the beat structure. In this beat and in the parallel beat at 1.5.128–41, where Juliet is left alone on stage with the Nurse and contrives to learn Romeo's identity, Shakespeare uses a question/answer/reaction format characteristic of many of his beats. Typically, he embodies the motivation that gives direction to the beat in a question, which appears at or close to the beginning of the beat (Juliet's "What's he that follows here, that would not dance?" serves the same function as Romeo's "What is her mother?"). The answer supplied by the responding character (here, in both cases, the Nurse) is followed by a reaction (not a new objective) from the original speaker. Coherence in this type of beat arises from the natural progression from question to answer to reaction.[5]

This summary, though brief, indicates that Shakespeare has organized a potentially chaotic sequence into a smoothly flowing entity by presenting each of the varied goals of the Capulets' guests within its own carefully structured beat. Each beat contains one dominating character whose will determines its direction and affects its length. All other motives in the beat are subordinated to that character's propelling motive.

Examples of beat motives thus far have been drawn from early plays which are highly formalized. Our last example is from Shakespeare's mature period. And to avoid creating the false impression that beats change only when characters change, we have chosen a passage in which the characters remain constant – *Hamlet* 4.7.

When scene 7 opens, Claudius is discovered with Laertes, who had broken into the palace two scenes back seeking revenge for the murder of his father Polonius. Claudius has managed to calm Laertes, eliminating immediate danger by deflecting Laertes' anger away from himself and toward Hamlet. As this new sequence begins, Claudius seems confident that with the report of Hamlet's death, expected any moment, Laertes will be satisfied. But suddenly the situation changes. Claudius discovers that Hamlet is alive and on his way to Elsinore. He dare not allow Laertes to meet Hamlet with an open mind and thus risk their joining forces: he must bind Laertes to his own cause first.

Between the exit of the messenger who brings news of Hamlet's return and Gertrude's entrance 120 lines later, Claudius and Laertes remain on stage together without interruption. Consequently, there is no obvious indication of smaller units, as there was in the *Romeo and Juliet* sequence where the spotlight was constantly shifting from one character group to another, making beat boundaries easy to locate. Is this long segment divisible into beats?

The four beats in which Claudius makes Laertes the instrument of a new scheme to murder Hamlet illustrate how closely character motivation is related to beat structure. Claudius's desires determine the beat divisions. Though a general or long-term goal of turning Laertes from enemy to ally provides continuity during the remainder of the sequence, the King exhibits four specific motives, successively directed toward the same responding character, in attempting to effect the desired reversal. Achievement of the smaller goals within the larger one not only creates the forward movement of the action but also brings the audience deeper into Claudius's character with each beat.

The first of these intensifying beats runs from the lines in which Claudius asks, "Will you be rul'd by me?" to the moment following Laertes' answer, "My lord, I will be rul'd," ten lines later. In this beat Claudius seeks Laertes' active compliance – not the polite but casual assurance of it offered in Laertes' "Ay, my lord" but a firmer, more lasting commitment. To obtain his end, Claudius hints at "an exploit" that will bring certain death to Hamlet, their mutual foe. He makes no mention of Laertes' involvement in the action; so circumspect is he in this regard that Laertes has to beg employment in the exploit:

> KING   If it be so, Laertes –
> As how should it be so? how otherwise? –
> Will you be rul'd by me?
>   LAERTES   Ay, my lord,
> So you will not o'errule me to a peace.
>   KING To thine own peace. If he be now returned
> As checking at his voyage, and that he means
> No more to undertake it, I will work him
> To an exploit, now ripe in my device,
> Under the which he shall not choose but fall;
> And for his death no wind of blame shall breathe,
> But even his mother shall uncharge the practice,

24

And call it accident.
LAERTES   My lord, I will be rul'd,
The rather if you could devise it so
That I might be the organ.
KING   It falls right.

(4.7.57–70)

Claudius begins by asking little. He simply begs Laertes to believe their goals are identical – a request that is easily granted. The request requires Laertes only to defer his action and accept advice from someone with the strength to give him benefit. It provides him with a powerful ally and protector. The effect of Laertes' "I will be rul'd" is far-reaching. The acquiescence diverts him from his earlier goal of rebelling against Claudius. And this of course is the King's real objective in the beat – to gain some measure of control over this rebel enemy. As soon as Laertes consents to the proposal, the King records his satisfaction with "it falls right," and the beat ends.

Shakespeare marks out the next beat (4.7.71–105) by references in its opening and closing lines to Hamlet's envy of Laertes and centers it upon the King's narration of Monsieur Lamord's "masterly report" of Laertes' excellence. Too frequently actors playing Claudius, lacking precise direction and viewing the lines about Lamord as exposition, merely relate the story of his visit as though the motive were to explain Hamlet's opinion of Laertes' fencing skills. But the motivation behind the speech originates with Claudius: his intention is to puff up Laertes' confidence in his own swordsmanship. Before venturing to suggest a match between Laertes and Hamlet, he wants to make sure Laertes will be receptive to the idea. Here is the flattery of a master. Without praising Laertes directly, Claudius conveys the impression that the whole world holds the young man in awe. The beat structure reveals that the actor should use every technique of the manipulator to charm Laertes and forestall him from declining a match with Hamlet on the ground of incompetence at the sport.

Claudius now takes a new tack: in the following beat he intimidates (106–28). The cunning of the King's approach is seen in the framing questions: "Was your father dear to you? / Or are you like the painting of a sorrow" and "What would you undertake / To show yourself indeed your father's son / More than in words?" He suggests that Laertes' will may not remain at the same pitch of fervor: his desire for revenge may flag. The subtle implication is that Laertes' threats against Hamlet may have no substance. The intention is to lock Laertes into a position from which he cannot later back off, to force him to accept the "exploit" even

25

before knowing what it is. Laertes is pinned down. He can respond in only one way to Claudius's question without seeming both an ungrateful son and a coward. Again the ending of the beat comes when the goal is achieved. "What would you undertake / To show yourself indeed your father's son?" Laertes makes the declaration Claudius requires, "To cut his throat i' th' church." With the King's macabre expression of approval, the unit is completed.

Only in the last of the four beats of his presentation does Claudius explain his exploit. Having tested his victim as he led him to the point of commitment, the manipulator can now introduce the gory details of the plot to murder Hamlet. This he does in a new beat. So cleverly managed was the preparation that the victim falls into the mood. Devices flow rapidly out of the brains of the plotters – to be stopped only by the change of beat that comes with the Queen's announcement that "your sister's drown'd."

This long passage from *Hamlet* 4.7 is uninterrupted by exits or entrances, and therefore lacks any character regrouping that would suggest unit divisions. Nevertheless, it is clearly organized into motivational units. In beat after beat the thought processes of the controlling character determine the beat structure. A significant change in the motive of the propelling character, then, proves to be a reliable indication of a change of beat – a more dependable indication in fact than exits or entrances.

How do these propelling motives relate to the multitude of secondary motives that exist within the beat? This distinction between dominant and secondary motives is crucial to any accurate conception of the beat. Usually, among the numerous elements compressed into any beat (stage directions, place indications, thematic imagery, versification, etc.) are many subordinate motives, intricate and personal, which the actor certainly must realize on the stage and which may give subtle indications of character without being structurally essential. These subordinate motives have their relevance strictly at the level of the speech or line. This is not to say they are unimportant – on the contrary. But their function is different.[6]

This hierarchy of motives can be studied in many places. In our *Romeo and Juliet* sequence, contrast the First Servant's desire to locate Potpan and Anthony (his beat motive) with the various subsidiary motives that give additional individuality to his character – his desire to sample the marzipan, for example. Contrast Capulet's significant desire to quiet Tybalt with the several minor objectives he pursues in the same beat as host of the party ("Well said, my hearts!" or "More light, more light!").

Contrast Romeo's desire to know who Juliet is – the central desire of the beat as well as the climactic one in the sequence – with the Nurse's wish to display her knowledge about Juliet's heritage. In each case the former motive is structural, the latter (whatever its dramaturgical rightness in the situation) remains an opportune enrichment.

The difference between beat and line motives is nicely displayed in a beat that introduces the Gadshill robbery in *I Henry IV*. The dramaturgical purpose of the beat is to set the scene. Shakespeare brings the thieves to the location early, deliberately leaving time between their arrival and that of their victims. He then invents a mini-action to engage the characters while they wait. In beat 2.2.1–47, Falstaff's motive is dominant: Shakespeare sends him on stage to demand the return of his horse. The Prince, who with Poins has previously hidden the animal behind a hedge, responds by putting Falstaff off. The beat motive threads insistently through Falstaff's discourse:

> The rascal hath remov'd my horse, and tied him I know not where.
> (11–12)

> Give me my horse, you rogues, give me my horse, and be hang'd!
> (29–30)

> What a plague mean ye to colt me thus? (37)

> I prithee, good prince – Hal! – help me to my horse, good king's son.
> (40–41)

Line by line, however, Falstaff has a succession of subordinate motives: to rest; to recapture his breath; to sit down; to succeed (should he sit down) in getting up again; to obtain revenge on Poins, then on Hal, for stealing the horse; to part company with them; to discover why he stays with them when they so plague him; to be back in the tavern where he could do without a horse – alternatives to searching for his horse enter his mind in almost every line. None of his line-to-line motives, though, go outside the governing motive constant throughout the beat – to recover that horse.

The actor playing Falstaff could take each of Falstaff's complaints and bleed it for laughs without regard to the context, as if Falstaff were a stand-up comic. Many of the lines, however, lose their humor if divorced from the frustration of being "unhorsed." In a careful production the throughline of the beat will be sufficiently highlighted: Falstaff must be seen as the butt of Poins and Hal's joke, for this beat subtly prepares the audience for the bluster but eventual vulnerability of Falstaff when he walks into the Boar's Head Tavern later with a string of complaints, having been robbed this time not of a horse but of the booty.

Line or speech motives can always be detected within any beat. But these motives usually seem more pertinent to character enrichment than to dramatic structure and could often be other than they are. In every instance they are distinctly subordinate to that motive of the dominant character which gives the beat its direction, justifies its conclusion, and, in doing both, provides its formal unity.

In isolating any beat, then, we should first discern its governing motive, that is, the principal objective of the currently dominant character. This motive inevitably provides a "container" for the subordinate elements within the beat, thereby uniting its disparate elements into a single whole. At the same time, that focusing motive gives the beat direction. It implies an end that lies somewhere in the future, something to be attained before the beat can conclude. As such it becomes a source of energy in the drama.

III

So far we have seen that each beat has some specialized role in the sequence, a function it must perform, and also that most beats contain one dominant motive which governs the direction of that beat and makes all of its other motives cohere. These two characteristics seem to have been, for Shakespeare, the necessary elements of the beat unit. But in many of his beats Shakespeare also strives for a high degree of rhetorical unity and in such cases language provides a useful key to beat boundaries.

For example, Shakespeare characteristically uses word relationships to link the lines of a beat together. Take a beat from the ballroom sequence, the highly formalized sonnet-dialogue in which Romeo begs a kiss from Juliet.

> Romeo If I profane with my unworthiest hand
> This holy shrine, the gentle sin is this,
> My lips, two blushing pilgrims, ready stand
> To smooth that rough touch with a tender kiss.
> Juliet Good pilgrim, you do wrong your hand too much,
> Which mannerly devotion shows in this:
> For saints have hands that pilgrims' hands do touch,
> And palm to palm is holy palmers' kiss.
> Romeo Have not saints lips, and holy palmers too?
> Juliet Ay, pilgrim, lips that they must use in pray'r.
> Romeo O then, dear saint, let lips do what hands do,
> They pray – grant thou, lest faith turn to despair.
> Juliet Saints do not move, though grant for prayers' sake.

28

ROMEO Then move not while my prayer's effect I take.

> [*Kissing her.*]

Thus from my lips, by thine, my sin is purg'd.

JULIET Then have my lips the sin that they have took.

ROMEO Sin from my lips? O trespass sweetly urg'd!

Give me my sin again.

> [*Kissing her again.*]

JULIET   You kiss by th' book.

> (1.5.93–110)

Because this exchange is regarded as a poem-within-the-play, it is commonly quoted as a fourteen-line passage, ending with the strong closing couplet of the sonnet that underscores the moment of the first kiss. The dramatic unit, however, contains eighteen lines: the beat continues for another quatrain as though the desire of the lovers had burst the bonds of the form, spun it out beyond itself, forced it to permit them that second forbidden kiss. In the eighteen-line entity Shakespeare seems to be playing with the tensions between the dramatic unit and the poetic unit.

One of the strongest unifying forces in this beat is its religious imagery. The words saint/pilgrim/palmer, prayer/faith/sin, plus the associated hands/palms/lips which perform the pilgrim's office of prayer, are woven into the dialogue in intricate patterns. Through them the beat receives continuity as well as coherence.

In the exchange between Olivia and the clown, Feste, in *Twelfth Night*, the witty manipulations of terms of address – madonna and fool – offer another example of Shakespeare's use of word repetition:

CLOWN Good madonna, give me leave to prove you a fool.

OLIVIA Can you do it?

CLOWN Dexteriously, good madonna.

OLIVIA Make your proof.

CLOWN I must catechize you for it, madonna. Good my mouse of virtue, answer me.

OLIVIA Well, sir, for want of other idleness, I'll bide your proof.

CLOWN Good madonna, why mourn'st thou?

OLIVIA Good fool, for my brother's death.

CLOWN I think his soul is in hell, madonna.

OLIVIA I know his soul is in heaven, fool.

CLOWN The more fool, madonna, to mourn for your brother's soul, being in heaven. Take away the fool, gentlemen.

> (1.5.57–72)

This is the small climactic unit of a sequence on the same subject (the banter about fools and folly occupies lines 1–98). But this small unit is

29

self-contained; Feste announces his intention to prove a certain point, succeeds in doing so, and has his final crow. After line 72 the subject changes; the next beat deals with Malvolio's puritanical response to foolery. The repetition of key words (madonna, fool) becomes an important binding device. These are but two examples of a device that is used to good effect in beats throughout the canon.

Another technique for marking out a beat unit through language also occurs regularly in Shakespeare's plays. Here a phrase or sentence from the beginning of the beat is repeated at or near its conclusion. For convenience we shall call this the technique of *enclosing*. The enclosing practice adds both clarity and order to the action and gives the beat a finished quality. There are examples of it everywhere. In the *Twelfth Night* beat excerpted above, the phrasing of Feste's opening line, "Good madonna, give me leave to prove you a fool," is echoed in his closing line, "Take away the fool, gentlemen." In the Claudius/Laertes beats examined earlier, where the beats are no longer differentiated by exits and entrances, Shakespeare employs the device to call attention to the logical stages of Claudius's persuasion. In every case, the opening lines reverberate in the closing lines of the beat:

> *Opening*: Will you be rul'd by me?
> *Closing*:   My lord, I will be rul'd.

> *Opening*: You have been talk'd of since your travel much,
>   And that in Hamlet's hearing for a quality
>   Wherein they say you shine. Your sum of parts
>   Did not together pluck such envy from him
>   As did that one. . .
> *Closing*:   Sir, this report of his
>   Did Hamlet so envenom with his envy. . .

> *Opening*: Laertes was your father dear to you?
>   Or are you like the painting of a sorrow,
>   A face without a heart?
> *Closing*: What would you undertake
>   To show yourself indeed your father's son
>   More than in words?

This finishing detail is most often discovered in finely wrought sequences where the beats have been developed with extreme care – but not only there. The routine entrance beat wherein Lucio seeks admittance into the convent in *Measure for Measure*, because of its simplicity and directness, also provides a lucid example of the enclosing technique:

> Lucio (*Within.*) *Ho! Peace be in this place!*
> Isabella   *Who's that which calls?*

FRANCISCA It is a man's voice. Gentle Isabella,
Turn you the key, and know his business of him;
You may, I may not; you are yet unsworn.
When you have vow'd, you must not speak with men
But in the presence of the prioress;
Then if you speak, you must not show your face,
Or if you show your face, you must not speak.
He calls again; I pray you answer him.   *Exit.*
    ISABELLA *Peace and prosperity! Who is't that calls?*

                                                          (1.4.6–15)

Here (and in similar beats throughout the canon) the enclosing is so distinct it cannot be accidental: Shakespeare is obviously indicating a beginning and an end.

Shakespeare's language often gives solid clues to beat boundaries and, in doing so, offers additional evidence that beats are his creations and not those of the director or critic. But while the rhetorical devices used to maintain coherence within the beat can reveal the seams between beat units, they rarely determine them. Beat function and beat motive are the more reliable determinants.

At this point we can pull together our definition of Shakespeare's beat. The beat is a group of lines joined together by a common purpose (generally to introduce, intensify, sustain, or conclude an action) and thereby distinguishable from other beats with which it is grouped. In each beat a single character is usually given the *active* or *propelling* role, this of course being differentiated from the secondary or *responding* role. The structure of the beat derives from the motive of that propelling character. This dominant motive, the *beat motive*, provides momentum and direction, linking the beat to adjacent actions. Additional motives may abound within any beat, speech, or line, but they always operate to support (not challenge) the motive that unifies the beat. Linguistic devices, such as the threading of a key word through the beat or the mirroring of an opening line in some closing line, are frequently added to give further coherence to the unit as unit. Not all of these indicators are present in every beat. But those that *are* work in combination to endow a beat with a readily detectable integrity as a unit.

3

Ancillary beats: the interval beat, the interpolated beat, the linking beat

I

If the sequence must be distinguished from the scene because the sequence contains the action the players must play, then sequence boundaries must also be located, for the actors cannot very well play an action without knowing exactly where it begins and ends. Only when the boundaries are made clear can the sequence be examined as a self-contained whole. And only when the sequence is seen as a whole can its own unique rhythms be accurately reproduced. How, exactly, does one locate a sequence?

The playwright did not intend each sequence to call attention to its independence, and part of the art of constructing sequences consists of joining them so smoothly that the transitions between them will not be noticed. There are few obvious end-stops: sequence boundaries are not meant to show in the finished production any more than in the printed text. Yet if the units are to be correctly articulated, if the performance is to convey to its audience the dramatic rhythms that make the play a play, then the people involved in the performance should have a sound awareness of where sequence boundaries fall. Any experienced play-reader will know instinctively that an action is unfolding long before he consciously isolates it. But while intuition will always remain essential to the analysis of action, much of the intuitive process can be raised to a conscious level. The next five chapters describe those playwriting devices that give the intuitive faculty its clues.

The three most reliable ways of discovering a sequence action are interdependent and applied simultaneously in practice. Nevertheless, for clarity's sake, they must be discussed one at a time. When an action is sensed, how can it be identified? The first method is to remove from the text all the extraneous, or "ancillary" beats, those that obviously have to do with some other action. All foreign matter is extracted: what remains constitutes a sequence. The second method is to study the introductory and concluding sections of the action. In them Shakespeare usually explains the goals of the sequence. The third and most organic method is to formulate the dramatic question upon which Shakespeare has structured the intensification. Every sequence has its own dramatic question, which fixes its direction and determines its length.

Though this process of identifying a sequence is a three-step one, it is not linear but circular. Each step depends on the others. Before the reader can identify ancillary material, he should comprehend the dramatic action the material is ancillary to – how it intensifies, what question holds it together. He cannot do this, however, without having thoroughly studied the introductions and conclusions that explain where the action is going. Yet an introduction or a conclusion may be overlooked if the sequence begins or ends with a series of ancillary beats. There seems to be no way out of (or into) this circle. Fortunately, in practice, the mind processes information from all three areas at once.

All three methods require close study, and we begin, in this chapter, with the first. Some sequences are weighted down with extraneous material. If those beats which are not integral to the action can be distinguished and set aside temporarily, the substance of the sequence will stand revealed. In interpreting Shakespeare's action it can be useful to identify and isolate the ancillary beats.

What is an ancillary beat? We have seen in chapter 2 that every beat has a function within the sequence to which it belongs. But beat functions fall into different categories. Actually, there are two species of the genus *beat* – the sequential beat and the ancillary beat. *Sequential beats* are those which advance the action of a given sequence or otherwise contribute to its development. Some introduce or summarize; some increase tension, sustain or release it; some simply help characters on or off the stage. All of these beat types work together *within the context of the sequence* to create the dramatic effect; remove any one of them from the sequence and you mar the whole. *Ancillary beats*, on the other hand, play no integral part in the build of a sequence but are inserted into it to solve other dramaturgical problems – to cover an interval of time, for example, or to supply information that, while not important enough to require development in a full sequence, is necessary to prepare the audience for some impending action; even (sometimes) simply to link one sequence more closely to another.[1]

Because ancillary beats create irregularities in sequence structure, they have the potential to confuse. It might even be said that their tendency to obscure the normal unit structure explains, almost by itself, why sequences have never been accorded a prominent place in structural analyses of Shakespearean drama.

II

Just as sequential beats have specialized functions, so also do ancillary beats. These functions are fairly obvious and often overlap, but here too things become clearer if the individual functions are distinguished. We shall examine three kinds of ancillary beat – the interval beat, the interpolated beat, and the linking beat.

What is the function of the *interval beat* and how does our awareness of it facilitate unit analysis? Consider the interval that occurs in the following sequence from *Antony and Cleopatra* and notice how Shakespeare creates a special beat to cover it. This sequence (four scenes long) runs from 4.10.1 to 4.13.10. At a certain point in the sequence Antony, seeking a better vantage point from which to observe the battle between his forces and Caesar's, announces to Scarus his intention to climb to "where yond pine does stand." He leaves the stage, then re-enters some moments later crying "All is lost!" Antony's temporary absence from the stage creates a gap of time that must somehow be filled. Shakespeare keeps Scarus on stage to carry on in soliloquy:

> Swallows have built
> In Cleopatra's sails their nests. The augurers
> Say they know not, they cannot tell, look grimly,
> And dare not speak their knowledge. Antony
> Is valiant, and dejected, and by starts
> His fretted fortunes give him hope and fear
> Of what he has, and has not.

$$(4.12.3-9)$$

Shakespeare takes advantage of the need to cover an interval by giving Scarus a speech that defines Antony's current psychological state, associates that state with Antony's declining position on Fortune's wheel, and by dwelling upon the "mighty opposites" of hope and fear weaves another strand into the play's pattern of paradoxes. All this is accomplished in only seven lines. The interval is short, yet long enough for us to believe that Antony's "All is lost!" and his deductions about Cleopatra immediately thereafter come in response to events actually witnessed from "yond pine." Yet because Scarus's lines are never heard by Antony, they remain relatively independent of the developing action. They certainly enrich the texture, but they do not affect the action. Whatever tension builds up here stems from our expectation of Antony's return, not from what Scarus says. Clearly, in Scarus's speech we have an ancillary beat. And that beat has a particular function – to fill an interval of time.

The value of the interval beat is nicely demonstrated in the opening scene of *Othello* where Iago and Roderigo inform Brabantio of his daughter's elopement. Brabantio receives the news on the upper stage and must then make an offstage descent from the balcony to the main stage below. As Brabantio leaves the upper level he announces his intention to "call up all my people" to help locate his daughter, and when he reappears on "the street" he comes accompanied by a band of "servants and torches." Not only must Shakespeare give Brabantio time to make the descent. He must also consider the expectations of the audience; they must feel that Brabantio has had time between his exit above and his entrance below to summon assistance.

The necessary interval beat is carefully provided: Shakespeare has Iago make use of Brabantio's absence from the stage to conclude his devious arrangements with Roderigo. Unlike Iago's previous dialogue in the sequence, this farewell speech to Roderigo (1.1.144–59) is not part of the sequential action. Not that the lines with which Iago fills the interval could be cut – far from it. They are, however, cleverly positioned to create the illusion of passing time. Sufficient theater time elapses during this conference so that no one is jarred when Brabantio appears with the beginnings of a search party already gathered.

A well-written interval beat expands not only stage time but stage space, for the audience, while listening to the dialogue that fills the interval, unconsciously accepts the fact that there is a sea battle going on and a hilltop from which Antony can view it, or that Brabantio's palace does indeed have inner chambers within which he is actively rousing his household. But though the interval beat enhances the stage illusion, that illusion is fragile: if the interval is inadequate, the illusion collapses. In order to believe that an offstage action is occurring in "real" time and in "real" space, an audience needs sufficient "psychological" or "theater" time to allow a completed action to recede, slightly, into the "past." Some distraction must occur to spread out time and space. The distraction must be absorbing enough to create the sense of a *lapse* of time, so that the interval is transformed, on the stage, into an indeterminate period and therefore becomes, in the drama, that period of time needed for the character to have accomplished his journey.[2]

The dramaturgical importance of the interval beat shows clearest when we see the effects of its absence. A serious flaw exists in *Hamlet* because too little adjustment-time is provided for the audience between the end of 3.3, where Hamlet leaves Claudius at prayer, and the beginning of 3.4, where Hamlet stabs the hidden Polonius and then asks "Is it the King?" Scholars and playgoers alike find it difficult to take

Hamlet at his word when he says of the Polonius he has just killed, "I took thee for thy better." Shakespeare certainly means us to believe Hamlet. We have difficulty in doing so, however, because Hamlet exits before Claudius does and re-enters almost immediately to Gertrude: Claudius would not have had sufficient "time" to reach the Queen's room before Hamlet does. Had Hamlet been detained for the space of an interval beat his lines would have greater credibility. Fortunately, such miscalculations are rare.

To become aware of how many familiar passages occur as interval beats is to appreciate their main advantage – while apparently only covering an interval they invariably enrich the dramatic texture. We might never have had Jacques's ruminations on the seven ages of man (2.7.136–66) had not Shakespeare had to fill a time interval while Orlando went out to fetch old Adam to the forest meal. Hamlet's controversial remarks to Horatio about the effects of "some vicious mole of nature" on a man's general reputation (1.4.7–38) come in a beat that marks time between the arrival of the two on the ramparts and the appearance of the Ghost. One of the most effective interval beats in Shakespeare occurs when Lennox describes the unruly night, the prophesying of "dire combustion and confused events / New hatch'd to th' woeful time" (2.3.52–63), while the audience awaits Macduff's emergence from the bloody chamber in which Duncan lies dead to reveal just how woeful the time indeed is. In these interval beats Shakespeare has redeemed time while marking it.[3]

Failure to make allowances for the auxiliary nature of the interval beat can lead to inadequacies in structural analyses of Shakespeare's action. When one of these beats creates enough lively activity in the middle of a sequence, for example, the tendency will be to view the action on either side of it as disconnected. This can result in the disruption of a dramatic action that is in fact whole. When analyzing the structure of the tavern scene of *I Henry IV* in terms of phases or dialogue units (but unmindful of Shakespeare's way with interval beats), Emrys Jones made this kind of error. Of the section in which Sir John Bracy turns up in search of Prince Hal, Jones writes: "Now the Hostess enters, and Falstaff goes out to see the 'nobleman of the court,' while Peto and Bardolph tell Hal of their stratagems (275–316). This is the bridge passage which effects a complete change of subject. Falstaff returns and announces the northern and Welsh rebellions (317–62)."[4] Jones has split the sequence in half. For him there are *two* dialogue-units (or sequences) here.

In fact this unit constitutes a single sequence. In it Shakespeare uses a variation on his typical "reporting" structure – a figure (Sir John Bracy) arrives from the court with a message, and, after enough delay to stimulate audience interest in the message, the report is finally given. The variation transforms this sequence from the routine to the satisfying. Instead of bringing the King's courier on stage, with all his dreary formality, Shakespeare has Hal send Falstaff out to hear the message, so that ultimately the report is delivered not by some dour official but by the mischievous fat rogue. A potentially dull "reporting" speech reaches the stage salted with Falstaffian witticisms, giving us a "sprightly . . . Douglas that runs a' horseback up a hill perpendicular," and so on. True, in the middle of this sequence structure there is a 26-line beat containing some delightful banter between the Prince and Bardolph (2.4.298–325), Jones's so-called "bridge passage." But this beat merely covers an interval. It provides psychological time for us to envision Falstaff interviewing Sir John Bracy out there "in the courtyard." If the critic fails to perceive this subordinate function of the interval beat, he may, like Jones, chop the sequence into arbitrary sections, missing completely the clear dramatic build from the arrival of the courier to the delivery of Falstaff's report.

Another lesson in Shakespeare's use of the interval beat and its relation to the sequential action is provided by 4.1.104–70 of *The Merchant of Venice*. Here Shakespeare dedicates an entire sequence (the second one of the scene) to the business of getting Portia onto the stage as Balthazar. The sequence begins when the Duke announces his intention to dismiss the court unless help comes from some "learned doctor," climaxes with Portia's entrance, and concludes when she takes her place in the courtroom. But Portia is as yet lodged at a nearby inn, while her "clerk," Nerissa, has arrived at the court so recently that the Duke remains unaware of her presence. To create this sequence successfully Shakespeare has to cover three intervals, allowing time for a messenger to admit Nerissa to the courtroom (111–18), for the Duke to peruse the letter Nerissa brings him (121–42) and for the dispatched escort to give Portia "courteous conduct to this place" (149–67). Consequently, intervals occupy an extensive territory in this sequence. Filling the first is a touching exchange between Bassanio and Antonio that proves their deep friendship. To fill the second, Shakespeare provides a contrasting (but comic) enmity, as Shylock whets his knife and Gratiano rails at his inhumanity. In the last, the Duke reads a letter to the court in which Bellario gives an account of the famous "Balthazar" Portia is impersonating. Given these three separate interval beats, two of them almost twenty lines in length, an accurate analysis of the dramatic thrust of Shakespeare's action will depend upon careful attention to beat function.

There are strong tensions operating here that are best worked out in rehearsal. But our interest in Shylock should not so dominate the sequence that the introduction of Portia becomes insignificant. Many a production has been muddied by a failure to articulate the throughline being developed here.

The interval beats discussed so far fill time gaps *within* the sequence; each has been culled from the middle of an action. Time lapses are more likely to arise between the conclusion of one action and the start of another, as in *Richard II*, where Aumerle must "travel" from the Duke of York's palace to Windsor Castle between the end of 5.2 and the beginning of 5.3. A useful interval of time is provided by the beat which divides Aumerle's exit from his re-entrance: in 5.3.1–22 King Henry is discovered complaining to his lords of "my unthrifty son." Another time lapse worth examining occurs between two sequences in the third act of *Othello* – 3.1.1–56 and 3.3.1–34. At the end of sequence 3.1.1–56, Cassio, who has been creating a stir outside Desdemona's house in an effort to obtain an interview with her, is admitted by Emilia. The following action, sequence 3.3.1–34, opens some while later. As Cassio's plea that Desdemona intercede for him need not be repeated on stage to an audience already well aware of the favor he seeks, Shakespeare depicts Cassio and Desdemona in the concluding stages of their conversation. The audience must be convinced, however, that enough time has elapsed for Cassio not only to have moved from the street into Desdemona's presence but also to have explained the reason for his visit. Thus, Shakespeare has inserted between the two sequences the beat labeled in the text as 3.2:

> *Enter* OTHELLO, IAGO *and* GENTLEMEN
> OTHELLO These letters give, Iago, to the pilot,
> And by him do my duties to the Senate.
> That done, I will be walking on the works;
> Repair there to me.
> IAGO   Well, my good lord, I'll do 't.
> OTHELLO This fortification, gentlemen, shall we see 't?
> GENTLEMEN We'll wait upon your lordship.
>
> *Exeunt.*
> (3.2.1–6)

This "brief but apparently irrelevant scene," as it has been called,[5] reminds us of the military and political world that will intrude, soon, into the domestic affairs of these characters, but it has an important function at the dramaturgical level as well, providing some very necessary psychological time between the two sequences.

In the *Othello* example, Shakespeare uses the interval beat to clarify the demarcation between sequences. But often the interval at the end of a sequence disguises sequence boundaries so that the juncture goes unnoticed. Awareness of this function of the interval beat clarifies transitional points and prevents the confusions that result when two adjoining sequences are erroneously staged as one. In *Twelfth Night* 1.5 there is a telling example of the transitional interval. The sequence in which Viola (as Cesario) plies her wit at the gate to obtain an audience with Olivia ends when Olivia finally sends Malvolio out to usher Cesario in. The illusion of offstage space so efficiently established through the dialogue would be dissipated if Malvolio and Cesario returned too quickly. Shakespeare concludes the sequence with a bit of stage business to cover the interval:

> OLIVIA Call in my gentlewoman.
> MALVOLIO Gentlewoman, my lady calls.   *Exit.*
>
> *Enter* MARIA.
> OLIVIA Give me my veil; come throw it o'er my face.
> We'll once more hear Orsino's embassy.
>
> (1.5.163–6)

Then – new sequence – Cesario enters. The beat in which Olivia dons her veil marks, or rather hides, the boundary between a sequence whose main purpose is to introduce Viola into Olivia's court (1.5.99–166) and a separate sequence in which Viola and Olivia actually meet (1.5.167–311).

Recognition of this frequently used method of effecting transitions so smoothly that one action flows imperceptibly into the next is of immense help both in detecting sequential actions and in pinpointing sequence boundaries.

III

The interval beat must be differentiated from the interpolated beat: the two are not necessarily identical. In the purest of interval beats, the content is often thoughtful, as in Scarus's reflection on Antony, or imaginative, as in Jacques's "ages of man" monologue: the lines could conceivably have been inspired by the need to stretch out time. This second type of ancillary beat has the more specific function of supplying required information.

Certain necessities of playwriting demand the insertion of information that is not strictly part of the sequential action. The need to foreshadow a

39

future event, to prepare for the entrance of a new character, to provide some information too unimportant to warrant extended treatment, to permit a character to voice unspoken thoughts – any of these necessities may require a digression. In such cases Shakespeare will use an *interpolated beat*, a beat which gives information that is pertinent but not organically related to the specific action of the sequence. Often the information is so skillfully blended into the sequence that only careful analysis of the surrounding action reveals its auxiliary nature.

An unmistakable example of the interpolated beat occurs in the final sequence of *Othello* 2.3, where Roderigo unexpectedly intrudes upon Iago. This sequence, occupying lines 259 to 388, contains the dialogue between Cassio and Iago in which the former laments the loss of his reputation and the latter advises him how to regain it, and it concludes with a coda where Iago, in soliloquy, informs us that he will arrange matters with Cassio so that "this honest fool / Plies Desdemona to repair his fortune" and thus undoes them both. No one is thinking about Roderigo, least of all Iago.

But the playwright cannot permit anyone to forget Roderigo. In a forthcoming sequence (4.2.172–245) Roderigo will threaten to expose Iago's treachery, and this insurrection of a formerly docile dupe cannot come out of nowhere. Shakespeare prepares us for it here in 2.3 with an interpolated beat. Iago's soliloquy is interrupted: Roderigo enters to express his discontent with Iago's treatment of him (2.3.362–82). Roderigo is livid – and rebelling. Iago easily dominates him, of course, and after ridding himself of the intruder continues with his thoughts as though there has been no interruption. It is almost as if the soliloquy had been written as a complete unit and the Iago/Roderigo beat inserted later, yet the interpolation is in no way jarring. The flow of events seems not only plausible but even more natural for the interruption. Still, in this brief beat, Shakespeare has deliberately interpolated extrinsic material to prepare us for Roderigo's role in act 4.

Sequences often contain implants of this kind. Caesar's immortal lines characterizing the "lean and hungry" Cassius form an interpolated beat (1.2.190–214) in a sequence where Casca's report of events in the marketplace constitutes the major line of action (1.2.178–322). Claudius receives the Ambassadors newly returned from Norway in a beat (2.2.58–85) carefully spliced into the sequence displaying Polonius's prolix revelation that he has discovered the cause of Hamlet's madness (2.2.40–170). The various announcements of offstage deaths at the end of *King Lear* – Gloucester's (5.3.180–200), Goneril's and Regan's (223–33), and Edmund's (296) – belong in the category. So, of course, does Brutus's revelation to Cassius of the death of Portia (4.3.143–58). If such interpolated beats are detected and temporarily set aside, the dramatic structure of any sequential action is more easily perceived.

This sampling of interpolated beats shows Shakespeare's versatility in working ancillary beats into sequential action. There are two dramaturgical situations, however, that actually invite interpolations. One is the interval required for adjustment-time. For this reason, the interval beat and the interpolated beat often appear in combination. Just as the time-gaps in the action facilitate the insertion of interpolated beats into the text, so also does any juncture between major units of action. To minimize the interruption, Shakespeare often slips interpolated beats in at such transitional points, especially where one sequence of action is ending and another just beginning. Thus placed, they offer the additional advantage of creating irregular patterns in the action, for this very irregularity increases the sense that events are unfolding in a spontaneous and therefore lifelike manner.

An obvious example, useful because the technique shows through so blatantly, is the 19-line passage in which Malcolm describes England's saintly King Edward (*Macbeth* 4.3.140–59). The material in this beat has no sequential role in the surrounding action; the beat is indisputably extraneous. Political and thematic considerations seem to have dictated its presence. The playwright, besides complimenting England in general and James I in particular, probably wished Edward's holiness to reflect favorably upon Malcolm – hence, the interpolation. Edward's goodness, like the dead King Duncan's, also provides one more touchstone against which Macbeth's atrocities can be judged. But why is the beat placed precisely here? What better place than at the boundary between two sequences! The interview between Malcolm and Macduff has just concluded; Malcolm has tested Macduff and found him trustworthy (4.3.1–139). Ross will enter shortly to report the slaughter of Macduff's family, initiating a new action (4.3.159–240). The beat is inserted at this convenient stopping point, where besides fulfilling its political and thematic functions it renders the abrupt joint between these two sequences less apparent.[6]

A more successful balance between sequence and interruption is achieved when Gertrude appears on stage to tell us how Ophelia died (4.7.162–84). Shakespeare does not allow the Queen's entrance to intrude, as it might in real life, into the skillful but risky manipulation of Laertes by Claudius. Rather, the action of that persuasion sequence is allowed to run its dramatic course. Only then does the Queen enter, the interpolated beat providing the impetus for Laertes to leave the stage, with Claudius following after him. Located thus, it also prepares us for the opening line of the next sequence: "Is she to be buried in Christian burial?" The news of Ophelia's drowning definitely constitutes an interpolated beat, thrust between two sequences. Yet the adjoining units blend together so well that the dominant impression is "how easily the action flows" rather than "how carefully the units have been ordered."

Interpolated beats, then, are employed most frequently to fill time-gaps and to mask the junctures between sequences. Both practices present possible pitfalls for anyone who is analyzing action. In the first case the danger is the same as with the interval beat: the interpolated beat, if dropped into the middle of a sequence, may be distracting enough on the page to give the impression that two sequences exist where there is only one. The second case involves the opposite danger. When it disguises a break between sequences, the interpolated beat may not seem distracting at all; separate actions may merge so smoothly that attempts will be made to play them as one, when they are really two. In either case the true rhythms of the action are distorted. Identifying interpolated beats helps prevent such errors.

IV

The insight that interpolated beats are often sandwiched between sequences may not in itself be startlingly new, but perhaps the awareness that grows from study of a sizable sampling of them is: the discovery of how much these beats teach about Shakespeare's habit of masking sequence boundaries. To broaden that awareness still further we will now investigate another of Shakespeare's masking techniques.

There remains a third type of ancillary beat, equally ubiquitous in Shakespeare's canon and used almost exclusively at transitional points between sequences. This is the linking beat. The *linking beat* is a beat that belongs to one sequence (called here the *parent* sequence) but has been lifted out of its expected location and set down into an adjacent sequence (the *host* sequence). Its function is to lock the host sequence tightly to the parent sequence. To hide the seams of his unit structure Shakespeare uses this linking technique far more deliberately than any other device.

In Shakespeare's multipartite scenes this third type of ancillary beat is often found in abundance, effecting smooth transitions between sequences. Take, for instance, *Julius Caesar* 2.1. The scene has three sequences. It opens with Brutus in the garden of his villa mulling over proposals made to him by Cassius. That meditation supplies the content for sequence 1 (2.1.1–85). Brutus goes on in sequence 2 (60–233) to receive the conspirators who are plotting Caesar's death; at this meeting they plan their strategies. Sequence 3 (233–309) brings in Portia, who begs Brutus to "make me acquainted with your cause of grief." The scene concludes with a fourteen-line epilogue (310–34). How does Shakespeare utilize linking beats in this three-sequence scene?

Take first the point of division between sequences 1 and 2. If we look only at those beats which bring sequence 1 to its conclusion, we find nothing unusual. Shakespeare climaxes the sequence with Brutus's decision to join the conspirators, then rounds out the action by revealing the anguish hidden beneath Brutus's apparently logical reasoning. This final section of the meditating sequence becomes a telling comment on all that has gone before. It unfolds in two beats – the first focusing specifically on internal terrors, the second on external ones. Examining the concluding beats in strict sequential order, we find nothing exceptional about the beat arrangement.

The same predictability is found if we examine *only* the introductory beats of sequence 2, the plotting sequence. To initiate that action Shakespeare writes a cue beat which foreshadows the entrance of new characters. He writes a second entrance beat that describes the clandestine behavior of the newcomers. As Brutus informs us, "They are the faction," and in the third beat of the sequence they all come in – Cassius, Casca, Decius, Cinna, Metellus, and Trebonius; Cassius makes the introductions.

Had the beats from each sequence appeared in this order, sequence boundaries would be patently obvious. But these beats do not occur in strict sequential order; Shakespeare has deliberately *altered* the normal beat order. Instead of completing one sequence before beginning the next, he chooses to insert the introductory beats from the new sequence between the concluding beats of the closing sequence so that, at the point of juncture, beats from the later sequence alternate with beats from the earlier one. Knocking is heard at the gate just after Brutus makes his climactic decision to strike down Caesar and before his concluding soliloquy, twenty-four lines before sequence 1 closes. Further, the conspirators' arrival is announced to Brutus not at the end of his soliloquy, as might be expected, but in the middle of it. The concluding soliloquy has been divided and the entrance beat for the conspirators placed between its two parts, so that the announcement of the new sequence provides the impetus for the closing beat of the preceding one. Far from running their separate courses, the two sequences keep intersecting:

LUCIUS *Sir, March is wasted fifteen days.* [*Knock within.*]
BRUTUS *'Tis good. Go to the gate, somebody knocks.*

(Beat 2.1.59–60)

BRUTUS Since Cassius first did whet me against Caesar,
I have not slept.
Between the acting of a dreadful thing
And the first motion, all the interim is
Like a phantasma or a hideous dream.
The Genius and the mortal instruments
Are then in council; and the state of a man,
Like to a little kingdom, suffers then
The nature of an insurrection.

(Beat 2.1.61–9)

LUCIUS *Sir, 'tis your brother Cassius at the door.*
Who doth desire to see you.
BRUTUS   *Is he alone?*
LUCIUS *No, sir, there are more with him.*
BRUTUS   *Do you know them?*
LUCIUS *No, sir, their hats are pluck'd about their ears.*
And half their faces buried in their cloaks,
That by no means I may discover them
By any mark of favor.
BRUTUS   *Let 'em enter.*

(Beat 2.1.70–6)

BRUTUS They are the faction. O Conspiracy
Sham'st thou to show thy dang'rous brow by night,
When evils are most free? O then, by day
Where wilt thou find a cavern dark enough
To mask thy monstrous visage? Seek none, Conspiracy!
Hide it in smiles and affability;
For if thou path, thy native semblance on,
Not Erebus itself were dim enough
To hide thee from prevention.

(Beat 2.1.77–85)

CASSIUS *I think we are too bold upon your rest.*
Good morrow, Brutus, do we trouble you?. . .[etc.]

(Beat 2.1. 86 ff.)

Shakespeare's technique here is to alternate a beat from one sequence with a beat from the other, effectively deflecting any expectation of full closure at the end of the meditating sequence. Sequences 1 and 2 are so successfully interlocked that the action appears to flow continuously from one to the other.

Notice that in the parent sequence the linking beat serves a normal sequential function; only in the *host* sequence does it become a *linking* beat. In the meditating sequence (2.1.1–85), beats 59–60 and 70–6 must be viewed as linking beats, for the news that the conspirators have arrived serves an ancillary function in that action: the announcement is in essence an interruption of Brutus's soliloquy. Similarly, in the plotting sequence (2.1.60–233), beats 61–9 and 77–85 are linking beats, for Brutus's soliloquy has little to do, technically, with the planning of Caesar's murder during the conspirators' meeting. Each linking beat has an ancillary function only in the sequence into which it has been inserted.

Such linking beats, concealed within sequences and therefore not normally detected, make sequence boundaries appear vague, even unstable, but they are not, even if they are meant to appear so. The superimposed illusion of shapelessness enhances the real-life quality of drama. But the clarity of the structure is easily detected once one realizes that this alternation of beats from different sequences at sequence boundaries is a standard feature of Shakespeare's technique.

Still more can be learned from the linking beats of *Julius Caesar* 2.1. Further examination of that scene suggests a need to broaden our definition of the linking beat slightly. There are times when Shakespeare moves the linking beat farther away from its parent sequence. The linking beat is occasionally inserted not *within* the host sequence but *before* or *after* it. In such cases a full sequence intervenes between the linking beat and the related action. Take, for example, beats 2.1.229–33, where Brutus muses again on the "fantasies / Which busy care draws in the brains of men," and 2.1.310–34, which treats of Brutus's meeting with Caius Ligarius. Both are concluding beats but each stands a full sequence away from the action which it concludes.

The Caius Ligarius beat with which Shakespeare ends this scene can hardly be considered the concluding beat of the Portia sequence it follows. That action dramatizes Portia's concern about her husband's odd behavior. It climaxes when, persuaded of Portia's worthiness, Brutus agrees to acquaint her with "all the charactery of my sad brows." By the time Ligarius enters, Portia has left the stage. Nor can the arrival of Ligarius be said to initiate a new sequence; he remains on stage for only one beat, and comes on as much to lead Brutus off as to strengthen the impression of Brutus's popularity. The beat has stronger affiliations with the plotting sequence than with the Portia sequence.

In fact, the beat links together all three sequences of the scene by forming a beat-length epilogue. Ligarius is first mentioned at the conclusion of sequence 2, where Metellus suggests to Brutus that "Caius Ligarius doth bear Caesar hard" and would probably support the conspiracy. The task of enlisting Ligarius is left to Brutus. But Shakespeare withholds the beat in which Ligarius is recruited. He reserves it for the end of the scene, in which position it revives and once more concludes the plotting sequence. Embraced thus by the linking epilogue, the Portia sequence is firmly locked into the scene. As the Ligarius beat indicates, a linking beat can stand a whole sequence removed from its parent sequence.

The classic example of such interlocking occurs in *Othello* 3.3, where Shakespeare inserts his linking beat ahead of the preceding sequence. The pertinent passage is well known:

> Iago Hah? I like not that.
> Othello　　　　　　　What dost thou say?
> Iago Nothing, my lord; or if – I know not what.
> Othello Was not that Cassio parted from my wife?
> Iago Cassio, my lord? No, sure, I cannot think it,
> That he would steal away so guilty-like,
> Seeing your coming.
> Othello　　　　　I do believe 'twas he.

(3.3.35–40)

This passage – a linking beat – forms the first beat of a sequence that will not begin until 3.3.93. But it has been inserted as Iago's comment on a sequence (3.3.1–34) whose principal business, in terms of the play's action, is to provide Cassio with Desdemona's assurance that once she "vows a friendship" she will "perform it / To the last article." Another whole sequence (3.3.41–92), where Desdemona urges Othello to recall Cassio, intervenes between the linking beat and the sequence it introduces.

Though the linking beat is positioned a full sequence early, the result is predictable. Sequence boundaries are disguised, the units locked together. This example illustrates the extraordinary effectiveness of Shakespeare's interlocking technique. How natural it seems that Othello and Iago enter as they do. We hardly notice the triple duty that their entrance in this ancillary beat performs – the beat provides the excuse for Cassio's departure, it puts Othello onto the stage for the sequence in which Desdemona will turn her promise to Cassio into action, and it brings on Iago so that he is ready at line 93 to begin the temptation. A single linking beat effects so smooth a transition that no one ever notices the several sequence boundaries in this vicinity.

Such interlocking devices, whether at the beginning or at the end of a sequence, wreak havoc with any system of unit analysis (James Hirsh's, for example)[7] that uses the cleared stage as the sole indication of unit boundaries. But if Shakespeare's linking beats are mentally removed and restored to their proper positions, the boundaries between sequences suddenly make perfect sense.

Before leaving this subject of linking and interlocking, we must point out that Shakespeare uses another method of disguising sequence boundaries that also involves interlocking. The method just examined might be called *alternate-beat interlocking* and the related method *fused-beat interlocking*. *Fused beats* are beats in which Shakespeare inserts lines from one beat into the middle of the beat immediately before (or after) it so that the two beats, rather than meeting end to end like railroad cars, are joined internally like the links of a chain. Shakespeare uses this device to interlock beats in the middle of sequences. The beats so joined, however, need not be in the same sequence. If the last beat of any sequence is fused with the first beat of the following sequence, this fused-beat technique will interlock not only the two beats but the two sequences as well.

The passage *Othello* 5.2.84–105 offers a striking example of sequences interlocked by the fusing of two beats: Othello's attempts to stifle the last gasps of Desdemona's breath bring the moving murder sequence to a close. Emilia's pounding upon their chamber door introduces a new sequence, the action of which will throw a different light for Othello on the "justness" of his deed. But the two beats are inseparably fused:

EMILIA *(At the door, [within].) My lord, my lord!*
What ho! my lord, my lord!
OTHELLO What noise is this? Not dead? not yet quite dead?
I that am cruel am yet merciful.
I would not have thee linger in thy pain.
So, so.
     EMILIA *(Within.) What ho! my lord, my lord!*
     OTHELLO   *Who's there?*
     EMILIA *[Within.] O, good my lord, I would speak a word with you!*
     OTHELLO *Yes, – 'Tis Emilia. – By and by.* – She's dead.
'Tis like she comes to speak of Cassio's death:
The noise was high. Hah, no more moving?
Still as the grave. *Shall she come in? Were't good?*
I think she stirs again. No. *What's best to do?*
If she come in, she'll sure speak to my wife.
My wife, my wife! what wife! I have no wife.
O insupportable! O heavy hour!
Methinks it should be now a huge eclipse
Of sun and moon, and that th' affrighted globe
Did yawn at alteration.

47

EMILIA [*Within.*] *I do beseech you*
That I may speak with you. O, good my lord!
OTHELLO *I had forgot thee. O, come in, Emilia. –*
Soft, by and by, let me the curtains draw. –
Where art thou? [*Unlocks the door.*]

(5.2.84–105)

By fusing the concluding beat of one sequence with the introductory beat of the adjacent one Shakespeare also effectively interlocks two sequences. But it should be borne in mind that fused-beat interlocking and alternate-beat interlocking, although similar in result, differ as radically as the line differs from the beat. The fused beat is created by dropping lines from one beat into another. The linking beat operates at a different level of magnitude, where whole beats are dropped into sequences (not merely lines into beats).

Certainly the impetus to distinguish first between sequential and ancillary beats and then between various forms of the latter comes not from a craving to categorize. Without an awareness of ancillary beats, precise decisions about sequence boundaries are impossible: the boundaries are too skillfully concealed. Awareness of ancillary beat functions eliminates perplexities arising from digressions that come in the middle of sequences and avoids confusion arising from devices used to mask sequence boundaries. It also makes one less apt, on one hand, to violate sequence unity, accidentally splitting an action in half by failing to subordinate some medial interpolation, and less prone, on the other, to run sequences together just because Shakespeare has cleverly disguised the joints between them.

4

Sequential beats: the introductory beat

I

In introducing an action every playwright has to solve the same familiar problems. Getting the characters onto the stage is one of them. Another is orienting the audience to these characters and their concerns. There is also the problem of credibility – supplying believable motives. The playwright can always send characters out onto the stage deep in pertinent conversation, but can he make this artifice seem natural? The problems are obvious, but their solutions should never be taken for granted.

Consider the problems of orientation. They are basic problems, sometimes easily resolved; still, the playwright has to confront them throughout the play. Because drama is an art that takes place in time, updating is a constant necessity. How much time has passed since the characters were last seen? Has anything significant occurred during their absence from the stage? How do matters stand now? Are the characters themselves of the same opinion or in the same state of mind as when last seen, or has some psychological change occurred that must be emphasized? If during the forthcoming sequence a character is to be moved from one state of mind to another, his starting position must be made clear in the introduction. When a character is making his first appearance late in the play, his relationship to the others has to be explained. Any number of details must be attended to in a period of orientation before an action moves forward. The playwright must also establish the new setting. Where are we now? In Venice or in Cyprus? In the palace or on the streets? In the great hall or in the private chamber? What time of day is it? This too is a task to be accomplished in the introductory beats.

What requires emphasis in this context is that Shakespeare creates an introduction not just for each new scene but for every new sequence. This means that one out of every ten or twelve beats in any Shakespeare play will be an introductory beat. It also means that if *Hamlet* 4.5 has two

49

sequences, we will find two different introductions in that scene, or if *I Henry IV* 2.4 has five sequences, we will find in it five separate introductions. This regular occurrence of introductory beats at the beginnings of sequences is further evidence that the sequence (not the scene) is Shakespeare's basic unit of action.

Some kinds of introductory beat can be noted without extensive comment. Scene-setting beats like those early ones in *Hamlet* that not only place the action but also supply the time and the temperature explain themselves (1.1.1–11, 1.4.1–6). So also do simple entrance beats like the one that brings Horatio and Marcellus into Barnardo's company on the battlements:

> MARCELLUS   Holla, Barnardo!
> BARNARDO   Say –
> What, is Horatio there?
> HORATIO   A piece of him.
> BARNARDO Welcome, Horatio, welcome, good Marcellus.
>
>   (1.1.18–20)

Shakespeare writes many such entrance beats: they halt the action momentarily while the characters exchange routine greetings. Equally transparent are introductory beats which profile a character appearing for the first time – Osric, for example, in the last act of *Hamlet*:

> HAMLET   Dost know this water-fly?
> HORATIO No, my good lord.
> HAMLET Thy state is more gracious, for 'tis a vice to know him. He hath much land, and fertile; let a beast be lord of beasts, and his crib shall stand at the King's mess. 'Tis a chough, but, as I say, spacious in the possession of dirt.
>
>   (5.2.82–8)

Or Sir Toby and Sir Andrew. The two-beat introduction to *Twelfth Night* 1.3 reveals a similar, if longer, focus on personnel. Shakespeare concentrates on acquainting us with a pair of new characters – Sir Toby, who is already present (1.3.1–15), and Sir Andrew, who will shortly appear (1.3.15–42). The more obvious introductory beats, then, set the scene, cover entrances, and profile new characters. While these three tasks may be handled in separate beats, they are sometimes all achieved in one.

What is more central to this study is the extent to which Shakespeare uses the introductory beat to establish the dramatic question of the sequence. If the sequence is an action, it should first tell us what that action is. Some directional signals should be provided. Our survey of sequence beginnings is therefore selective: it will demonstrate the care

Shakespeare takes to establish the subject of each sequence before moving into the rising action.

II

Shakespeare's concern that his audience be properly oriented is indicated by the length of time he is willing to take to set up an action. Let us look first, therefore, at an extended introduction, one long enough to illustrate several different principles. Our example comes from *Coriolanus* 3.3, which begins just after Volumnia has persuaded her son to go back to the Roman people whom he had insulted and apologize. Shakespeare takes us to the marketplace before Coriolanus gets there. On stage are the Tribunes, who will be dominant in this sequence, already planning their strategies. They are to press the charges. Shakespeare next brings in the defendant. And finally he supplies an "audience," the plebeians. Of the 143 lines in the sequence, the first forty are introductory. This is one of Shakespeare's longer introductions. How does he order it?

Shakespeare first introduces Brutus and Sicinius, the Tribunes, who have thirty of the forty lines in the introduction. This section contains three beats. The most important of them, in which Brutus reveals his objectives privately to Sicinius, supplies the motivation for the sequence:

> *Enter* SICINIUS *and* BRUTUS
> BRUTUS In this point charge him home, that he affects
> Tyrannical power. If he evade us there,
> Enforce him with his envy to the people,
> And that the spoil got on the Antiates
> Was ne'er distributed.
> . . .
> Put him to choler straight, he hath been us'd
> Ever to conquer, and to have his worth
> Of contradiction. Being once chaf'd, he cannot
> Be rein'd again to temperance; then he speaks
> What's in his heart, and that is there which looks
> With us to break his neck.
>
> (3.3.1–5. . .25–30)

Brutus is of course speaking about Coriolanus. From Brutus's "Put him to choler straight" we gather that the Tribunes mean to antagonize their enemy, knowing that once aroused he will lose all self-control. Thus is the conflict of the sequence set up. Coriolanus has promised his mother he will speak not "th' matter which your heart prompts you" but soft and gentle words. The Tribunes intend to push him till "he speaks / What's in his heart."

But more exposition is required, some by way of updating, some to foreshadow the planned outcome. Shakespeare therefore inserts in the beat containing Brutus's monologue the Tribunes' conversation with an Aedile, so that Brutus's remarks form an enclosing frame around this section of the introduction. Through the exchange between the Tribunes and the Aedile, Shakespeare provides more introductory information.

In beat 3.3.5–11, the Aedile serves Shakespeare in several ways. First, Shakespeare uses him to smooth the way for Coriolanus's entrance. He presents the Aedile as a messenger, whose role is to report to his superiors. As such, the Aedile helps to bridge the gaps of time and distance between Coriolanus's departure from Volumnia's house and his arrival here. The Tribunes are informed and so is the audience. We are made to picture Coriolanus and certain Senators traveling through the streets of Rome toward the marketplace. When they enter, they will seem to have come from another part of the city, not from the wings of the theater. At the same time Shakespeare uses the Aedile to reveal how actively the Tribunes are pursuing their stated goal:

> SICINIUS   Have you a catalogue
> Of all the voices that we have procur'd,
> Set down by th' pole?
> AEDILE   I have; 'tis ready.
>
> (3.3.8–11)

This again is exposition. The Tribunes' questions indicate that since we last saw them they have been issuing subversive orders to their subordinates. Beyond the mental preparations shown in the Tribunes' private exchanges, these public exchanges with the Aedile reveal that Brutus and Sicinius have made much practical preparation for the forthcoming encounter.

While beat 3.3.5–11 reviews the immediate past, beat 3.3.12–24 hints at the future. Once more the Aedile is useful: satisfied that their previous orders have been carried out, the Tribunes now give the Aedile new instructions, through which Shakespeare makes apparent the Tribunes' determination to manipulate the people and also explains in advance the plebeians' role in the sequence:

> SICINIUS Assemble presently the people hither;
> And when they hear me say, "It shall be so
> I' th' right and strength a' th' commons," be it either
> For death, for fine, or banishment, then let them,
> If I say fine, cry "Fine!"; if death, cry "Death!"
> Insisting on the old prerogative
> And power i' th' truth a' th' cause.
> AEDILE   I shall inform them.

Sequential beats: the introductory beat

BRUTUS And when such time they have begun to cry,
Let them not cease, but with a din confus'd
Enforce the present execution
Of what we chance to sentence.
AEDILE   Very well.
SICINIUS Make them be strong, and ready for this hint
When we shall hap to give't them.
BRUTUS   Go about it.

[*Exit Aedile.*]
(3.3.12–24)

By the time this introductory glance at the Tribunes draws to a close, much has been revealed about their motives and methods. However spontaneous the disruptive events they cause in the sequence may seem, the audience knows that little has been left to chance.

Shakespeare next provides an entrance beat for Coriolanus and his escort:

MENENIUS Calmly, I do beseech you.
CORIOLANUS Ay, as an hostler, that for th' poorest piece
Will bear the knave by th' volume. Th' honor'd gods
Keep Rome in safety, and the chairs of justice
Supplied with worthy men! plant love among 's!
Throng our large temples with the shows of peace,
And not our streets with war!
I SENATOR   Amen, amen.
MENENIUS A noble wish.

(3.3.31–8)

But the beat does more than effect the hero's entrance. In it Shakespeare also establishes the position he will move Coriolanus away from during the sequence. Before allowing the sequence to proceed, he brings forward the promises Coriolanus made in his recent interview with Volumnia. Since this interview has only just ended, the reminder can be brief, yet it is essential. Notice the action Shakespeare has invented to give this position extra emphasis. It is centered on "persuading." Shakespeare makes Menenius active in the beat by setting him up as a persuader. As representative of all the Senators, he beseeches Coriolanus to keep calm. In response Coriolanus agrees to be as obsequious "as an hostler." Shakespeare provides a hint of the shakiness of Coriolanus's resolution in the tone of his "prayer," which has the ring of a desperate attempt to remember his commission more than of sound determination to capitulate. This parental concern of the Senators that Coriolanus "keep calm" and Coriolanus's automatic submission constitute the action upon which the fourth introductory beat is structured.

53

The introduction has presented the objective of the prosecution, to anger Coriolanus, and the objective of the defendant, to remain calm. It now summons in the plebeians, the jury which will pass judgment. This final section of the introduction, beat 5, contains a pure example of the entrance beat: the role of the plebeians in this sequence having been explained by Sicinius in advance (12–24), the plebeians have only to rush in. Even here, though, Shakespeare thinks in terms of action. He does not write *"Enter the Aedile with the Plebeians"* and leave it to the crowd to get itself on stage. He creates a context. He requires the plebeians to pour onto the stage with a thunderous babble, and gives the Aedile the task of hushing them:

> SICINIUS Draw near, ye people.
> AEDILE List to your tribunes. Audience! peace, I say!

> (3.3.39–40)

To guard against a sudden and too artificial silence, he lets this hubbub of the entrance beat spill over into the following beat, thereby interlocking the introduction with the body of the sequence – the crowd must be hushed again at line 41 by both Tribunes ("Peace ho!").

This is a long introduction. Shakespeare is already several beats into the sequence but – notice – the action proper has yet to begin. It starts only with the sixth beat, where Coriolanus interrogates the Tribunes as to the nature and finality of this trial (3.3.41–7). By the end of the sequence Coriolanus will be "proved" guilty and banished. But everything up to line 40 is preparatory.

The standard purposes of a sequence introduction have been accomplished in the five introductory beats. First, the participating groups – Tribunes, Senators, Citizens – have been brought onto the stage in good order and with adequate motivation. Second, the scene has been set. But, above all, the conflict to be developed during the sequence has been established: the Tribunes have declared their intention to make Coriolanus "speak / What's in his heart," and Coriolanus has declared his intention to make a show of peace. Everything is in readiness. When extensive preparation is necessary Shakespeare does not skimp.

III

From an expanded introduction we move to a compressed one. Our second "beginning" features the earnest Polonius in a sequence from the middle of act 2, scene 2. It is the second of six sequences in the scene, coming immediately after Claudius has explained to Rosencrantz and Guildenstern "the need we have to use you" and immediately before

Polonius accosts Hamlet in the fishmonger sequence. Sequence boundaries occur at lines 40 and 170. The motivation behind the action of this unit derives from Polonius, who comes to Claudius and Gertrude to report that he can answer the question currently perplexing Claudius, why is Hamlet mad? Though the question that interests the characters in this sequence is, what is the reason for Hamlet's strange behavior?, the question that the playwright is working with, the question that determines the sequence structure, is slightly different. The playwright catches the interest of his audience with a more specific question, *how will Claudius respond to Polonius's report?*

Consider what this introductory beat must do and how it does it. First, entrances. The King and Queen are already on stage, holding court, but Shakespeare must bring on Polonius, as well as Voltemand and Cornelius, two Ambassadors who are waiting to see Claudius. Motives must be supplied for these entrances, motives which take protocol into consideration. Polonius's desire to apprise the King of Hamlet's love for Ophelia would not be sufficient cause for intruding on royalty; better if Shakespeare gives him access to the King in some other way and then introduces that subject. By arranging matters so that Voltemand and Cornelius arrive from Norway to deliver their report just at this moment, Shakespeare provides a more natural reason for Polonius to approach Claudius: to announce the Ambassadors. By assigning Polonius the "task" of preparing the way for the arrival of Voltemand and Cornelius, Shakespeare makes the Ambassadors' entrances plausible as well. This is a deftly crafted entrance beat.

Second, orientation. Since the Ambassadors' business remains an ancillary matter and occupies but a single beat (2.2.58–85), the audience must be warned that the sequence as a whole focuses on Polonius's report, not the Ambassadors'. Shakespeare employs a characteristic technique here. Though he supplies Polonius with an official motive for entering the state apartments, he handles that motive in the enclosing lines of the beat. Nested within that framework of motivation is a broader statement of purpose:

> *Enter* POLONIUS
> POLONIUS *Th' ambassadors from Norway, my good lord.*
> *Are joyfully return'd.*
> KING *Thou still hast been the father of good news.*
> POLONIUS *Have I, my lord? I assure my good liege*
> I hold my duty as I hold my soul,
> Both to my God and to my gracious king;
> And I do think, or else this brain of mine
> Hunts not the trail of policy so sure

As it hath us'd to do, that I have found
The very cause of Hamlet's lunacy.
KING O, speak of that, that do I long to hear.
POLONIUS *Give first admittance to th' ambassadors;*
My news shall be the fruit to that great feast.
KING *Thyself do grace to them, and bring them in.*
[*Exit Polonius.*]
(2.2.40–53)

Polonius proclaims to Claudius that he has more revealing news than what he has just delivered – and here Shakespeare announces the real subject of the sequence. Polonius believes he has "found / The very cause of Hamlet's lunacy." Shakespeare adds a further touch of realism by making this information so important to Claudius that he elects to hear Polonius out before admitting Voltemand. The wily Polonius, however, prefers to hold the King in suspense. Much to the advantage of the sequence structure, Polonius's explanation of the love affair is temporarily postponed. The beat ends with Polonius going out to fetch the Ambassadors.

This introductory beat nicely demonstrates the principle of compression, for several matters are addressed in a single beat. It explains two separate entrances and announces a sequence subject.

An interesting point about Shakespeare's attitude toward sequence introductions is illustrated when he follows up this beat by stating the subject a second time. It appears that Shakespeare has compressed so much material into the introductory beat that he fears that slower members of the audience might miss the main point. Beat 54–8, which follows, seems designed to ensure that everyone will be focused on the target.

Notice how Shakespeare emphasizes the key information. The old counsellor's exit in search of the Ambassadors creates the need for an interval beat that will use up enough stage time to make that offstage action appear probable. Shakespeare could have filled this interval with almost anything. But note what he does. He has Claudius repeat Polonius's claims to Gertrude:

KING He tells me, my dear Gertrude, he hath found
The head and source of all your son's distemper.
QUEEN I doubt it is no other but the main,
His father's death and our o'erhasty marriage.
KING Well, we shall sift him.

(2.2.54–8)

There is no pressing need for Claudius to repeat this to Gertrude, for Gertrude was on stage with them and heard it herself. That Claudius does so indicates both his tenderness toward his wife and his own curiosity: his mind continues to dwell on the subject. Through the Queen's response the beat also tells us that Gertrude already sees the cause of Hamlet's madness more clearly than Polonius ever will. But there is also an important structural reason for the repetition: with so much early emphasis on the Ambassadors, the real subject of the sequence might get lost. In serving its function of filling the interval this second beat therefore repeats the subject for anyone who may have missed it – Polonius's claim to have "found / The head and source of all your son's distemper."

IV

Much can be learned by comparing a selection of similar beats from different plays. This approach reveals not only the more common dramaturgical needs but also less familiar ones.

Take the problem of character positioning. The most interesting of Shakespeare's introductory beats are those designed to acquaint the audience with some change in a character's emotional state. In Shakespeare a character continues to "live" and "breathe" even when he is offstage, not because he is a living person who has a complete life but because Shakespeare shows his characters developing as if their minds had been active during the intervals between the scenes in which they appear. When he wishes us to understand that changes have been wrought in the character's psyche between an exit and a later entrance, he usually has the character reveal his altered position at the start of the new sequence.

The introductory beat to the seduction sequence in 2.4 of *Measure for Measure* illustrates character positioning well. Shakespeare structures the beat as a soliloquy for Angelo. Why a soliloquy? When we last saw Angelo at the end of the companion sequence 2.2.1–186, he had fallen prey to sexual temptation. He was surprised and appalled by his lustful feelings for the beautiful nun Isabella but had not yet chosen to act upon his passion. No one seeing the play for the first time could be sure how Angelo would act. But now he has made his choice. If we are to believe that Angelo can place the proposition he does before a young nun and at the end of the seduction sequence say, "Now I give my sensual race the rein. / . . . Redeem thy brother / By yielding up thy body to my will," we must first be shown the change that has taken place in him. Shakespeare must write an introductory beat for this new sequence that positions the character.

Thus, when Angelo reappears at the beginning of 2.4, after he has succumbed to temptation, he delivers this soliloquy:

When I would pray and think, I think and pray
To several subjects. Heaven hath my empty words,
Whilst my invention, hearing not my tongue,
Anchors on Isabel; heaven in my mouth,
As if I did but only chew his name,
And in my heart the strong and swelling evil
Of my conception. The state, whereon I studied,
Is like a good thing, being often read,
Grown sere and tedious; yea, my gravity,
Wherein (let no man hear me) I take pride,
Could I, with boot, change for an idle plume,
Which the air beats for vain. O place, O form,
How often dost thou with thy case, thy habit,
Wrench awe from fools, and tie the wiser souls
To thy false seeming!. . .

(2.4.1–15)

Consider first what the beat does not do. During the sequence Angelo will attempt to persuade Isabella to sacrifice her chastity in exchange for her brother's life, using a sophistic reasoning that redefines sin as charity. Yet nothing of his method and little of his intention are revealed in the opening beat. Angelo says only that his heart is full of "the strong and swelling evil / Of my conception"; he does not spell out what his conception is – simply that it appalls him. Presumably he has no method yet worked out, for Shakespeare presents the seduction as a series of spontaneous responses to the developing situation.

In this introductory beat Shakespeare is concerned solely with presenting Angelo's state of mind. How does he do this? The introduction is cast in the form of a meditation. Angelo does not speak directly to the audience: instead, Shakespeare shows him in conversation with himself, remarking upon the transformation that has occurred within his psyche. In "case," in "habit," Angelo appears unchanged. His imagination, however, "anchors" on Isabella, activating the passions. For Angelo this is a new experience, and though he retains enough awareness to know that he does not like the rift lust has created between the inner man and the outer man, his blood drives him on: he can only watch himself being taken over by himself. This presentation of Angelo's most intimate thoughts makes us feel the force of the passion that has taken over Angelo's will. With its propelling character firmly in position, the sequence can now move forward.

Another example of character positioning occurs in an introductory beat that connects the two temptation sequences of *Othello* 3.3. The beat brings the Moor back to the stage after a strategically crafted dinner-interval. When we last saw Othello two sequences back (that is, in sequence 3.3.93–279), he was uncertain which way to move. He had just been shaken by Iago's report that his wife had taken a lover and, left to make a choice that would affect his future life, was vacillating between two courses of action – to accept Iago's story or to put his faith in Desdemona. Shakespeare arranged matters so that the sequence ended with Othello in the latter position. His direction was a positive one: "If she be false, O then heaven mocks itself! / I'll not believe 't." Could he hold himself fixed on that true point?

A beat or two into the second temptation sequence (3.3.333–480) the Moor will be in a rage, issuing his famous challenge to Iago: "Villain, be sure thou prove my love a whore; / Be sure of it." But Shakespeare does not permit this challenge to emerge from nowhere. He first establishes the position Othello has moved into. In his introductory beat (3.3.333–58) he discloses a new Othello who, as Iago tells us, "already changes with my poison." This introductory beat reveals a husband who recoils from his wife's lips because he fancies he sees another man's kisses there, who already imagines the general camp "had tasted her sweet body," and who, consequently, feels himself stretched upon the rack. Gone is content, gone the tranquil mind. Not until he has established Othello in this new position by constructing a psychologically revealing introductory beat does Shakespeare allow him to initiate further action by demanding "ocular proof" of Desdemona's infidelity.

Expository updating remains a constant function of sequence introductions, and clarifying the character's starting position is a necessary form of it; such current information makes the character's subsequent actions plausible.[1] But character-positioning beats often have a more specific purpose: Shakespeare almost always writes one for a sequence in which he employs a reversal structure. In such sequences the character who is to undergo the reversal is clearly placed at the beginning of the sequence in the stance that he will be moved away from, and the justification for the polarity between the initial and the final positions may stem as much from dramaturgical as psychological considerations.

Take the reversal dramatized in 2.3.1–264 of *Much Ado About Nothing*. Here Benedick, in a concluding soliloquy, states that he "will be horribly in love" with Beatrice. To begin this sequence Shakespeare brings Benedick on stage early and writes for him a long introductory beat that sets out in detail Benedick's belief that a "man is a fool when he dedicates his behaviors to love" (2.3.7–35). Benedick's opening statement makes his initial position not only concrete but seemingly firm. It also highlights the rapidity of his subsequent departure from it.

In reversals effected in some key character by the delivery of important news Shakespeare depends upon this emphatic introductory positioning to give impact to the subsequent alteration. Examples abound in *Romeo and Juliet*. After Romeo has killed Tybalt, for instance, Juliet must be told of it. This news, conveyed to her by the Nurse, will convert her nuptial joy to "sour woe." To introduce the sequence in which the reversal takes place Shakespeare creates a Juliet as impatient for Romeo's arrival as a "child that hath new robes / And may not wear them," her anticipatory joy made apparent through her ecstatic apostrophe to the "gentle, . . . loving, black-brow'd night" that will bring Romeo to her. Against this background of expectation, rendered through a soliloquy that positions the character (3.2.1–31), Shakespeare lets Juliet react to the news that Romeo has been banished. In the apothecary sequence two acts later, Romeo's initial position is established in the same way. News of Juliet's death will send Romeo at the close of the sequence to buy poison to end his hapless life. Almost by way of habit Shakespeare goes back to the beginning of the sequence and positions Romeo at the most widely divergent point from that to which the news of Juliet's burial will bring him:

> My dreams presage some joyful news at hand.
> My bosom's lord sits lightly in his throne,
> And all this day an unaccustom'd spirit
> Lifts me above the ground with cheerful thoughts.
>
> (5.1.2–5)

In this last instance the technique appears at its baldest.

A final example of the introductory beat that prepares for a reversal by establishing the position a character will be moved away from occurs in the sequence in which Lady Macbeth persuades her husband to murder Duncan. In the first twenty-eight lines of this action Shakespeare works Macbeth to a decision to "proceed no further in this business." As a unit, Macbeth's soliloquy has been viewed in many ways. It has often been performed in isolation from the surrounding text, and in at least one case has been perceived as the ending of the preceding series of actions.[2] Beat 1.7.1–28 is not a conclusion, however, but an introduction. Macbeth will shortly abandon his own stand against "deep damnation" to embrace his wife's attitudes. How much less effective Lady Macbeth's victory would have been had Shakespeare not begun the sequence by having Macbeth judge the arguments against the murder of his kinsman, king, and guest more weighty than the urgings of his "vaulting ambition." Here, as in all of the examples cited above, when a character is to be turned round during the course of a sequence, Shakespeare's introductory beat normally records the radically opposing position from which that character will be starting.

V

Introductory beats are ubiquitous but not always obvious. They are easier to detect when they follow a change of location, for the clearing of the stage prepares one for new beginnings. There is greater difficulty when no change of location or vacated stage gives warning of the change of sequence. It will be useful to review the introductions to the various sequences of a multi-sequence scene to see from still another point of view how deliberately Shakespeare works with introductions as well as to show how frequently introductions come in the middle of scenes. The introductory beats discussed in the next section all come from the five sequences of *I Henry IV* 2.4.

In 2.4 the Falstaff plot moves from the open road to the interior of the tavern. The robbery at Gadshill has already been staged – Falstaff and his cohorts have held up the coach, and Prince Hal and Poins in turn have stolen the booty from Falstaff. They now meet Falstaff again for the first time since the robbery. The entire scene – 550 lines – takes place in the Boar's Head Tavern.

To establish the atmosphere of the tavern fully, Shakespeare uses a whole sequence to set the scene, placing the Prince and Poins in the tavern well before Falstaff reaches it, and leaving Hal among the drawers for approximately 100 lines. But even though this entire sequence is introductory, it still has its own introductory beat, just like any other sequence. Shakespeare takes 33 of the 100 lines to set up the sequence.

This introductory beat works hard to get the sequence moving. Ned Poins's question, "Where hast been Hal?" permits the Prince to describe his activities for the past fifteen minutes, during which he has been fraternizing with Tom, Dick, and Francis, the "leash of drawers." By amassing minute observations of the manners and language of the taproom, the beat supplies a wider view of the tavern than is available to the viewer's eye; in fact, in this introductory beat Shakespeare furnishes a complete architectural orientation, deliberately depicting many other rooms than the one Hal occupies – the "fat room" Poins is called from and goes back to, the cellarage where the hogsheads of wine are stored, and so on, so that we accept the expanded space and feel it buzzing with activity.

But this overview is supplied within the context of a sense of play. Notice what happens in the enclosing lines of the beat, where

Shakespeare narrows the action to make Hal focus on a single tapster, the bewildered Francis. In lines 1 and 2 Shakespeare announces Hal's motive – Hal summons Poins to lend his hand in effecting a practical joke – and in the beat's last lines Hal explains the particulars. The beat is thus structured around an activity – plotting a practical joke. By arranging matters so that Hal engages Poins in that activity within our hearing, Shakespeare informs us of the exact nature of the trick that will be played upon Francis. From then on Hal can indulge – and display for us – his sense of humor.

Hal's exposure of Francis as a simpleton becomes a prelude to his exposure of Falstaff as a coward. This second sequence (2.4.113–283) is the main sequence of the scene as well as Falstaff's biggest scene in the play; consequently, the introductory section is suitably grandiose.

In the previous sequence, entrances and introductions were handled simultaneously. In the coward sequence, however, not only is the entrance handled separately from the introduction but it also takes Shakespeare several beats to effect it. Sir Jack's impending arrival is hinted at in the beat discussed above, where Ned and Hal are said to jest with Francis merely "to drive away the time till Falstaff come," but Falstaff does not appear just yet: we are made to wait a whole sequence for him. Even then it will take three separate entrance beats to get Falstaff to the stage. As the opening sequence nears its end, the Vintner interrupts the Prince's sport with Francis to announce Falstaff's arrival:

> VINTNER My lord, old Sir John with half a dozen more are at the door, shall I let them in?
> PRINCE Let them alone awhile, and then open the door.
>
> (2.4.82–5)

Falstaff is not admitted. Poins is called back in, and there is a further teaser:

> PRINCE Sirrah, Falstaff and the rest of the thieves are at the door; shall we be merry?
> POINS As merry as crickets, my lad.
>
> (2.4.87–9)

But the two are still absorbed in their game. Falstaff is forced to wait through the concluding remarks of the Francis sequence. He must wait, too, while Hal interpolates a few witty lines about Harry Percy, "the Hotspur of the north." Only when Hal is fully ready is Falstaff actually summoned.

> PRINCE I prithee call in Falstaff. I'll play Percy and that damn'd

brawn shall play Dame Mortimer his wife. *"Rivo!"* says the
drunkard. Call in ribs, call in tallow.

(2.4.108–12)

There is of course sound playwriting logic behind the delay – in terms
of both plot structure and character development. Because of Falstaff's
status, his entrance is no mean matter, to be got through as quickly as
possible. On the contrary, Shakespeare teases us with expectation. The
last we saw of Falstaff, he had been held up, robbed of his booty, and was
tearing away in a panic. What will he have to say for himself when he
reappears? Behind this sound playwriting logic there is also sure
motivation. Shakespeare has set up the tavern as Hal's court, and the
action as a series of interviews with those who seek an audience. This
arrangement guarantees (among other things) that the motivation will
appear to come from the character rather than from the playwright
himself. By allowing Hal this power to permit or deny Falstaff access to his
presence, Shakespeare also subtly reinforces the audience's sense that in
spite of the affinity between them, Hal always remains superior to and in
control of proud Jack.

After so much preparation, strung out over three beats and threaded
through a sequence, Falstaff's entrance must be suitably striking. The
introductory beat (2.4.113–56) gives Falstaff the exuberance that so
elaborate an entrance calls for. He struts on stage full of the curse that is
the keynote of this beat, "A plague of all cowards!" The refrain line
berating cowards, ever on Falstaff's lips, effectively ties these forty-four
lines together into one beat. But it does more. It embodies in its implied
sense of outrage the essence of Falstaff's counterattack. Hal and Poins
mean to prove Falstaff a coward. Fat Jack, exhibiting his characteristic
gall, comes out not in submission but in full battle array, charging that
Hal and Poins are the cowards. And of course to the very end of the
sequence, Falstaff insists upon his own valor. The more we feel the force
of the position established in this strong and carefully structured
introductory beat, the better we will appreciate Falstaff's refusal to
abandon it.

This forceful presence has temporarily driven from Prince Hal's mind
the fancy he had expressed to Poins of casting Falstaff as Dame Mortimer.
The idea of staging a play has been planted, however, and will come to
fruition in a later sequence.

The introduction to the scene's third sequence (2.4.284–372) is
interesting because it introduces a character who never makes it out of
the wings and onto the stage, Sir John Bracy. Shakespeare writes an
entrance beat for him:

Enter HOSTESS

HOSTESS O Jesu, my lord the Prince!

PRINCE How now, my lady the hostess! what say'st thou to me?

HOSTESS Marry, my lord, there is a nobleman of the court at door would speak with you. He says he comes from your father.

PRINCE Give him as much as will make him a royal man, and send him back again to my mother.

FALSTAFF What manner of man is he?

HOSTESS An old man.

FALSTAFF What doth gravity out of his bed at midnight? Shall I give him his answer?

PRINCE Prithee do, Jack.

FALSTAFF Faith, and I'll send him packing.   *Exit.*

(2.4.284–97)

Hal refuses to give this emissary from his father an audience, and so we never meet Sir John Bracy.

The time has come in the play for Hal to leave the carefree world of the tavern, as serious affairs – a rebellion in the kingdom – require his presence at court. This sequence brings the summons that calls Hal back home. The playwriting problem here is to construct an action that will inform Hal of the uprising. Someone must bring him a report. With characteristic daring Shakespeare has set himself the challenge of delivering this information to Hal at a moment when he is most absorbed in pleasure: Gravity comes knocking at the door of the House of Levity. How is the playwright to convey this somber message without destroying the tone of a scene that is, after all, dedicated to displaying the Rabelaisian qualities of Jack Falstaff? Shakespeare structures the action in a way that gives the nobleman's scene to fat Jack. He shows in the introductory beat that Hal's and Falstaff's attitudes toward the courier are identical and has Hal employ Falstaff to send his father's emissary away. When Falstaff returns he brings with him the message Sir John Bracy would have delivered. As Shakespeare has devised things, the message, far from disrupting the tone of the scene, provides Falstaff with new and greater opportunities to exercise his scandalous wit.

Sequence 4 (2.4.373–485) contains the two playlets staged by Hal and Falstaff, with Falstaff first representing King Henry and Hal playing himself, and then, in a reversal of roles, with Hal as the King and Falstaff as the rebellious Prince. For several reasons Shakespeare can slip quickly into this sequence without much ado. For one thing, no entrances or exits are required. For another, the idea of staging a play had been suggested earlier by Hal, so the audience is already prepared for it when the Prince recalls the idea now. Because so little preparation is necessary, the exact point of division between these two sequences is difficult to mark. The movement from one subject to the other is effected through certain connections made in Falstaff's mind. It occurs to him that with "three such enemies as that fiend Douglas, that spirit Percy, and that devil Glendower" Hal ought to be "horribly afraid." Then he imagines the chiding Hal will receive from his father when he returns home, a thought he finds worth playing with: "If thou love me, practice an answer." Suddenly we are in a new sequence. Hal improves on Falstaff's hint and the play is on.

Despite the smooth and rapid transition, the introductory beat is easy to spot. It is a beat of scene-setting. Once the characters have decided to stage a play they begin to prepare a stage:

> FALSTAFF Well, thou wilt be horribly chid tomorrow when thou comest to thy father. If thou love me, practice an answer.
>
> PRINCE Do thou stand for my father and examine me upon the particulars of my life.
>
> FALSTAFF Shall I? Content. This chair shall be my state, this dagger my sceptre, and this cushion my crown.
>
> PRINCE Thy state is taken for a joint-stool, thy golden sceptre for a leaden dagger, and thy precious rich crown for a pitiful bald crown!
>
> FALSTAFF Well, and the fire of grace be not quite out of thee, now shalt be mov'd. Give me a cup of sack to make my eyes look red, that it may be thought I have wept, for I must speak in passion, and I will do it in King Cambyses' vein.
>
> PRINCE Well, here is my leg.
>
> FALSTAFF And here is my speech. Stand aside, nobility.
>
> (2.4.373–89)

Falstaff gathers props, improvises a costume, prepares his face, and kindles a passion for the task before him. After this introductory beat in which the subject is announced and the scene set, the action of the sequence proper – the play-within-the-play – unfolds.

Reality is forever intruding on the careless pleasures of the tavern, reminding us that there is a world of law and order outside this realm of sack. Hal has been summoned back to that real world, but the play sequence between "father" and "son," "king" and "prince," lets him live for a while longer in the carefree state of Falstaff's world. A summons now comes for Falstaff himself; the play sequence is interrupted by the arrival of the Sheriff. This last of the scene's five sequences requires Shakespeare to write still another introduction:

Enter the HOSTESS

HOSTESS O Jesu, my lord, my lord!

PRINCE Heigh, heigh! the devil rides upon a fiddlestick. What's the matter?

HOSTESS The sheriff and all the watch are at the door, they are come to search the house. Shall I let them in?

FALSTAFF Does thou hear, Hal? Never call a true piece of gold a counterfeit. Thou art essentially made, without seeming so.

PRINCE And thou a natural coward, without instinct.

FALSTAFF I deny your major. If you will deny the sheriff, so, if not, let him enter. If I become not a cart as well as another man, a plague on my bringing up! I hope I shall as soon be strangled with a halter as another.

PRINCE Go hide thee behind the arras, the rest walk up above. Now, my masters, for a true face and a good conscience.

FALSTAFF Both which I have had, but their date is out, and therefore I'll hide me.

(2.4.486–505)

There are both parallels and differences between the introduction written for Sir John Bracy and this one written for the Sheriff. First the parallels. Both intruders are announced by the Hostess, whose own sense of crisis enhances the stature of the visitor without destroying the comic tone. Both involve an action in which the Prince must decide whether to admit the intruder. In both, Falstaff influences the choice.

Now the differences. To vary the structure, Shakespeare employs the technique of the false start. In the Sir John Bracy introduction the Hostess entered breathlessly to announce the visitor, and so she does here. But this time, Bardolph runs in ahead of Mistress Quickly and breaks the news first (2.4.482–5). Of course Bardolph is silenced: Falstaff insists on continuing the play sequence. But the interlocking here is effective, for Falstaff's desire to "play out the play" permits a natural spillover of the play sequence into the Sheriff episode that creates a stronger sense of sudden interruption. Announcing the Sheriff's arrival twice not only avoids making the parallel too exact a copy of the Bracy one but also has the effect of doubling the excitement. Another difference is that whereas Falstaff and Hal acted in unison in the Bracy introduction, shutting out the intrusion, here they are humorously at odds: the action depends for its effect on Falstaff's fear that Hal will betray him to the law. Finally – one more difference – while Bracy was "sent packing," the Sheriff is admitted.

The distinctions between Shakespeare's introductions to these two sequences and his introduction to the more central coward sequence are worth bringing forward. In the coward sequence Shakespeare wrote several brief entrance beats to bring Falstaff onto the stage as well as a lengthy introductory beat to establish the position from which Falstaff was to be moved. In these less important sequences, in contrast, Shakespeare uses the same technique of compression that we glanced at in the introductory beat which conveyed Polonius into the state apartments: the entrance and the introductory functions are handled in the same beat.

This single scene from *I Henry IV*, then, contains more than a single introduction. Because Shakespeare uses five sequences in this scene, there are five separate introductions, each constructed of one or more beats and each unique. The fact that each of these introductions provides information from which an action can move forward offers further support for our contention that the sequence is the primary unit of action in Shakespeare. Even when Shakespeare clusters his sequences within the confines of a long scene, he feels obliged to give each sequence a separate introduction, just as he gives each sequence its own intensification and its own conclusion.

5

Sequential beats: the concluding beat

I

Categories in beat analysis are useful only so long as they avoid rigidity, and nowhere is this more true than in the category of concluding beats. The range and variety are wider even than in introductory beats. Yet a close study of their functions can be revealing.

Some of the most famous lines in *Hamlet* appear in beats that conclude sequences:

> Thanks, Rosencrantz and gentle Guildenstern. / Thanks,
> Guildenstern and gentle Rosencrantz.

> At such a time I'll loose my daughter to him. . .

> You cannot take from me any thing that I will not more willingly
> part withal – except my life.

> I am but mad north-north-west. When the wind is southerly I know
> a hawk from a hand-saw.

> Dost thou hear me, old friend? Can you play *The Murder of Gonzago?*

Even the unforgettable "What a piece of work is a man, how noble in reason, how infinite in faculties. . ." appears in a concluding beat.

Interestingly, these lines have all been drawn from a single scene – *Hamlet* 2.2 – so that to examine their concluding functions is to make sense of that scene's complex sequence structure: the scene has six sequences. Gertrude's courtesies to Guildenstern and Rosencrantz close sequence 1, in which the two friends have been commissioned to spy out the cause of Hamlet's madness (2.2.1–39); Polonius's decision to make a decoy of Ophelia ends sequence 2, in which he too adopts the role of detective (2.2.40–170); and Hamlet's expressed willingness to part from Polonius completes sequence 3, in which Polonius tries to gather evidence by observing the method in Hamlet's madness, much to Hamlet's dismay (2.2.170–221). As Polonius exits, the work of sifting Hamlet goes on: Rosencrantz and Guildenstern undertake in sequence 4 the commission they were given in sequence 1 (to "glean, / Whether aught to us unknown inflicts him thus"). To our amusement they find themselves, instead, being interrogated by Hamlet, admit they were sent for, and receive an answer to their query before they ever make it – the long description of Hamlet's melancholy: his "What a piece of work is a man" monologue concludes that sequence.

> I will tell you why, so shall my anticipation prevent your discovery, and your secrecy to the King and Queen moult no feather. I have of late – but wherefore I know not – lost all my mirth, forgone all custom of exercises; and indeed it goes so heavily with my disposition, that this goodly frame, the earth, seems to me a sterile promontory; this most excellent canopy, the air, look you, this brave o'erhanging firmament, this majestical roof fretted with golden fire, why, it appeareth nothing to me but a foul and pestilent congregation of vapors. What a piece of work is a man, how noble in reason, how infinite in faculties, in form and moving how express and admirable, in action how like an angel, in apprehension how like a god! the beauty of the world; the paragon of animals; and yet to me what is this quintessence of dust? Man delights not me –
>
> (2.2.293–309)

Shakespeare makes this beat a concluding beat by taking advantage of Rosencrantz's inability to rise to Hamlet's level. Hamlet's "Man delights not me" reminds Rosencrantz of the arrival of some actors from the city, and he responds only with "If you delight not in man, what lenten entertainment the players shall receive from you." This change of subject aborts Hamlet's original train of thought, turning the conversation from the philosophical to the practical; thus, Rosencrantz's announcement that the players are "hither coming to offer you service" begins sequence 5 (2.2.309–79). In this fifth sequence Shakespeare builds to the flourish that trumpets the arrival of the players at court, then rounds out the unit with its own concluding beat, as Hamlet turns his thoughts back to Rosencrantz and Guildenstern:

> HAMLET Gentlemen, you are welcome to Elsinore. Your hands, come then: th'appurtenance of welcome is fashion and ceremony. Let me comply with you in this garb, lest my extent to the players, which, I tell you, must show fairly outwards, should more appear like entertainment than yours. You are welcome; but my uncle-father and aunt-mother are deceiv'd.
>
> GUILDENSTERN In what, my dear lord?
>
> HAMLET I am but mad north-north-west. When the wind is southerly I know a hawk from a hand-saw.
>
> (2.2.370–9)

The scene's sixth and last sequence – occupied by the players themselves – is the major sequence of the scene; consequently, it ends with an important series of concluding beats: in one Hamlet sends the players away with Polonius in charge (2.2.522–36), in the second he confers with the First Player about a performance of the Gonzago play (537–46), in the third he provides for the exit of Rosencrantz and Guildenstern who are still on stage (546–9), and in the last he delivers his "What a rogue and peasant slave am I" soliloquy (549–605). If one develops an eye for concluding beats, one has yet another tool for locating the sequences in any long scene.

The primary function of the concluding beat is fairly obvious, but it will do no harm to review it. The concluding beat sums up the preceding action – not just at the end of an act or at the end of a scene: Shakespeare writes concluding beats at the end of every sequence. As *Hamlet* 2.2 with its six sequences indicates, sometimes there are six conclusions in a single scene. The concluding beat also gives the unit a sense of closure: we know that Shakespeare has said what he wanted to say about this subject and is now going on to something else. He may diffuse that sense of closure but he nevertheless puts it in. And in concluding beats tensions are being released: these are the beats that form the decrescent stage of the sequence.

But concluding beats do more than conclude. Ironically, it is possible to present a series of concluding beats that point toward the future and (despite such apparent "beginnings") declare them typical endings. Most concluding beats contain lines calculated to create new expectations in the audience, hints of actions to be rendered in some forthcoming sequence: Polonius here conceives the plot for the later nunnery sequence, Hamlet arranges to have the Gonzago play performed before Claudius. In one way or another Shakespeare indicates in the concluding beats of a sequence the direction his action will take as a result of the action just completed.

The concluding portions of the sequence also serve a third function – to remove superfluous characters from the stage. Many concluding beats have the single purpose of effecting an exit. Exit beats often display a practical brevity:

> KING   Let's follow, Gertrude.
> How much I had to do to calm his rage!
> Now fear I this will give it start again,
> Therefore let's follow.
>
>   *Exeunt.*
>   (*Hamlet* 4.7.191–4)

Brevity notwithstanding, Shakespeare generally supplies the exiting characters with a credible motive for their departure and where possible a stated destination, so that they exit into defined space.

That the concluding beat provides for exits does not mean that sequence boundaries can be located solely by marking out characters' departures and arrivals. The boundaries of completed actions are not determined in that way. At the end of the sequence pitting Rosencrantz and Guildenstern against Hamlet, nobody leaves the stage, for all the characters are needed in the subsequent sequence. There need not be exits at the end of a sequence; in fact, characters may come or go at any point within a sequence. Exit or entrance beats are possible but never fully reliable clues to unit divisions. Many an exit nevertheless takes place in the concluding section of the sequence, and such exit beats can be considered specialized forms of the concluding beat.

II

The functions of concluding beats – to summarize the action just completed, to foreshadow new directions, and to cover the necessary exits – can be handled separately, so that a single sequence may have two or three or even five concluding beats. The less important the functions, however, the more likely are they to be compressed into one concluding beat.

The principle of compression noted in introductions operates even more strongly in conclusions. To demonstrate just how economical Shakespeare can be in writing a concluding beat, we shall examine three in which he has tidied up all the pending concerns at once: *Hamlet* 1.4.87–91, *As You Like It* 1.3.33–138, and *Coriolanus* 2.1.193–204.

Several of the end-of-sequence functions mentioned above turn up in the concluding beat of *Hamlet* 1.4. Hamlet has just broken away from Marcellus and Horatio to follow the Ghost, against their protests, for they would gladly be quit of it. When Hamlet charges after the Ghost, they are left on stage to conclude the sequence:

> HORATIO He waxes desperate with imagination.
> MARCELLUS Let's follow. 'Tis not fit thus to obey him.
> HORATIO Have after. To what issue will this come?
> MARCELLUS Something is rotten in the state of Denmark.
> HORATIO Heaven will direct it.
> MARCELLUS   Nay, let's follow him.
>   (1.4.87–91)

Each of these lines addresses a different dramaturgical problem. Two remarks reflect on the action just completed. Horatio's "He waxes desperate with imagination" suggests the tremendous impact the Ghost has had on Hamlet, while Marcellus's "Something is rotten in the state of Denmark" hints at larger causes for this disruption in nature. The remaining lines point to the future. "To what issue will this come?" and "Heaven will direct it," thoughts assigned to Horatio, are broad in their outlook. One creates suspense, the other reassures, but both enlarge the scope of this particular event. They are still reverberating in the play's final act. To Marcellus Shakespeare assigns the task of thinking for the more immediate future – What shall be done about Hamlet? Shall he be abandoned to the Ghost? Marcellus's speech, "Let's follow. 'Tis not fit thus to obey him," prepares us for the sequence at 1.5.113–90 where these loyal friends rejoin Hamlet and are sworn to secrecy. The decision of Marcellus and Horatio to go in pursuit of their prince clears the stage for the return of Hamlet and the Ghost.

So many diverse elements. How does Shakespeare unify them? Is this really a single beat? The unity of the beat comes from the motivating desire – to follow Hamlet. The beat contains many thoughts but only one action. Marcellus is the first to suggest that action; believing Hamlet needs protection, he says "Let's follow" the Prince. Horatio agrees: "Have after." Strictly speaking, this is an exit beat; the characters' desire to follow Hamlet will get them off the stage. The experience, however, has been so overwhelming for Marcellus and Horatio that they cannot help speculating upon its meaning. Partly because of the shock and partly because there is no dramatic point in their discussing this matter in the wings, they remain in place for a moment or two, so that their speculations are heard by the audience. Once all of these concluding remarks have been made, Marcellus again urges the action – to follow Hamlet – and they leave. To emphasize this unifying element Shakespeare has positioned the lines in which Marcellus expresses the motive at both the beginning and the end of the beat, "Let's follow" being very nearly the first words spoken and a variation of the phrase, "Nay, let's follow him," being the last. Marcellus's motive not only controls the direction the action will take but acts as a binding force that unifies the disparate concluding elements that must be compressed into this beat.

The final beat of the sequence 1.3.90–138 in *As You Like It* works in the same way. The sequence itself dramatizes the reaction of Rosalind and Celia to Duke Frederick's irrational banishment of Rosalind, from whom Celia refuses to be separated. As it unfolds the two girls agree on a plan of escape from the palace. At the end of the sequence, in its concluding beat, Celia decides that they ought to make their move:

> Let's away,
> And get our jewels and our wealth together,
> Devise the fittest time and safest way
> To hide us from pursuit that will be made
> After my flight. Now go we in content
> To liberty, and not to banishment.
>
> (1.3.133–8)

In one of its manifestations, this is an exit beat. It disguises the bare fact that the two characters must leave the stage by suggesting that they have a specific task to complete elsewhere in the palace. Celia's motive is stated and restated in the enclosing lines – "Let's away . . ." and "Now go we in content . . ." Here again, though, in the very sentences that cover the exit other problems relating to the sequence conclusion are resolved. Celia's concerns that in their offstage moments they "devise the fittest time and safest way" to hide from their pursuers foreshadows the action to come after they have escaped from the palace, for in 2.2 a pursuit is indeed made. Celia's "Now go we in content / To liberty, and not to banishment" strikes a note of harmony that makes this unit satisfying as a concluding beat: between the nearly divided friends there is now total agreement and a fresh sense of hope. Much information is compressed into this concluding beat. Nevertheless, Celia's wish to put their plan into effect provides the force that holds the other elements together.

Having noted the pattern we can appreciate a more richly structured use of it in the "going on" beat at *Coriolanus* 2.1.193–204:

> HERALD Give way there, and go on!
> CORIOLANUS [*To Volumnia and Virgilia.*] Your hand, and yours!
> Ere in our own house I do shade my head,
> The good patricians must be visited,
> From whom I have receiv'd not only greetings,
> But with them change of honors.
> VOLUMNIA   I have lived
> To see inherited my very wishes
> And the buildings of my fancy; only
> There's one thing wanting, which I doubt not but
> Our Rome will cast upon thee.
> CORIOLANUS   Know, good mother,
> I had rather be their servant in my way
> Than sway with them in theirs.
> COMINIUS   On, to the Capitol!
> *Flourish, Cornets. Exeunt in state, as before.*
>
> (2.1.193–204)

This beat concludes the sequence of procession in which the nobility of Rome joyfully receive the returning hero. The chorus of welcomes delivered, the procession must relinquish the stage: Shakespeare needs it for the Tribunes, who initiate a new sequence at line 205.[1]

The unifying motive in this beat is so simple that it would normally go unnoticed: the Herald announces it in the opening line, "Give way there, and go on!" As usual the characters need additional nudging before the exit is effected and so at the beat's end Cominius adds his authority to the Herald's: "On, to the Capitol!" The beat derives its structure from this need to move the characters along.

In this case Shakespeare attaches other levels of meaning to the idea of going on and weaves them into the beat to provide unity at an even deeper level. For the Herald and Cominius, to "go on" means little more than to move on down the street in the direction of the Capitol. For Coriolanus, to "go on" means something slightly more elevated: fulfilling a duty. He would prefer to go home, but first "the good patricians must be visited," for he has received honors from them and must pay them due respect. Coriolanus accepts the necessity of going on, following along with the procession to its final destination. For the moment at least his will is aligned with the actions required of him by the state. For Volumnia, to "go on" has a third meaning, one that indicates the direction in which the play will develop: "Only / There's one thing wanting, which I doubt not but / Our Rome will cast upon thee." Volumnia means that Coriolanus must "go on" to become consul.

Here at this moment of triumph, Shakespeare introduces the seed of the conflict that will destroy Coriolanus. Coriolanus's virtues are the virtues of a soldier; he is a great general. In this role, he is both successful and content. Rome – and Volumnia is the very spirit of that Rome – means to cast greater honors on her servant, but, for those honors, will demand of Coriolanus a service he is by nature incapable of performing. In this exchange, a conversation in the streets overheard before the procession and the play itself "go on," where both characters speak from their hearts about the movement toward greater honors, Shakespeare gives us a sense of the future danger that "going on" entails.

This technique for completing a sequence is second nature to Shakespeare. One character suggests a removal to some definite offstage location. His motive is stated in the enclosing lines of the beat so that it receives sufficient emphasis, and the characters act upon this motive. The stage thus seems to be cleared as a result of the characters' own initiatives, the playwright's sure hand remaining deftly hidden. Yet in the conversation that falls between and around these enclosing lines the characters clear up any pending matters and speculate upon the future. The foregoing examples not only prove the rule but also demonstrate the freshness Shakespeare manages to achieve while repeating the technique.

III

Most of the sequences considered so far have been preparatory for some more dramatic sequence; in them, Shakespeare has not wanted to expand the ending to majestic proportions. The concluding beats of major sequences will of course exude a stronger sense of finality. This is true even when the major sequence is itself preparatory.

Take, for example, the ending Shakespeare constructed for 3.3.93–279 of *Othello*. This is the familiar sequence in which Iago initiates his plot to make Othello jealous. Iago's first and crucial step, to get Othello even to consider the idea of Desdemona's infidelity, is a major undertaking. Before daring to express the thought, Iago has first aroused Othello's interest in his opinion of Cassio, has then pretended that his opinion was too uncharitable to discuss, and, when pressed to explain, has declared that nothing can force him to speak of such matters – the entire exchange culminating in Iago's feigned reversal. Immediately prior to the passage to be examined, Iago has done what he vowed never to do – he has revealed his thoughts to Othello, revealed them, he claims, "to show his love and duty." Of course the thoughts in question amount to the grossest calumny: Iago has accused Desdemona of taking Cassio as a lover.

After this climactic revelation the sequence enters a phase of decrescence. The change of pace occurs with Iago's "I see this hath a little dash'd your spirits" (3.3.214). Iago has achieved his present goal, and everything is being pulled together – from here on there is a sense of closure. In what ways do the six beats in this sequence conclusion end an action, even though the larger action within which this one nests will continue for two more sequences? How are we prepared for future developments so that the conclusion supplied does not become *too* final? And how are the characters' exits made credible?

First, let us notice what Shakespeare does not do. By peaking the action at Iago's revelation, Shakespeare raises an important expectation that he must fulfill for the audience; such a dramatic revelation gives him the opportunity to construct a dramatic response from Othello. But Shakespeare has arranged matters so that the full force of Othello's response occurs two sequences later (3.3.333–480), where it forms the central climax of the play: Othello's fury, when it matures, is so powerful that it will take a whole new sequence to contain it. Here, Shakespeare limits himself to depicting the initial shock that numbs Othello.

There is one response, however, that Iago must at all costs prevent – Othello could seek verification of the story by confronting the offending parties with it. This brings up the second expectation Shakespeare must address. What will Iago do next? How will he retain control of the situation? Can he keep his lie alive – and undiscovered? In these concluding beats Shakespeare focuses on Iago, who remains the propelling character until he exits; the concluding action takes its direction from his desire to press his advantage.

Yet since the challenge here at this supreme moment is to give the ending sufficient magnitude, Shakespeare creates a situation in which the emotions aroused by the climax can be sustained for several beats – Iago must protect himself. He must be sure, for example, that Othello remains convinced of his honest reluctance to condemn the lovers. He has insisted upon his selfless integrity from the beginning of the sequence, but this is also one of the leitmotifs of his concluding sentiments: in the first of the concluding beats, in fact, he develops the idea that "what is spoke / Comes from my love" (3.3.214–26). Iago must fortify his position in another way: before he can risk a parting or allow Othello to think on his own, he must be absolutely certain that the idea of Desdemona's infidelity has taken firm hold in Othello's imagination. Consequently (beat 3.3.227–38), Iago reminds Othello how unnatural it was for Desdemona to marry one not "of her own clime, complexion, and degree," and in beat 3.3.244–57, he implants in Othello's mind the idea that Desdemona's attempts to secure the reinstatement of Cassio as Othello's lieutenant will be signs of her guilt. To reiterate, to repeat, to rub in – repetition is Iago's major concluding tactic. The conclusion is drawn out, but its extension takes shape from Iago's attempts to consolidate his position.

Shakespeare, then, gives Iago the motives that propel the concluding action. Iago's calculated attempts to advise Othello provide a running commentary on the "meaning" of his revelation that Desdemona is unfaithful. By adopting Iago's perspective, Shakespeare finds a psychologically effective way to sustain the emotions aroused in the body of the sequence and thereby to give the closure an appropriate magnitude.

How does Shakespeare's treatment of Iago help the audience to experience Othello's emotion? Notice that in beat 214–26 Iago's comments fill a void. Othello is speechless, possibly even in a state of shock. This is clear from Iago's choric observations, which function as stage directions for the actor playing Othello:

I see this hath a little dash'd your spirits.

I do see y' are moved.

My lord, I see y'are moved.

In time, though, Othello is allowed to speak for himself, through a common device in Shakespearean endings, the concluding soliloquy. Othello's sentiments themselves are well known. What is of interest for our purpose is, first, the integral relationship of Othello's soliloquy to the sequence that precedes it and, second, why Shakespeare split that soliloquy into two parts.

In what sense does the soliloquy *conclude* the temptation sequence? Scholars often speak of such soliloquies as though they existed independently of the preceding action – indeed, as though all action stops when the lone character is engaged in a meditation,[2] but it is wrong to overemphasize that isolation at the expense of sequence unity. Othello's soliloquy grows directly out of the action being concluded and forms an integral part of it. This soliloquy is the last of several carefully crafted concluding beats, in an ending specifically applicable to the action of a single sequence.

As we suggested earlier, one of Shakespeare's principal tasks in writing this conclusion is to satisfy the viewer's need to learn more about Othello's response to the news of his wife's infidelity. All of the points Othello touches on in this soliloquy are uttered in response to that report. Notice, though, how much Othello's thoughts tend to echo Iago's. The soliloquy demonstrates the extent to which Iago has been able to dictate the contents of this meditation – Othello's self-consciousness about his color and his age, his belief that the offense Desdemona is accused of is so common in women as not to be unlikely in her, and above all his certainty that Iago is a man "of exceeding honesty" who "sees and knows more, much more, than he unfolds," all of these notions originate with Iago. Their presence in the soliloquy tells us something else we need to know before the sequence concludes – that Iago has succeeded in creating exactly the impression he had hoped for.

As in the other concluding beats, the summarizing elements of the soliloquy exist in tension with hooks into the future. In this soliloquy Shakespeare shows us Othello's predilection to loathe Desdemona (should she prove guilty) as he loathes the lust she stands accused of, and he hints at her ultimate fate. The forward thrust given the conclusion by such lines leaves an opening to Othello's more violent response in the last sequence of the temptation. At the same time the playwright indicates that his protagonist has not yet lost all reason. Having ranged through his innermost feelings and expanded on the subject in the direction suggested by Iago, Othello shows himself capable of pulling back. At the sight of Desdemona he regains his faith: "If she be false, O then heaven mocks itself! / I'll not believe it." In these final lines of the soliloquy Shakespeare establishes the position Othello chooses to take at that time. He is a step away from the total commitment of his earlier statement, "When I love thee not, / Chaos is come again." But for the moment hope remains that he will have faith in Desdemona.

The last challenge for the playwright as he wrote this sequence was to assign motives that would remove both characters from the stage. One of his solutions was to give Iago two exits, and the motivational structure developed to effect these exits achieves much in the way of character revelation. Shakespeare does not choose to have Iago and Othello go off together at the end of the sequence as they will in symbolic unity at the end of the scene. On the contrary, he has Othello dismiss his Ancient as soon as he regains enough composure to do so:

> OTHELLO   Farewell, farewell!
> If more thou dost perceive, let me know more;
> Set on thy wife to observe. Leave me, Iago.
> IAGO [*Going.*] My lord, I take my leave.

(3.3.238–41)

Shakespeare uses Iago's first exit to further the impression that Othello is upset and wants to be alone.

While the dismissal gives us a clue to Othello's distress, its placement between Iago's key concluding speeches (3.3.227–38 and 3.3.244–57) reinforces what we already know about Iago – that Iago cannot yet allow Othello to think for himself. Iago has been definitely dismissed and in order to deliver his final speech must force himself once again into Othello's presence. Iago's reappearance interrupts the soliloquy Othello had begun at his departure. By placing Iago's initial exit early in the sequence, then allowing him to intrude upon Othello's meditation, Shakespeare renders in a playable form Iago's reluctance to permit Othello to reason for himself at this critical point and also displays Iago's audacity.

Othello's exit is also interestingly managed. To forestall any feeling that Othello remains on stage merely to deliver a soliloquy Shakespeare delays his exit. It occurs in the opening beat of the following sequence, and to effect it Shakespeare writes one of those exit beats in which he brings a character onto the stage (here Desdemona) to accompany another character (Othello) off. The device is useful, for Desdemona's appearance at the end of the concluding soliloquy, as we have seen, demonstrates the ability of her chaste presence to dispel illusion, even as her accidental loss of her handkerchief here sets the next sequence going; moreover, the delay in Othello's departure smooths over the juncture between the two sequences.

Clearly, Shakespeare writes concluding beats not just at the ends of acts and of scenes but at the ends of sequences as well. A standard feature of Shakespeare's sequence is that the action passes into a decrescent stage where tensions are released. Every sequence has its own conclusion, whether compressed into five or six lines or extended over five or six beats, and any scene will have in it as many sets of concluding beats as it has sequences. Concluding beats, in other words, are appropriately spaced throughout the scene, not simply at its end.

6

Sequential beats: the intensifying beat

I

Analyzing intensifying beats is by far the most rewarding part of the work on a sequence, as well as the most important, for these are the beats in which the rhythms of its action are determined. Toward what event is the action pushing? How slow or how fast does this particular sequence move to get there? Does the pace change at any place? How much of a crescendo will be appropriate? Where are the turning points? How much emphasis should they be given? When is the climax reached? Is it a momentary or a sustained climax? And so on. The problems to be resolved in any study of the intensification section of a sequence can be fascinating.

If the introductory beats of a sequence raise a dramatic question, the intensifying beats pulse toward the resolution of that question; therefore, an examination of the intensifying beat as well as of the common patterns of intensification is prerequisite to any meaningful analysis of Shakespeare's use of dramatic questions as the structural underpinnings of his sequences. Every sequence must be given direction; in some way the action builds toward a goal, and before the unit runs its course, characters are moved to a different position. Let us look in this chapter, then, at how Shakespeare uses the beat to simulate that sense of movement customarily referred to as the "rising action."

Intensifying beats do not occur singly, but comes in sets. Their very function of increasing tension requires that they must somehow suggest stages in a sequence of events, as in the opening sequence of *King Lear*, where Shakespeare has Lear interview first Goneril (beat 1.1.53–67), then Regan (67–82), and finally Cordelia (82–107). Each conversation represents a single stage in the intensification and consequently a separate intensifying beat. The result is a string of intensifying beats, all closely related, which seem inseparable.

An interesting factor, good to pinpoint before going any further, is that intensifying beats themselves can be far more complex in their structure than other beats, that is, they sometimes contain an additional level of nesting. The beat between Lear and Cordelia just mentioned is a case in point. The patterning established in the intensification section of that sequence is obvious and regular: Shakespeare gives each sister a full beat in which to declare her love. Yet Cordelia's beat displays a complexity absent from the earlier beats. Instead of a single question with a single answer, as in the Goneril and Regan beats, Lear puts a *series* of questions to Cordelia, for he finds her initial answer incomprehensible. This results in an unusual segmentation. The Cordelia beat appears to break down into six segments, each segment (A through F) having a semblance of independence:

A

LEAR   Now, our joy,
Although our last and least, to whose young love
The vines of France and milk of Burgundy
Strive to be interess'd, what can you say to draw
A third more opulent than your sisters? Speak.
      CORDELIA Nothing, my lord.

B

      LEAR Nothing?
      CORDELIA Nothing.

C

      LEAR Nothing will come of nothing, speak again.
      CORDELIA Unhappy that I am, I cannot heave
My heart into my mouth. I love your Majesty
According to my bond, no more nor less.

D

      LEAR How, how, Cordelia? Mend your speech a little,
Lest you may mar your fortunes.
      CORDELIA   Good my lord,
You have begot me, bred me, lov'd me: I
Return those duties back as are right fit,
Obey you, love you, and most honor you.
Why have my sisters husbands, if they say
They love you all? Happily, when I shall wed,
That lord whose hand must take my plight shall carry
Half my love with him, half my care and duty.
Sure I shall never marry like my sisters,
To love my father all.

E

LEAR But goes thy heart with this?
CORDELIA   Ay, my good lord.

F

LEAR So young, and so untender?
CORDELIA So young, my lord, and true.

(I.I. 82–107)

But the divisions A through F make more sense if understood as sub-
sections and not as independent beats. Neither the beat function nor its
subject nor Lear's propelling motive has changed. His questions simply
confirm the truthfulness of Cordelia's response, which is explained and
accented. Lear's probing questions bring him a fuller understanding of
Cordelia's position, but the whole section is best explained as a single
beat.

What should be remembered about the Cordelia beat is that
Shakespeare occasionally finds it necessary to add an additional level of
nesting. Ordinarily the beat nests within the sequence, the line within the
beat. But now and then some crucial beat may itself be constructed of
segments.

But what are the larger patterns through which Shakespeare
organizes his intensifying beats into sequences? Although Shakespeare's
sequences are highly individualized, certain organizational patterns
recur with some frequency, and these provide the best context for a
discussion of the interior portions of the sequence. Of these organizing
forms, three stand out as most significant – the *chronological intensification*, which relies heavily upon the story itself to build the action; the
cumulative intensification, which is more consciously rhetorical and
depends for its effects upon deliberate repetition; and the *motivated
intensification*, where the energies of the propelling character become the
force that pushes the action to its climax (the principles in the motivated
sequence are exactly the same as those we have detected in the motivated
beat, except that those principles are now controlling a larger unit).

We shall examine each type of sequence intensification in greater
detail. But this, let us emphasize, will be a linear, rather than a thematic
study. In any aspect of human life there are two crucial elements – depth
and direction – and both are present in the mirror Shakespeare holds up
to nature. In the sequence the element of depth is achieved in many
different ways, characteristically profound imagery being one of them.
Were there space, this book would include a chapter on another – the
way the narrative structure of an action gives rise to and often

determines meaning. But thematic concerns remain outside our scope, for we are approaching drama at that preliminary point at which narrative or story is transformed into play and are therefore dealing with the elementary organization of events. The task is to demonstrate how Shakespeare gives his action direction. The focus will be on the body of the sequence, but on its linear rather than its thematic elements.

II

The most basic way of organizing beats to increase tension is to arrange discrete episodes in chronological order so that they tell a story. *Basic* in this context does not mean unsophisticated, for the chronological intensification underlies one of the most complex sequences in Shakespeare, that in which Duncan's body is discovered in *Macbeth*. Our intention here is only to make apparent the significant difference between a sequence in which events are organized merely by the flow of time, like the discovery sequence just mentioned, and the kind of sequence in which the motives of Macbeth himself actually govern the entire action. Though all *beats* take their direction from the objectives of the character who happens to be in the ascendant, this is not true of all *sequences*. Shakespeare's chronological sequences move along without any central controlling figure. Because direction in these sequences is imposed from outside the characters, it is usually futile to search the action for the will that brings it to its culmination. All that can be said about the source of the movement in such sequences is that the events occur in chronological order. The direction originates from the narrative itself rather than from some specific human will.

How does this *chronological*, or *narrative*, sequence work? In these sequences the selection and ordering of the incidents is the paramount factor. Each beat is constructed as a vignette – a short, descriptive, and self-contained "slice of life," deliberately realistic in detail. Progression occurs because of the consecutive placement of these beats: joined together they tell a story. Shakespeare, of course, evokes the feeling that no selection has been made, that these events unfold naturally, as events do in life.

Because the narrative is organized as a series of discrete events, chronological sequences tend to involve a mixture of characters. These characters come and go not just at the ends of the sequence but throughout; if they do not actually leave the stage, they at least tend to circulate – characters group and regroup. The beat structure reflects such regrouping, beat boundaries usually occurring where characters enter or exit.

If there is no obvious motivational throughline in this kind of sequence, where then is the motivation? At this point the value of the beat as a motivational unit is apparent. As we have already seen, in Shakespeare the beat normally contains a propelling character whose motives give it direction. That character becomes the focus of the beat action, and the beat action advances the action of the sequence one step further. It is a characteristic of chronological sequences that in general each beat will have a different propelling character (think of the ballroom sequence of *Romeo and Juliet*).[1]

Because its action seldom follows a single character, the chronological intensification can go anywhere. The episodes occur as if by chance – so much so that in many of these chronological sequences the ending cannot be predicted from the beginning. This may seem a truism: no action worth its salt will lack some element of surprise. But in cumulative and motivated sequences there is something specific at stake from the beginning so that whatever surprises develop occur within predictable limits, as we shall see later on. Not so in the chronological sequence. The action here gives a stronger sense of spontaneity.

It will be helpful to examine these principles as Shakespeare applies them in specific sequences. The Gadshill sequences in *I Henry IV*, 2.1.1–97, for example, epitomize the kind of external realism best captured by arranging discrete beat-length vignettes into a continuous narrative sequence. Shakespeare has written sequence 2.1.1–97 to create the rural setting that makes the robbery of the next sequence credible. It transports us out of London to some place on the Rochester road and through it the stage is transformed into an inn yard. A sense of immediacy is established.

To create this sequence Shakespeare takes individual narrative incidents and strings them together. In the first episode (1–31) he depicts an encounter between two carriers and an ostler. The latter is never seen, but his ineptitude provides the impetus for the action of the beat, as its enclosing lines clearly indicate. In these enclosing lines, spoken by the First Carrier, Shakespeare supplies both drivers with a motive for appearing on stage: eager to be off on their day's journey, they need their horses saddled, and the negligent ostler is apparently not up or, if up, hardly moving. Their task is to get the ostler hustling. Between attempts to raise the ostler the carriers engage in conversation, the natural topics being how each spent the previous night, and where each is heading that day. In this interior section of the beat, details thus emerge that fill out the picture. The inn itself is apparently not well tended, being "the most villainous house in all London road" for discomforts, with the horses treated as shabbily as the guests. One of the carriers has a wagonload of live turkeys which, like the horses, the servants have not fed. The details of this miniature action structured upon the attempt of two carriers to rouse a lazy ostler create a vivid sense of early morning at an inn.

This is Shakespeare's introductory beat. How is this action intensified? Shakespeare has told us where we are but not where we are going. In the second beat (32–46), in fact, he gives us a new mix of characters – Gadshill (the man, not the place) enters the sequence. Action no longer focuses upon the carriers' motives; rather, the initiative in this beat lies with Gadshill. Clearly a rogue and a thief, Gadshill attempts to mingle with the carriers, who do not trust him and break away. The beat depicts only a brief episode in the inn yard – a meeting between the coachmen whose carts are about to be robbed and the scout sent by the thieves to spy on them – another vignette. But with this encounter we move a step closer to the robbery.

When Gadshill summons the Chamberlain a third cameo sketch begins (beat 3, 47–97). It provides the climax of this inn-yard sequence. Again the enclosing lines give the actors the clue to their tasks in the beat: Gadshill, dominant, seeks a report from the Chamberlain, who proves to be in the employ of the thieves and who identifies for Gadshill the wealthiest of the inn's overnight guests with realistic detail: "there's a franklin in the Wild of Kent hath brought 300 marks with him in gold" and an accountant "that hath abundance of charge too." In return for the tip-off, the Chamberlain is promised "a share in our purchase." Between these enclosing lines Shakespeare adds a round of jesting that instills character into Gadshill's part, expands the humor of the sequence, and keeps Prince Hal before the audience while he is offstage (Gadshill boasts of the royal company whose presence will grace the adventure). The style of this third beat is the same: another episode in the inn yard that this time identifies the victims of the proposed robbery.

The intensification in this chronological sequence, then, proceeds through a series of vignettes, each more or less self-contained, but each contributing to the sense of the impending robbery. The beat boundaries are easily determined, because there is a change of characters between each unit. In each beat a single character dominates. But dominance changes. Initially it belongs to the First Carrier, later to Gadshill. And Gadshill drifts from group to group. The constant regrouping of characters gives a panoramic quality to the sequence, in the sense that Percy Lubbock might use the word: the action is viewed from a distance, outside of the characters. Emphasis is on the developing story (and here its setting) rather than on the inner workings of the characters' minds.

Though in drama the playwright cannot stand back from his scene and describe it through the voice of a narrator, he can suggest a larger whole by treating, in chronological order, a series of events occurring in the same setting, thus suggesting movement toward a goal and a consequent increase in tension. The chronological unfolding of the narrative lends the individual beats just enough unity to allow the audience to perceive them as a piece.

This is of course an enjoyably comic sequence, preparatory in function and deliberately subordinate to the robbery sequence which follows it. Structurally, however, the robbery sequence unfolds in a similar way – in vivid episodes, each a beat: after the introductory taunting of Falstaff, who for the course of the first beat must search for his lost horse (2.2.1–47), there is, second, the notice that the victims are approaching, with the consequent scurrying about to be masked and in position (48–77); third, the robbery (78–92); and finally – the action this chronological intensification has been leading up to – the robbing of the robbers (93–111).

The events staged in the handkerchief sequence of *Othello* are primarily domestic; nevertheless, as at Gadshill, there is a constant change of characters, each usually signaling a change of beat. Again the vantage point is external (we observe the characters as if from a slight distance), and the form is highly representational. One has the sense that events are unfolding as they do in life. However, because the element of chance is heightened as Desdemona's handkerchief changes hands, the feeling of spontaneity is even greater than in the robbery sequence.

Compare this sequence with those adjacent to it in *Othello* 3.3, for it differs markedly from the surrounding ones. In the two immediately preceding sequences a single character determines the direction the action will take. In 3.3.41–92 Desdemona conducts the entire action; throughout the sequence she begs Othello to be reconciled with Cassio. In 3.3.93–279 Othello propels the sequence, questioning Iago about Cassio's honesty. In both cases the direction remains constant from start to finish; moreover, the possible conclusions are limited. In 3.3.41–92 Othello must say either "no" or "yes" to Desdemona's plea. In 3.3.93–279 Iago must either conceal his thoughts or (even if falsely) reveal them.

In the handkerchief sequence, by contrast, everything appears to happen by chance. No single character controls the entire action; new characters keep appearing on stage, and control shifts from one to another. In beat 3.3.279–89 Desdemona is the propelling character; in beats 290–9 and 300–13, Emilia; in beat 313–20, Iago. Not only do new characters keep appearing; they are there (seemingly) by accident. But for the dropped handkerchief, Emilia would have followed Desdemona out. Iago just happened to pass by at that moment. And finally, the end is not so closely determined by the beginning. Nothing said between Desdemona and Othello in the introductory beat indicates how this sequence is going to continue, let alone how it might end. When they go off to dinner, the action could go anywhere. The rising action of this sequence unfolds episode by episode, each episode following on as if by chance.

Yet the episodes exist within a very tight structure. Behind the apparently random series of events lies a skillfully designed action, held together by the dramatic question the actors must be playing (even though the audience cannot have recognized it yet), *What will happen to Desdemona's handkerchief?* At the end of the first beat the handkerchief lies alone on the stage, the focus of audience attention. It lies there long enough to be noticed, then Emilia picks it up. The next three beats are intensifying beats. Emilia's thought that "my wayward husband hath a hundred times / Woo'd me to steal it. . .What he will do with it / Heaven knows, not I" introduces an element of danger. By now we know far more than Emilia does about Iago's scheme; her speculations stimulate both fear that he will get the prize and suspense as to how. With Iago's entrance in the next beat the threat becomes stronger – the handkerchief is dangled before his coveting eyes – "Look, here 'tis." Iago's desire for the object is established as the final stage of the intensification: "Good wench, give it me." The climax occurs when he snatches the handkerchief from Emilia. Shakespeare heightens the dramatic impact by making us aware, beforehand, that the worst possible place for the handkerchief to end up would be in Iago's pocket. Once Iago gains the prize all tensions are released. The sequence must close. Shakespeare concludes it with a decrescent beat in which Iago gloats upon his "victory."

Intensification obviously does not just happen. Even in sequences built up through the juxtaposition of individual episodes there is always a controlling force – the playwright. The writer must control the beats in order to create the desired thrust. Tension arises naturally, simply because the audience experiences movement in the flow from a beginning toward an end. The story itself gives direction, with the intensification occurring as a movement toward the most pertinent episode.

The disparate events that make up the action of a chronologically organized sequence may be given forward motion through the addition of any number of subtle elements superimposed upon the structure. The sense of time is the most natural of these intensifying devices. Any progression from present to future always implies a question about what the future holds. Tension mounts as the future is approached. In the ballroom sequence from *Romeo and Juliet* Shakespeare capitalizes on this chronological advantage by spreading the action of the Capulet ball over the course of an evening. He begins with the arrival of the guests and builds from there. So with the *Henry IV* robbery sequence, which starts at dawn and advances with the day. Within the time element is another option, that of timing. Intensification may be created through acceleration. Long, slow episodes may give way to short, quicker ones, as they do in the sequence which brings on a plodding, unhorsed Falstaff to grumble for a beat of forty-seven lines and ends with the thieves scattering in a beat of eleven lines. Greater energies are created as the action speeds up. In the sequence in which Volumnia returns from Coriolanus's camp to Rome (5.4.1 to 5.5.7) ordering is spatial. Intensification occurs because the movement progresses from far to near. The closer Volumnia comes to Rome, the more excited the characters awaiting her return become, and her actual arrival supplies the climax. Another way of creating a sense of growing significance that will intensify a chronologically structured action is to use minor characters in early beats and major characters in later ones. Chronologically ordered sequences benefit from such additional strengthening. In them, the forces advancing the action are limited to the most basic forces available to the dramatist – the chronological sequence of events and the progress of the narrative itself toward an end – with no reinforcement from a unifying and strongly motivated psyche. Little wonder that additional intensifying devices are superimposed upon the narrative structure to increase the forward thrust.

Yet an intensification structured in the chronological form can exude great power. Consider the sequence from *Macbeth* in which Duncan's death is discovered (2.3.42–146). A look at the playwright's purpose in writing this sequence explains why the action is best cast in the episode-by-episode form. The sequence asks how all of the characters – but especially the guilty couple – will respond to the news of Duncan's murder. Given such a question, the action can *only* unfold spontaneously. No one, not even the guilty Macbeths, knows what will happen until the time comes when it has to happen. Significantly, no one character in the sequence has a motive that dominates the whole and drives it forward. Shakespeare shifts the focus throughout from character to character, capturing the individual response of each one, until at last occasion lets all eyes turn toward Macbeth.

The sequence unfolds as a series of relatively independent beats. These beats suggest a constant flux both in character and situation that underscores the chaos engendered by the murder. In the introductory section Macduff calls to rouse the King (beat 45–52). As soon as he goes into Duncan's chamber the action begins to intensify. While Macduff remains offstage there is an intriguing interval of suspense, during which an unsuspecting Lennox reports the dire omens of the past night to Macbeth (beat 53–63). Then Macduff bursts in to announce the death of the King (beat 64–73). As Lennox and Macbeth disappear into the death chamber, Macduff sounds an alarm that raises the household (beat 73–80). Next he informs Lady Macbeth and Banquo that Duncan is dead (beat 81–90). Macbeth returns, bringing the action to a critical moment: Duncan's murderer must now respond publicly to the murder. Will he escape detection? The spotlight shifts from Macduff to Macbeth, who delivers a lament for Duncan that gets him through this crisis (beat 91–6). Tension continues to mount as Macbeth and Lennox describe the murder to Duncan's sons, for their questions are probing (beat 97–119), and is finally released by the ruse that allows the guilty couple to exit in safety – the well-timed swoon of Lady Macbeth. Motivation changes even more rapidly in the concluding beats: Malcolm and Donalbain decide to flee (119–25), Banquo calls for a formal meeting to discuss the situation (125–34), and Malcolm and Donalbain make their escape (135–46).

The style is panoramic rather than psychological. Macbeth does not think aloud. We can only guess that Lady Macbeth planned her swoon. We are not made privy to the Macbeths' relief at surviving the crisis. The emphasis is instead upon the announcement of Duncan's death – the painful eulogy Macduff delivers upon emerging from the murder chamber, the startling alarums, the violence, the horror, and the grief. Against this background of sincere grief, the Macbeths display the false faces that win them temporary acquittal. Through Macbeth's act confusion "hath made his masterpiece"; in this sequence, Shakespeare has made a masterpiece of confusion. The chronological narrative style works as well with major climactic sequences as with minor ones.

III

Intensifying beats may be linked together in more obvious ways, and we turn now to another form of sequence organization found throughout the canon, intensification through accumulation. The intensification of the sequence still unfolds in episodes – each episode a separate beat. But in amassing these intensifying beats Shakespeare creates a sense of repetition rather than of spontaneity. A general might receive three different messengers, each delivering a crucial report. A king holding court might hear petitions from three different subjects. A justice might decide three different cases. Three is a favorite number in such sequences (two episodes would not establish the notion of a series, four could prove too many). In planning his rising action, Shakespeare takes advantage of the cumulative impact of any series of repetitions: he stresses the parallels but subordinates the earlier episodes to the later to produce the effect of movement from the least important to the most important.

To give the sequence additional coherence Shakespeare calls upon some dignitary to preside over the individual episodes. This character will dominate the introductory and concluding beats. His presence throughout the intensification is both a unifying and a direction-giving factor. The addition of a single governing figure changes the character of the sequence considerably: with his advent a new level of motivation comes into play – the sequence motive. In the chronological intensification, motivation remains primarily within each beat. Beat motives do not disappear in the cumulative intensification, but a unifying motive is superimposed upon them. Because the action of the intensifying beats unfolds in response to the will of that guiding figure, his motive gives direction to the incidents not only individually but also as a series; the subordinate characters act in response to his desires. Also, with a presiding figure there is a greater potential for psychological depth: the way the ruling character reacts to what occurs in the episodes will reveal his own attitudes and goals. Finally, there is greater opportunity for a strong impact, for the will of the ruling character may be thwarted. When impact is desired, the climax is managed by creating opposition in the third or final interview. The first two respondents obey; the last rebels.

Repetition is the key to the intensifying beats of sequences unfolding through the cumulative pattern. The peacemaking effort at the court of King Edward examined in chapter 2 depends for its effect on the repetition of closely related episodes. In that sequence Edward engages several different groups, successively, in the same action – swearing perpetual amity. As each group capitulates to Edward's will, the harmony being established appears more and more complete. The cumulative technique is apparent again in two of Shakespeare's most familiar sequences, one from *Hamlet* and one from *King Lear*. In *Hamlet* 1.2.1–159 he depicts Claudius presiding over his court. The King addresses various issues of state, and the order of business supplies the order for the intensifying beats:

17–41   Claudius dispatches Voltimand and Cornelius to Norway to negotiate about the Fortinbras affair.

42–63   Claudius hears and grants Laertes' petition that he might return to France.

64–128 Claudius and Gertrude urge Hamlet to cast aside his grief.

First Fortinbras, then Laertes, then Hamlet – one issue per beat – and, presiding over all, King Claudius. Repetition of this sort is the method of the fairy tale, and it is used to memorable effect in the opening sequence of *King Lear* (1.1.1–139); there are three sisters and each speaks her piece.

In all these situations a rising action develops through the movement from the least to the most important business. There is less interest in a handshake between Hastings and Rivers or in a kiss between the Queen and Buckingham than in the assurance of Richard of Gloucester that his soul is at odds with no man's. There is less complexity in the affairs of Cornelius and Voltemand or of Laertes, who are easily dispatched on their respective journeys, than in the affairs of Hamlet, who has lost both a father and a throne. There is less drama in the flattery of Goneril or Regan as they soothe their father's vanity than in Cordelia's refusal to love publicly and on cue. As with the chronological narrative, the cumulative structure has an inherent tendency toward drama that need only be developed and pointed. Two lesser figures shape expectations regarding a more central third figure. The effect of that figure is naturally dramatic, and the impact is doubled if he shatters the expectations established in the earlier intensifying beats.

The third episode in the cumulative series is always the episode toward which the action is moving and it always holds the greatest interest. Thus, while each of the first two elements in the series will usually be treated within the space of one beat, the third sometimes requires more space. Hamlet's section is drawn out longer than either Fortinbras' or Laertes', Cordelia's more than Goneril's or Regan's. This suggests an important point. Though the cumulative style is based on a situation that unfolds in three stages and though any single stage may be handled in a single beat, this is not an inviolable rule. The third stage in particular may contain either a single beat with a highly complex, multipartite structure or an expansion of the final stage into more than one beat. The more powerful the sequence, the greater the likelihood that all three episodes will be expanded.

The *Hamlet* and *Lear* sequences have been analyzed in many places. Let us instead watch Shakespeare using this cumulative technique of intensification to shape two minor sequences – one from *Coriolanus* and another from *Othello* – and then a major sequence from *Richard II*.

Coriolanus offers us a minor sequence that reveals Shakespeare playing with this cumulative method of intensifying an action (4.5.1–49). The sequence occupies one-third of a scene. Coriolanus has come to Antium hoping to confer with Aufidius. That conference takes place in the scene's central sequence, the lighter sequences before and after it being populated by the servants of the household.[2] In order to obtain an audience with Aufidius, Coriolanus, in the action we are examining, must breach this defensive wall of servants.

The flurry of activity among the serving men in beat 4.5.1–6 is introductory. It establishes the interior of the house and makes the point, already mentioned in 4.4, that this night Aufidius "feasts the nobles of the state." While the whole sequence prepares us for the important meeting in which Coriolanus offers his services to Aufidius, this introductory beat acquaints us specifically with the servants Coriolanus will encounter when he steps inside the house.

The cumulative intensification begins with Coriolanus's appearance. The action is slight, even humorous. The Volscian servants prove as cantankerous as the Roman citizens. Coriolanus's intrusion elicits from them a natural response – the impulse to cast him out – which unifies and gives life to the series of repeated episodes that comprise the intensification. In episode 1 the First Servant orders this apparent beggar to leave:

> 1 SERVANT What would you have, friend? whence are you?
> Here's no place for you; pray go to the door.　　　　*Exit*
> CORIOLANUS I have deserv'd no better entertainment
> In being Coriolanus.
>
> (4.5.7–10)

The Second Servant pursues the same objective in episode 2, but with more fervor. By way of intensification Shakespeare substitutes for the preoccupation of the First Servant the annoyance of the Second:

> 2 SERVANT Whence are you, sir? Has the porter his eyes in his head, that he gives entrance to such companions? Pray get you out.
> CORIOLANUS Away!
> 2 SERVANT Away? Get you away.
> CORIOLANUS Now th' art troublesome.
> 2 SERVANT Are you so brave? I'll have you talk'd with anon.
>
> (4.5.11–18)

In the third effort to remove Coriolanus, force is applied. The Third Servant attempts to push Coriolanus out the door. He finds stronger resistance than he expected:

> 3 SERVANT What fellow's this?
> 1 SERVANT A strange one as ever I look'd on. I cannot get him

out o' th' house. Prithee call my master to him.

3 SERVANT What have you to do here, fellow? Pray you avoid the house.

CORIOLANUS Let me but stand, I will not hurt your hearth.

3 SERVANT What are you?

CORIOLANUS A gentleman.

3 SERVANT A marv'llous poor one.

CORIOLANUS True, so I am.

3 SERVANT Pray you, poor gentleman, take up some other station; here's no place for you. Pray you avoid. Come.

CORIOLANUS Follow your function, go, and batten on cold bits.

Pushes him away from him.

3 SERVANT What, you will not? Prithee tell my master what a strange guest he has here.

2 SERVANT And I shall.

Exit Second Servingman.

(4.5.19–36)

In order to increase our sense that serious pressure is now being put upon Coriolanus to leave, Shakespeare spreads this last stage of the intensification over two beats. In beat 19–36, just quoted, the Third Servant is naive: he must experience what the others have already learned – that this stranger is not easily brushed off. This beat has an interesting set of enclosing lines – the cue lines for Aufidius: "Prithee call my master" (21) and later, "Prithee tell my master what a strange guest he has here" (34–5). When the beat ends, the Second Servant rushes off to fetch Aufidius. Beat 37–49 takes place as we await the master's arrival. The Third Servant, now more scornful, continues to bait Coriolanus, who responds with condescension, the sequence ending in a climactic bit of slapstick in which the Third Servant is beaten from the stage.

The action builds distinctly from a casual command to the intruder, flung back over the shoulder of a servant who is hurrying out, to a bodily attempt to remove him. The climax occurs when scuffling breaks out. Though Coriolanus is not directing the action but resisting it, his presence as the force that defies the efforts to remove him gives meaning and unity to the repeated episodes. By the end of the sequence it is clear that even as a stranger and exile in Antium Coriolanus remains a formidable presence.

The cumulative technique lends itself well to situations in which some important personage must acquire information from outside his immediate environment. In such cases the playwright brings on a series of messengers with news from the wider world. Take the sequence that

93

introduces the Duke of Venice, who will soon try Brabantio's case against Othello before the Senate council (1.3.1–47). This council has met for other reasons: its primary concern is not Othello's marriage to Desdemona, which will occupy it shortly, but the report of a Turkish attack on Cyprus. The Senators are at first intent upon analyzing the movements of the enemy fleet. Their analysis proceeds from three successive reports. If we understand the purposes of this sequence, we see how appropriate the cumulative technique is to its meaning. By casting the Duke of Venice as the controlling figure Shakespeare dramatizes an act of judging. The Duke passes from doubt to certainty during the sequence.

Ralph Berry describes the ultimate purpose of this action nicely:

> Now what is the point of this military miniature? It is not in Cinthio, and is a genuinely Shakespearean piece of business. It hardly adds to the theatrical excitement of the crisis, and apparently slows up the real action. Its purpose is to maintain the theme before the audience, and demonstrate by contrast the capacity, so unlike Othello's, to weigh and sift evidence and from it deduce the workings of the mind . . . The Venetian leader represents admirably the character of his people when, in reply to Brabantio's wild allegations, he says:
>
> > To vouch this is no proof,
> > Without more wider and more overt test
> > Than these thin habits and poor likelihoods
> > Of modern seeming do prefer against him.
>
> And the consecutive incidents of the Council's business figure to us the play's main affair – the determining of truth upon a just consideration of all available evidence.[3]

This is the ultimate meaning. But there is a more immediate one. Seeing the play for the first time we certainly would not find the Duke "so unlike Othello" here, for at this point (1.3) what little we have seen of Othello gives us every reason to believe that his own judgments would be as sound as the Duke's. The thematic mirroring that Berry describes would be detected later, after careful thought about the production or, more likely, after additional readings of the play. But here we do notice the wisdom of the judges. The sequence's immediate effect on the audience is to prepare us to trust the Duke to decide wisely in Othello's case through this demonstration of his repeated good judgment. In this first impression it is not Othello but the emotional Brabantio who suffers in our estimation from the contrast.

This action, then, has both hidden and obvious reasons for demonstrating the methods of good judgment. To recognize either tells us what effect the sequence should have on the audience. But how are these effects achieved? Berry's "consecutive incidents" comprise the intensifying section of the sequence, which builds through cumulative repetition. In the first beat (1.3.1–12) the Senators review the information already at hand. They have several letters, all stating that a Turkish fleet is approaching Cyprus, but some report 107 galleys, some 140, some 200. This inconsistency requires a judgment: is the discrepancy in the secondary evidence important enough to justify dismissal of the primary claim that the Turks mean to attack Cyprus? The first beat shows the Senators confronting a problem raised by contradictory reports and resolving it.

A report followed by a judgment – this structure is repeated in beat 2 (1.3.12–31). A messenger enters with new information: "The Turkish preparation makes for Rhodes." The inquiry is intensified. Earlier the fleet had seemed to be "bearing up to Cyprus." The question now is, can this new evidence be believed? The councillors weigh the evidence against the knowledge they already possess and decide that reason dictates one conclusion only – "'tis a pageant / To keep us in false gaze."

Beat 3 (1.3.32–43) confirms that truth will out. A messenger arrives from Montano (here a symbol of reliability) to report that the Turkish fleet remained at Rhodes only long enough to pick up additional ships, then changed course, and now heads openly for its true destination. The careful judgments of the council have proved sound: "'Tis certain then for Cyprus." The cumulative effect provided by the repetition of three beats, in each of which a report is offered and its contents judged, leaves us with the feeling that the Duke and his advisors are admirably prudent.

This minor sequence is handled with the utmost economy. Its first beat sets up the situation, while the second and third intensify and resolve it. The climax comes with the moment of certainty. Shakespeare writes a three-line concluding beat to suggest that the Senators are ready to take action, but (again for economy's sake) he makes it an aborted beat; Brabantio arrives to change the direction of their inquiries. By this time, however, the audience has been readied by the cumulative effect of the sequence to trust the council's judgment of Othello more than Brabantio's.

This cumulative pattern is used for a related purpose in *Richard II* 3.2.1–218, where poor judgment is exposed. As in the example from *Othello*, three reports are brought to a presiding figure, in this case King Richard himself, who is about to learn that rebel forces under Henry Bullingbrook have occupied his kingdom. In segment 1 (3.2.63–90),

Salisbury brings word to Richard that "all the Welshmen, hearing thou wert dead, / Are gone to Bullingbrook." In segment 2 (90–177), Scroop brings further tidings of calamity: the King's favorites, Bushy, Green, and the Earl of Wiltshire, have been defeated by the rebels and beheaded. One hope remains. Threaded throughout the sequence are references to the saving power of the great Duke of York, Richard's loyal uncle. In segment 3 (178–203), Scroop announces that York, too, has joined with Bullingbrook. Three reports, each more damaging than its predecessor, are delivered to Richard, the repetition proving the means of intensifying the action of the sequence. Again each report elicits a response from the presiding character and again it is to the cumulative thrust of the responses that Shakespeare directs our attention. But while the responses in the *Othello* sequence portrayed wisdom, these reflect incompetence. Richard's reactions substitute naiveté for acumen, emotion for judgment, and rhetoric for action.[4]

Shakespeare offers us one more example of Richard's weakness, and on a grand scale. Where both the *Coriolanus* and the *Othello* sequences prepared the ground for the more central actions that succeeded them, this sequence stands at a turning point in the play. In it Shakespeare imbues the form with the intensity and power suitable to so climactic a moment. In this round of cumulative intensification every potential of the form is realized.

The most important step Shakespeare takes to give this sequence stature is to add a reversal. By the end of the sequence Richard's youthful optimism will have degenerated into the pessimism of despair. Shakespeare thus constructs a long introductory section to establish not just the setting (3.2.1–26) but Richard's current expectations as well (3.2.27–62). The King has just returned from Ireland. He is aware that rebel forces are in arms, yet his confidence is strong:

> Not all the water in the rough rude sea
> Can wash the balm off from an anointed king;
> The breath of worldly men cannot depose
> The deputy elected by the Lord.

> (3.2.54–7)

Knowing the source of his authority he expects it to continue unchanged, with no effort on his part. News of his return will by itself make Bullingbrook "sit blushing" and, "self-affrighted, tremble at his sin." This beginning establishes Richard at the point from which he is to be moved. Beat by beat the King's confidence evaporates, until at the end of the sequence Richard will discharge his followers and embrace "that sweet way" of despair:

Go to Flint castle, there I'll pine away –
A king, woe's slave, shall kingly woe obey.

Examination of this structure reveals an interesting fact about Shakespeare and reversals. Often it is not so much that the character himself is changing that abruptly – the 180-degree turn is more a matter of structure. This occurs over and over again. In *Macbeth* 1.7, for example. Despite appearances Macbeth does not change from white to black within eighty lines. After all, just before Duncan's arrival at Inverness, Macbeth has acquiesced, at least in thought, in the urgings of his "dearest partner in greatness." The full reversal occurs because Shakespeare moves Macbeth a step backward in the introductory beat, gives him last-minute scruples, so that the "reversal" confirms in a dramatic way a position he was inclined to take all along. The same here. Richard is ready in the first beat to fly into a state of despair. The marvel of the structure is not so much that Richard changes positions as that Shakespeare skillfully keeps him from doing so sooner. In this sense we have to admire the use the playwright makes of Carlisle and Aumerle as counterforces that repeatedly buoy Richard up.

Another technique Shakespeare employs in this sequence to produce the essential magnitude is to expand each unit of intensification beyond the confines of a single beat. The action unfolds in the usual three stages, each containing a report and Richard's response. But whereas in the lesser sequences just examined each step of the intensification is generally presented in one beat, here more has to be accomplished in each segment. The episodes become more elaborate: each stage of the intensification has several beats. Stage one unfolds in three beats (3.2.63–74, 75–81, 82–90), stage two in four beats (90–121, 122–42, 143–4, 144–77), and stage three in two beats (178–91, 192–203). To achieve Richard's reversal, Shakespeare has added an extra level of nesting – not between the line and the beat (as in the Cordelia beat of *King Lear*) but between the beat and the sequence: here beats are grouped into phases, which in turn form the sequence.

Despite this expansion, the beat groups never become full sequences in their own right; they remain phases of a cumulative action. And despite the additional level of nesting the standard cumulative pattern remains fundamental. There is still the repetition of three closely related episodes, and the repeated episodes effect a change in the character whose presence binds them together. The extended treatment given to the cumulative pattern here arises from the importance of the sequence, and the pattern proves itself able to carry so important a charge.

Intensification produced through repetition, with the desired effect being built up cumulatively, is a traditional device but effective as Shakespeare uses it. As with the chronological method, this one requires a fairly full stage, for though there is a single character dominating the sequence and giving it direction by pursuing his own goals, there must be at least three subordinate characters – three assorted Messengers; First, Second, and Third Servingman; Fortinbras, Laertes, Hamlet; Goneril, Regan, Cordelia – and all these sequences (with the exception of the one from *Coriolanus*), populate the stage with a full assortment of peripheral characters.

IV

In the final method to be studied, the motivated intensification, the focus narrows considerably. Here Shakespeare generally engages only two characters: the controlling character focuses all his attention upon one subordinate character. It is as if a single beat of one of the previous types had been expanded to occupy an entire sequence. Throughout the sequence a propelling character has a single objective, and the energies of the sequence derive from his attempts to attain it. When the beats change, it is because of some alteration in his tactics. Intensification now occurs not through some accident of chronology or narrative, not through some formal device like repetition, but through the intentional play of one psyche upon another.

In pitting one psyche against another Shakespeare selects some fundamental human activity as the basis for his sequence structure – for example, observing, reporting, interrogating, persuading, or disputing. Let us concentrate for now on persuading, an activity which has begun to receive attention from theorists and which is used throughout the canon. What interests us here is the way one character's objective can span a sequence and thus give direction to its intensifying beats.

Critical discussions of Shakespeare's persuading actions generally focus upon *Macbeth* 1.7, Lady Macbeth's powerful persuasion being viewed as the classic example of the type.[5] For variety's sake, we have selected instead the intensification Shakespeare invents for *Othello* 1.3.301–404, where Iago attempts to influence Roderigo. Though this *Othello* sequence occupies only the last 103 lines of a 400-line scene, it is constructed on the very same principles as those found in *Macbeth* 1.7, a full scene: in it Shakespeare gives Iago a significant objective, to persuade Roderigo to continue his pursuit of Desdemona, and that objective shapes the action of the sequence. An analysis of Shakespeare's handling of Iago's motives in this action will help us to understand how Shakespeare organizes intensifying beats in a motivated sequence.

Notice first the difference in perspective between this type of sequence and those we have been examining. The other sequences offer a very wide view. Each beat is full of action, and there are many beats. Much material is covered. Now we get a closeup. Shakespeare gives us "direct access to an imagined consciousness," as Matthew Black puts it – the consciousness of Iago. "The character is not just enunciating propositions or even persuasive arguments: he is creating a sense of himself meaning to do these things but also giving us himself; and this self of his is felt with an intimacy that we do not often feel in life."[6] The sequence penetrates deeply into Iago's psyche. All sequences reveal character, but in sequences structured on motivation character revelation is a major purpose. Here Shakespeare wishes to reveal the malignant nature Iago so carefully hides from Othello and Desdemona. To do so, he puts Roderigo in Iago's way, then shows how naturally Iago slides into manipulation.

Second, the sequence is basically a duet – it involves only two characters, in other words two conflicting motives. One of these characters exerts the dominant force and therefore controls the action; the other responds. Iago acts, Roderigo reacts – *throughout* the sequence. Dominance does not change from episode to episode but remains with Iago to the end of the sequence.

The sequence takes its structure from the motive of the propelling character: the task given to (or, as it seems, chosen by) Iago is to persuade. The introductory and concluding beats make that framing action clear enough, especially in the enclosing lines of the sequence. Roderigo approaches Iago moaning "I will incontinently drown myself," and leaves after promising to abandon this intention:

> IAGO No more of drowning, do you hear?
> RODERIGO I am chang'd.[7]
>
> (1.3.378–9)

As Roderigo's "I am chang'd" indicates, Iago's persuasion is successful (could he so change Othello, and not succeed with this gull?). And his is the mind we must follow throughout the sequence.

This is not to say that anyone should take seriously Roderigo's threat to drown himself. He obviously adopts an attitude, but his talk about drowning is purely metaphorical. It means something like "I am despondent," and Iago's task is not to stop Roderigo from dashing into deep water but to move him from despair to hope. Implicit in Roderigo's despair is his belief that Desdemona, having married, is lost to him; further pursuit of her would be absurd. Also implicit in the situation is Iago's awareness that Roderigo will no longer be useful if he abandons his pursuit of Desdemona: better for Iago that Roderigo's expiring hope remains alive. The tensions of the sequence stem from this difference in objectives, a difference their contrasting attitudes to the projected drowning render concrete.

But what determines the beat structure? In the chronological intensification the individual episodes of the narrative provide material for beats. In the cumulative intensification the repeated incidents supply natural divisions. What organizing mode underlies the beats in an intensification that follows the direction of a mind? Here the beats are shaped by the individual motives through which the larger objective is sought. The sequence objective is achieved through a series of subtle and always subordinate motives that nest within it and advance the persuader's cause, one step at a time. The intensification developed within this particular persuading structure spreads out over four beats, all controlled by Iago, who, in working Roderigo around, first ridicules, next reproves, then offers hope, and finally reassures. These beat motives, taken together, create the persuading action.

Iago knows that before he can instill hope, he must shatter the despair. Therefore, in the first two intensifying beats, Iago attacks the cause of that despair – Roderigo's lovesickness. Not that he wants Roderigo to give Desdemona up. But Roderigo will gain nothing by puling. Iago begins with ridicule – he attempts to convince Roderigo that no woman is worth dying for (beat 1.3.311–18). With the assuredness of experience addressing youth, Iago tags Roderigo a fool whose talk of drowning himself "for the love of a guinea hen" is absurd. Roderigo counters feebly that "it is not in my virtue to amend it."

Roderigo's protest that he cannot change shifts Iago onto a new tack, provoking a diatribe that moves away from light-hearted ridicule. In the second beat (1.3.319–34), Iago rebukes. What incenses him is the word "virtue." As Bernard Spivack points out, we miss the point of his lecture if we fail to understand that by virtue Roderigo means "divine grace flowing into the otherwise helpless nature of man, creating there the power toward good."[8] Iago is arguing against Roderigo's assumption that human actions are guided by a force that transcends human reason. For Iago, human reason by itself gives us "the power and corrigible authority" to order our lives. A key passage for the study of Iago's psyche, this discourse reveals a deficiency in Iago's outlook that aligns him with Shakespeare's rationalists, Edmund and Richard III. But it should not be approached as a set piece, isolated from the rest of the sequence. Shakespeare makes it one phase of an ongoing persuasion. Iago implies that Roderigo could do more to achieve his end by activating his will than by drowning in his own sensuality.

Having sufficiently chastised Roderigo, Iago switches tactics. In the third beat of the intensification (1.3.335–61), he extends hope. He now attempts to convince Roderigo that Desdemona is not lost to him forever.

> It cannot be long that Desdemona should continue her love to the Moor . . . nor he his to her.

> These Moors are changeable in their wills . . . the food that to him now is as luscious as locusts, shall be to him shortly as acerb as the coloquintida.

> She must change for youth; when she is sated with his body, she will find the error of her choice.

"Thou shalt enjoy her," promises Iago, for all that lies between Roderigo and success is "sanctimony and a frail vow." This vulgar account of a pure love serves Iago's purpose well in prodding Roderigo toward acquiescence. In this third intensifying beat, Iago instills hope.

In the fourth and last beat of the intensification (1.3.362–72), the reversal begins: Roderigo is about to seize the hope offered him. Shakespeare suggests Roderigo's change of mind obliquely by making him hesitant ("Wilt thou be fast to my hopes, if I depend on the issue?"): Roderigo needs to be convinced that if he acts upon Iago's suppositions and follows Desdemona to Cyprus Iago will indeed support him; thus, in the final stage of the persuasion Iago reassures: "I have told thee often, and I retell thee again and again, I hate the Moor. My cause is hearted; thine hath no less reason. Let us be conjunctive in our revenge against him." Having Iago's reassurance, Roderigo reverses his stand.

Of course these long passages effectively reveal Iago's character, but in addition, they are intensifying beats put together to create a rising action. Iago ridicules, he rebukes, he instills hope, and finally he reassures.

Shakespeare handles the persuading structure not like a formula but like a recipe, transforming it at each making by varying the ingredients. How different in effect is the sequence in which Desdemona begs Othello to overlook Cassio's offense, yet the energies in it, too, stem from persuading. The sequence runs from 3.3.41 to 3.3.92, and since there is total honesty on both sides it unfolds with quiet simplicity. Desdemona is the propelling character, Othello the resisting one. Desdemona has one objective throughout, to persuade Othello to call Cassio back. She announces that goal immediately: "Good my lord, / If I have any grace or power to move you, / His present reconciliation take." This objective not only unifies but gives direction to the four intensifying beats, propelling the action toward the moment at which Othello grants her suit ("Let him come when he will; / I will deny thee nothing," 75–6) and, so that no one can miss his decision, reaffirms it (83).

Persuading is the governing motive of the sequence but again there are subsidiary motives involved, each providing just enough force to propel a beat, and of course that force always originates with Desdemona. The initial plea in beat 45–55 takes the form of a defense. Desdemona urges Cassio's obvious honesty, the accidental rather than willful nature of his offense, and his deep grief; she would impress Othello with Cassio's merits. Othello's tendency to procrastinate causes Desdemona to intensify her persuasion: in this second beat (56–68) she has a more specific goal – to set a date for Cassio's pardon. At line 68 her whole tone changes perceptibly, so that in the third beat the appeal becomes more personal and Desdemona now expresses surprise that her request could meet with such resistance (one might even say she remonstrates):

> I wonder in my soul
> What you would ask me that I should deny,
> Or stand so mamm'ring on. What? Michael Cassio,
> That came a-wooing with you, and so many a time,
> When I have spoke of you dispraisingly,
> Hath ta'en your part – to have so much to do
> To bring him in! By'r lady, I could do much –
>
> (3.3.68–74)

This third plea succeeds, bringing us to the beat in which Shakespeare moves the sequence to its climax (75–83). Desdemona makes one last point: even as Othello grants her favor she insists that the plea was "as I should entreat you wear your gloves, / Or feed on nourishing dishes." In this climactic beat she defends the naturalness of her proposal. Thus each of these four subsidiary motives advances the action a step. The intensification comes from the attempts of Desdemona to bring Othello to the desired end, and her will determines the beat structure.

This example proves exceptionally valuable, in that a careful study of the beat motives and their outcome explodes a common misconception: because Cassio and Othello are *not* reconciled many people consider Desdemona's persuasion unsuccessful. On the contrary, Shakespeare constructs the sequence as a reversal; Desdemona moves Othello from refusal to acquiescence. He goes back on his promise later, when Iago urges him to "hold Cassio off a while"; however, at the end of this sequence, the lady has won Cassio a reprieve. Except for Iago's interference, all would have been well.

The motivated intensification, obviously, works quite differently from either the chronological or the cumulative intensification. In exploring it we have concentrated on the motive of persuading, but Shakespeare employs other motives when they are more pertinent – reporting, for example, or quarreling or commanding; motives other than persuading can also give direction to a sequence. Since the motivated intensification is by far the most interesting of the three forms and deserves more detailed study, in later chapters we shall examine the way Shakespeare handles some of these alternative motives.

But in the meantime, this survey of Shakespeare's intensifying beats illustrates how Shakespeare gives movement to a sequence by combining beats. Although a combination of two or three introductory beats or of the same number of concluding beats could conceivably be fairly static, intensifying beats are not. Each sequence has its own action, and the function of the intensifying beat is to build that action; therefore, any combination of intensifying beats will always have both movement and direction.

V

Little has so far been said about climactic beats or the way Shakespeare structures sequence climaxes. What exactly is the relationship between the sequence climax and the beat structure? Or, more specifically, does Shakespeare ever write "climactic beats"? How useful, how exact, is that term?

Naturally every sequence works its way toward some climax: intensification cannot go on indefinitely. The time comes when, as the Tribunes say to Coriolanus, "H'as said enough!" The goal has been reached. But intensification will be recognized as intensification only if there *is* some goal in view: in the chronological intensification the goal lies in the episode that finally reveals the outcome of the story; in the cumulative intensification there will be a revelation in the third episode affecting the presiding figure; in the motivated intensification the goal is reached when the objective of the propelling character is achieved (or thwarted). Each intensification obviously has built into it the expectation that the suspense being generated will somehow be resolved.

Though there is always a climax, there is not always a climactic beat: Shakespeare often effects the sequence climax abruptly. When the climax does require a full beat, there are perceptible reasons for sustaining the emotional pitch. The climactic moment may require clarification, for example, or even confirmation, if it has been so subtle that someone might have missed it. Or Shakespeare may be striving for dramatic power by sustaining the impact longer. The climax itself is the most subtle and elusive of moments, difficult to capture (for many playwrights, impossible).

This subtle quality of the climactic moment in sequences is best illustrated by climaxes which are not spelled out, where the printed text is searched in vain for a climactic beat. Take the Roderigo sequence recently examined. The action builds to this point:

> RODERIGO Wilt thou be fast to my hopes, if I depend on the issue?
>
> IAGO Thou art sure of me – go make money. I have told thee often, and I retell thee again and again, I hate the Moor. My cause is hearted; thine hath no less reason. Let us be conjunctive in our revenge against him. If thou canst cuckold him, thou dost thyself a pleasure, me a sport. There are many events in the womb of time which will be deliver'd. Traverse, go, provide thy money. We will have more of this tomorrow. Adieu.
>
> (1.3.362–72)

There is no fanfare at the moment of Roderigo's reversal, no line, not even a word, to cover his acquiescence. There is his hesitant question in the fourth beat of intensification ("Wilt thou be fast to my hopes?") marking Roderigo's inclination to turn, then Iago's awareness that he has won, manifested by his readiness to let Roderigo go. At some unspecified point during Iago's speech, Roderigo joins causes with Iago, because an exit beat for Roderigo follows:

> RODERIGO Where shall we meet i' th' morning?
> IAGO At my lodging.
> RODERIGO I'll be with thee betimes.
> IAGO Go to, farewell.
>
> (1.3.373–6)

Only as Roderigo leaves (and that only in the quarto version), does Iago demand confirmation:

> IAGO Do you hear, Roderigo?
> RODERIGO What say you?
> IAGO No more of drowning, do you hear?
> RODERIGO I am chang'd.
> IAGO Go to, farewell. Put money enough in your purse.
>
> (1.3.376–81)

Shakespeare makes it obvious with Roderigo's "I am chang'd" that the reversal has taken place. But this beat strikes us as a statement after the fact, a clarification for those in the audience who missed Roderigo's subtle surrender. This method of depicting the reversal reflects Roderigo's weak character, for he is less apt to make a forceful choice than to drift into a position because he lacks the will to oppose it. Yet the example also demonstrates that climactic moments often occur, quite literally, between the lines.

In *Macbeth* 1.7 sensitivity is also needed to discern the moment at which the hero falls victim to his wife's persuasion, for Macbeth makes the climactic decision to murder Duncan well before he expresses it in words. The reversal is complete by the time he says, "I am settled, and bend up / Each corporal agent to this terrible feat": this statement has the finality of a conclusion. The actual decision is probably made just before the final beat of intensification, when Macbeth cries out, "Bring forth men-children only! / For thy undaunted mettle should compose / Nothing but males." In this case the climax occurs in a pause between beats.

Not all climactic moments occur between the lines. An interesting question to ask of anyone rehearsing *Othello* 2.3 is where exactly does the climax occur in the scene's second sequence, where Iago plies Cassio with wine knowing that drink will render his rival "full of quarrel and offense," Iago's intention being to disgrace Cassio publicly. We refer not to the scene as a whole, only to that part of the scene which might be tagged the revels sequence (2.3.64–168).⁹ Sequences climax at the moment when the controlling character's objective is achieved. When is Iago's goal of disgracing Cassio achieved? There are so many possibilities and thus a real danger of staging the climax too early. The question is also relevant to our search for a climactic beat.

Where does the revels sequence climax? Is it when Cassio tries to demonstrate that he can "stand well enough, and speak well enough" but reveals himself too drunk to do either (2.3.110–20)? Is it when Iago's accomplice, Roderigo, succeeds in drawing Cassio into a quarrel (2.3.144–50)? When Cassio goes farther than Iago could have wished and attacks Montano, Cyprus's most prominent official (2.3.151–6)? Or perhaps when Roderigo rushes out and "cries a mutiny" that raises the town (2.3.157–63)? Surely the ringing of the alarm bell summoning the whole island to witness Cassio's "ingraft infirmity" might fittingly signal Iago's success. It ought to be easy to locate a climactic beat in a sequence that ends in a brawl, but the crisis grows ever more intense, and even with the clanging of the bell, its climax is not reached.

The climax comes not with the "barbarous brawl" Iago has staged, but with the entrance of the party for whom Iago staged it – the governor of Cyprus, Othello. Shakespeare most certainly means the action to climax at Othello's "What is the matter here?" (2.3.164). With Othello's appearance, authority intrudes upon the chaos. The fighting ceases, and all risk that the incident might be covered up, with Iago's trouble going for naught, vanishes on the instant.

Is there a climactic beat? Here the climax becomes the matter of a single line – Othello's "What is the matter here?" Shakespeare accompanies the climax with a brief additional skirmish between Montano and Cassio, but only to display Othello's ability to halt it. His climactic line ends both the brawling and the sequence.

Othello's "What is the matter here?" leads directly into a new action, an interrogating sequence with Othello as judge, and Montano, Cassio, and Iago as witnesses. In this sequence too the climax occurs as a riveting line at the end of a long intensification. After restoring order Othello makes an inquiry into the cause of the commotion, learns from Iago that Cassio is at fault, and responds to the Ancient's report with "I know, Iago, / Thy honesty and love doth mince this matter, / Making it light to Cassio. *Cassio, I love thee, / But never more be officer of mine.*" The action both of the sequence (2.3.169–258) and of the whole scene peaks with Othello's judgment. But despite the larger context, the full force of the climax is still concentrated in that one powerful line which terminates the interrogation: "Cassio, I love thee, / But never more be officer of mine." In that single line is revealed both the power of Othello, who, seeing the problem, moves immediately to effective action, and the victory of Iago, whose plot to discredit Cassio finds its ultimate resolution in this judgment.

But of course Shakespeare creates longer climaxes. The impact of the climax to Othello's trial before the Senate council is sustained for a full beat:

> BRABANTIO God be with you! I have done.
> Please it your Grace, on to the state affairs.
> I had rather to adopt a child than get it.
> Come hither, Moor:
> I here do give thee that with all my heart
> Which but thou hast already, with all my heart
> I would keep from thee. For your sake, jewel,
> I am glad at soul I have no other child,
> For thy escape would teach me tyranny,
> To hang clogs on them. I have done, my lord.
>
> (1.3.189–98)

But notice how Shakespeare constructs the "climactic" beat. The impact occurs at the moment of Brabantio's recognition that he cannot prove that "spells and medicines" and "practices of cunning hell" seduced his daughter. As soon as he realizes his case is lost, he gives up: "God be with you! I have done." The climactic statement is as sharp as any we have seen. In this instance, however, the moment of reversal is expanded. Brabantio delivers the key line twice, and between his initial expression of defeat and its echo, Shakespeare allows him to vent his disappointment, so that the emotions of the climax are sustained for a full beat.

The opening sequence of *King Lear* provides in its final beat another example of a sustained climax. Again there is an electric line that defines a moment of decision – Lear's "Let it be so: thy truth then be thy dow'r!" And again Shakespeare develops the climactic statement with lines that expand the emotion, clarify the intent, and sustain the force. But while both fathers build upon their initial statement, Lear goes further than Brabantio. Lear adds a curse:

> Let it be so: thy truth then be thy dow'r!
> For by the sacred radiance of the sun,
> The mysteries of Hecat and the night;
> By all the operation of the orbs,
> From whom we do exist and cease to be;
> Here I disclaim all my paternal care,
> Propinquity and property of blood,
> And as a stranger to my heart and me
> Hold thee from this forever. The barbarous Scythian,
> Or he that makes his generation messes
> To gorge his appetite, shall to my bosom
> Be as well neighbor'd, pitied, and reliev'd,
> As thou my sometime daughter.
>
> (1.1.108–20)

The climactic beats written for Brabantio and Lear can be usefully contrasted in yet another way, for in the *Lear* example Shakespeare draws out the climax one stage further. While the *Othello* sequence has a climactic beat, the *Lear* sequence has a climactic beat that spills over beyond the standard beat form. This device is generally used to depict a character who has lost control. Some interrupting cry "Enough!" fails to register on the raging character, and his tirade continues when it should instantly cease. Notice that as Lear concludes his curse Shakespeare moves the Earl of Kent to intervene:

> KENT   Good my liege –
> LEAR Peace, Kent!
> Come not between the dragon and his wrath.
>
> (1.1.120–2)

Kent has interrupted with the equivalent of the rational "Enough!" Not only the beat but the sequence is about to change at this moment. Shakespeare is ready to move on to Kent's defense of Cordelia (sequence 1.1.139–87). But Kent's appeal cannot still the torrent of abuse. Kent is silenced rather than Lear, whose diatribe continues:

> LEAR I lov'd her most, and thought to set my rest

On her kind nursery. [*To Cordelia.*] Hence, and avoid my sight! –
So be my grave my peace, as here I give
Her father's heart from her.

(1.1.123–6)

It seems as if these last four lines have burst the boundaries of the beat. Here the climactic rage is not only sustained for a full beat: the unsuccessful attempt to interrupt it creates the impression that that rage is too fierce to be confined.

How accurate, then, is the term climactic beat as a description of Shakespeare's technique? It seems to us reasonably safe to say that every sequence has its own climax and beyond this that the common factor in sequence climaxes is a climactic moment, occurring toward the end of the intensification and (usually) before the concluding and exit beats. That moment may be effected in a sharp compelling line or it may occur in some subtle unstated motion of the will, in which case it will be brought out primarily by the skill of the staging and the ingenuities of the actor. But, frequently enough, Shakespeare does extend the climax for the space of a full beat, this extended climax being found most often in sequences that are of sufficient magnitude to require that the dramatic impact be sustained beyond that electric instant at which the sequence peaks. For this reason, the term *climactic beat* may be useful.

Let us remark, before closing this chapter, that the climactic beat should be differentiated from the *sustaining beat*. Such a distinction proves its value in making sense of the last few beats of the nunnery sequence in *Hamlet*. The nunnery sequence climaxes with Hamlet's sudden inquiry to Ophelia, "Where's your father?" (3.1.129), almost immediately after which Shakespeare begins to effect Hamlet's exit. Normally, when characters begin to exit a sequence passes into its decrescent stage, yet Hamlet's two farewell beats are among the most important beats in the sequence, those in which Hamlet vents his anger upon Ophelia (3.1.134–41 and 142–9). These beats are not climactic in themselves, but they do very effectively sustain the climax. Only thereafter does Shakespeare withdraw Hamlet from the stage and let the concluding section begin.

7

The dramatic question

Shakespeare's units of action are not snapshot stills, episodes caught and frozen in time, as Mark Rose has suggested, or "a cycle of narrative paintings" on a museum wall.[1] However useful it may be to isolate beats or sequences temporarily from their context, they are not static, like paintings. We do not stroll at our own pace past Shakespeare's sequences: they unfold before us. They are pregnant with change, thrusting forward restlessly toward experiences that lie in the future. As units of action sequences are characterized by movement, or – to use a more specific term – by *direction*.

Because in every sequence direction is itself a major structural factor, our third method of discovering the boundaries of the sequence entails plotting that direction. If the reader realizes where the sequence is going, he will be more aware of when and how it ends. In case this seems simplistic, we offer a more sophisticated statement of the principle – the sequence (to apply to it a definition proposed by Bernard Beckerman) "embraces a phase of action which contains a development, crux, and decrescence. The balancing of projects and resistance as extensions of the precipitating circumstances reveals the vector of a segment. By tracing the vector to its resolution, the reader can determine the conclusion of one segment and the commencement of another."[2]

Tracing the vector of a sequence is not merely a tedious academic exercise. The vector, or dramatic question, is the element which unifies the beats and gives the action of the sequence its form. People preparing a play for production certainly must train themselves not only to recognize but also to formulate the dramatic question Shakespeare is working with in any sequence, for these dramatic questions must be articulated in a production if the audience is to experience the aesthetic rhythms of the play. Theater critics need similar skills, for they have to judge the degree and quality of this articulation. Casual readers may never take time to locate the dramatic question of every sequence, but they too can benefit from a familiarity with the general purposes of the dramatic question.

I

Although the concept of the dramatic question is commonplace, we make two original assertions: first, that every sequence has its own dramatic question; second, that special benefits accrue if that question is located and precisely formulated for each sequence. True, the dramatic question of any sequence can usually be intuited more or less accurately. For the casual reader this may be sufficient. But for anyone who wants to be certain of the emotional arc of each unit of action, intuition (though often brilliantly right) can be backed up by analytic exactitude. Each sequence is structured not around a set of vague feelings or expressions but around a specific dramatic question. Accurate re-creation of the thrust, pitch, tempo, and tone of each sequence, either on the stage or in the mind, calls for a solid assessment of its dramatic question.

But how do we find the dramatic question? Any sequence structure has two dynamic elements: a propelling force, or intention, and a goal, or climax – the intention provides the question, the goal its answer. The shortest route to the dramatic question is to go straight to the climax of the sequence, where the question is answered, and work backwards from the resolution to the question. Nothing really valuable can be said about the action of a sequence until its resolution is made clear. But from the vantage point of the sequence climax it is easy to determine what is significant about the introductory and intensifying beats, that is, how Shakespeare is setting up his action.

It helps of course to have some idea of where the sequence begins and ends, and the techniques presented earlier can be utilized in the search for the dramatic question. Any distracting ancillary beats should be lifted out of the sequence temporarily, and the pertinent introductory and concluding beats should be identified. It also helps to be alert to those statements of intention through which Shakespeare foreshadows his sequences, many of which appear not in the introductory beat but in preceding sequences. But the fundamental skill needed here is the ability to pinpoint the moment at which the intensification climaxes.

The basic procedure is fairly obvious. It is in essence the procedure of all valid interpretation: read through to the end, find out what is at stake – then go back and read again, this time with hindsight. The process itself is obvious, but its application requires sensitivity, insight, and above all precision. First impressions of "what is at stake" may not be entirely accurate.

It is possible to get very close to the playwright's dramatic idea and yet miss it. If one formulates a sequence's dramatic question too loosely, the finer points of the action get lost. It is therefore worth striving to recapture the original idea with precision. What then are the principles underlying the carefully formulated dramatic question?

In theater practice it is a commonplace to teach that dialogue units in a play should be described with a verb rather than a noun. Verbs describe actions, and actions can be acted. The practice can be applied to the sequence, and one wants of course the most precise verb available.

But there is more to a dramatic question than a verb: that verb must be attached to a subject. Whose action is the verb describing? We come back to the notion of dominance. As in motivated beats, so in motivated sequences: one motive dominates all others. The dramatic question should reflect not only the action but also its *source*, the character with the dominant intention. Who is the propelling character?

We have seen this practice applied to isolate beats – in 1.3.301–404 of *Othello*, for example, where in successive beats Iago ridicules, Iago rebukes, Iago instills hope, Iago reassures: it takes both a subject *and* a verb to define each beat. Iago is also the propelling character of the sequence as a whole, and his action, the action that supplies direction to these beats over the duration of the longer unit, is persuading. Subject and verb, then, for the *sequence*, too: Iago persuades.

To define a sequence adequately, however, more is needed. Certainly the responding or resisting character should be identified as the recipient of the action. Iago persuades Roderigo. But more, even, than that. At the sequence level there is a rising action involved, and the formulation should point to the moment at which the tensions of that persuading action are released. Since these tensions break when the propelling character either achieves or fails to achieve his objective, the dramatic question must be framed so that it assumes that objective. *Can Iago persuade Roderigo to continue pursuing Desdemona?*

Much more is thus involved in formulating the dramatic question than tagging the unit with a verb, but we do not mean to downplay the importance of that verb. The verb must describe the *means* being taken by the propelling character to reach his desired end. Iago is neither interrogating nor reporting, he is persuading.

What in sum are the principles that will help one to arrive at a carefully formulated dramatic question? Assuming of course that the sequence is a motivated sequence and thus one controlled by a single character, the properly formulated question will identify four things: (1) the active or propelling character; (2) that character's objective, toward the fulfill-ment or failure of which the entire sequence is moving; (3) the means he has chosen to pursue that objective; and (4) the character he is acting upon. These precepts will need further refinement when in later chapters we explore the notion of means more fully, but they will serve well enough here.

A few illustrations may clarify these precepts. The necessity for proper framing of the question can be demonstrated in the sequence between Claudius and Laertes analyzed earlier – *Hamlet* 4.7.1–194. It opens after an offstage parley between the two characters. Having just informed Laertes that Hamlet was the murderer of Polonius, Claudius has himself received news that Hamlet is en route to court. Claudius and Laertes discuss their future course of action.

There are a number of alternative ways of formulating the question that underlies this sequence. Some are just plain wrong. *Can Claudius survive Laertes' wrath?* This question was resolved in a previous sequence (4.5.96–220), when Laertes agreed to binding arbitration; no longer is this an absorbing question. *Will Hamlet return?* This question will be answered in the graveyard sequence, not here. Other possibilities are limited. *How will Claudius respond to Hamlet's letter? Will Laertes become the King's accomplice?* Both are valid questions, pertinent to this sequence. But each leaves out one of the main parties to the conflict. The first ignores the fact that Laertes is in the sequence, the second misses the fact that Claudius's motives direct the action, and both fail to describe the relationship between the two characters: Claudius is the dominant figure and Laertes the secondary or responding one. Furthermore, neither of the latter questions describes the activity that propels the sequence. The action lies in persuading. All these facts should be taken into account in the formulation of the question.

The question might better read, *Can the King persuade Laertes to kill Hamlet?* It now reflects more accurately the relationship between the characters, as well as the means through which the dominant character will act upon the subordinate one. But this version is still imprecise. The imprecision stems from vagueness as to the goal of the persuasion. Claudius will have little difficulty persuading Laertes to kill Hamlet; Laertes has pronounced for vengeance at the beginning. Claudius's object is more subtle. He must persuade Laertes (who has so recently accused him of murder) to become his ally in a dishonorable plot, without revealing his own reasons for fearing Hamlet. This objective displays itself in Claudius's opening remark to Laertes, "Now must your conscience my acquittance seal, / And you must put me in your heart for friend" (4.7.1–2). It is stressed more strongly still in the question with which the King begins his manipulation, "If it be so, Laertes –" (that is, if Hamlet is now returned) "will you be rul'd by me?" Claudius has a use for Laertes' wrath and wants to channel and control it. The dramatic question is not, then, *Can the King persuade Laertes to kill Hamlet?* but rather *Can the King persuade Laertes to become his accomplice, his henchman, in effecting Hamlet's death?* This phrasing of the question extracts precisely the dramatic idea Shakespeare was working with when he constructed the action.

If loose formulations of the dramatic question are carefully avoided (precision being the target here), the deeper energies governing the action will stand revealed. As further evidence, let us consider the dramatic question in *As You Like It* 1.3.90–138, where Celia and Rosalind confront the problems raised by the Duke's banishment of Rosalind. Celia's grief over her cousin's misfortune expresses itself in poignant questions:

> O, my poor Rosalind, whither wilt thou go?
> Wilt thou change fathers?

> Prithee, be cheerful: know'st thou not, the Duke
> Hath banished me, his daughter?. . .
> Shall we be sunder'd? Shall we part, sweet girl?

> Why, whither shall we go?

Provocative questions, these, and they might at first be mistaken for dramatic questions. But the characters' own questions are not necessarily reliable expressions of the dramatic question: their perspectives on the action are too narrow. Since the dramatic question is always the question the playwright is working with, rather than one the characters are entertaining, the characters lack the ability to express it fully in words. The dramatic question is beyond their ken.[3]

None of the quoted questions gives shape to the sequence. In this action the dramatic question is not *Will the two girls be parted?*, nor is it really *Where will Rosalind go?*, deeply though both questions may concern the characters. Compare these questions with another, *Can Celia comfort Rosalind?* This comes much closer to describing an action.

The third formulation is better than the other two. It informs us which girl is the propelling force in the sequence and which the recipient of the action. Celia is of course dominant. Even though Rosalind is the play's heroine and though she is the one banished, she herself has been stunned into inaction by the time this sequence begins. Moreover, Celia has the stated intention. Her desire is that Rosalind "devise with me how we may fly, / Whither to go, and what to bear with us," with the additional proviso that Rosalind "not seek to take your change upon you, / To bear your griefs yourself, and leave me out." Celia is clearly controlling the course the action will take. She initiates the moves.

Formulated as *Can Celia comfort Rosalind?* the question has an additional advantage. It describes a playable action – comforting. Celia's statement of intention goes beyond the simple search for a destination. All her moves to find a solution to Rosalind's problem are intended to relieve Rosalind's distress. Celia even charges her friend to "be not more griev'd than I am," begs her to "be cheerful." This phrasing of the dramatic question, *Can Celia comfort Rosalind?*, would be a closer description of Shakespeare's action.

But the formulation can be made more precise. Comforting, by itself, does not necessarily produce much action, beyond a smile, an embrace, a few tears. The activity that injects drama into this sequence is in fact persuading. In order to console Rosalind, Celia first persuades her that in banishing one of them Duke Frederick has banished both. Celia's offer to accompany Rosalind into exile is more than an offer: Shakespeare assigns Celia the task of making Rosalind believe she means it. Celia must also deflect Rosalind's objection that the projected trip to Arden could be full of dangers. True enough, both objections are quickly countered; this, after all, is a short and simple sequence from a gentle comedy and hardly requires the kind and degree of persuasion that Iago or Lady Macbeth might bring to bear on a question. Still, the very fact that Celia changes Rosalind with her arguments transforms into drama a phase of exposition that handled otherwise could have remained a mere dialogue. The persuasion moves Rosalind from despair to hope.

The more precise phrasing of the dramatic question might be, then, *Can Celia persuade Rosalind that together they can transcend adversity?* The precise formulation of the dramatic question moves one much closer to the heart of the action. One discovers energies placed in the sequence by Shakespeare that give the actors more intense motives, which motives, realized on stage, render the relationship between the two characters far more dynamic than would have been possible given the initial, more superficial formulation.

There is another significant reason for formulating the dramatic question in this way: the formulation renders quickly apparent Shakespeare's heavy reliance on the reversal to effect a climax. For him the reversal seems to be the essence of drama, and here at the sequence level he uses it constantly. To read Shakespeare's sequences without detecting these reversals is to cheat oneself of the enjoyment of experiencing their full dramatic potential. To stage his sequences persistently without articulating them is to cheat the audience.

Keeping the reversal in mind, we can consider another potential dramatic question, *Can Viola gain access to Olivia's court?* Let us see how precise this formulation is as a description of the sequence action constructed in *Twelfth Night* 1.5.99–166 and, more particularly, whether it accurately reflects the reversal that the actors must articulate. (Notice, by the way, that Viola's interview with Olivia takes place in the succeeding sequence and is not pertinent here.)

The dramatic question as formulated is based on a consideration of stated intentions. In the light of Orsino's instructions to Viola in 1.4, it seems an accurately formulated question. This certainly will be the question the audience is asking, for they have watched Orsino giving Viola motives for the sequence:

> Therefore, good youth, address thy gait unto her,
> Be not denied access, stand at her doors,
> And tell them, there thy fixed foot shall grow
> Till thou have audience
> . . .
> Be clamorous, and leap all civil bounds,
> Rather than make unprofited return.
>
> (1.4.15–22)

Following his counsel Viola sets her "fixed foot" at Olivia's door and demands access. From what is reported to Olivia we know that Viola has chosen to "be clamorous and leap all civil bounds" rather than return unadmitted. *Can Viola gain access to Olivia's court?*

Yet this question fails to reflect the conflict Shakespeare establishes and thus precludes the possibility of a reversal; it needs to be rephrased. Still viewing the action from Shakespeare's foreshadowing of it, we might try, *Can Viola persuade Olivia to admit her?* A conflict has been added, for Viola is now acting upon Olivia. But is Viola persuading? The movement of the sequence comes in fact only indirectly from Viola's will. Far from operating as the dominant character engaged in a persuading action, Viola never appears on stage in this prelude to her meeting with Olivia. Shakespeare stations her at an offstage gate throughout the sequence and develops the entire action from another point of view – that of Olivia. Olivia's will is the governing will in this action.

As usual it is more practical to work retrospectively. Once we know where the sequence ends (it climaxes with Olivia's decision to "Let him approach") we can find what is significant in the introduction, and that is Olivia's initial attitude – to send Orsino's advocate away. As in the other two sequences of this group Shakespeare wants to work a reversal. But Olivia's will, not Viola's, is reversed. The dramatic question, to reflect the reversal as the playwright planned it, is more usefully stated thus: *Will Olivia send Viola away?*

With the dramatic question so stated, the sequence reveals its internal structure. The initial response to Viola's request for admittance is a spontaneous "no" from the presiding figure, the Lady Olivia. Her "If it be a suit from the Count, I am sick, or not at home – what you will, to dismiss it" (1.5.108–9) stands as her position statement. Then follows the intensification, which develops in a classic cumulative pattern. Three reports about the young ruffian at the gate are brought to Olivia, the first by Maria, the second by Sir Toby, and the third by Malvolio, each more intriguing than the last. The third report effects a reversal in Olivia: she now grants the audience she had so adamantly refused.

Had the dramatic question been framed with Viola at the center, there would have been only confusion. In fact the alternative formulation, *Can Viola persuade Olivia to admit her?* contains several important errors. These errors cannot be justified as "subjective choices." They are objective and easily verifiable errors: (1) since, being offstage, she has no lines in the scene, Viola is hardly the propelling character; (2) nor is Olivia the responding character; and (3) the reversal is effected through reporting, not persuading.

These examples should demonstrate that more is needed than vague intuition or good intentions when it comes to expressing the dramatic question. That question must reflect the structure of the action accurately. It must reveal the flow and direction of the human energies Shakespeare has activated. It must show actors and actresses playing the sequence where the intensification peaks and how to build it. A properly formulated dramatic question encapsulates the central action.

Finally, we need to consider whether these precepts apply to all three types of intensification – the motivated, the cumulative, and the chronological. We began by saying that when the sequence is propelled by a single character, the properly formulated question will identify four things: (1) the propelling character; (2) his intention; (3) the means through which he will attempt to reach the desired goal; and (4) the responding character. These precepts apply to sequences intensified through character motivation. They also apply to sequences intensified through repetition, provided there is a presiding figure with a definable intention. But what about the chronological intensification? Such sequences typically lack a controlling figure. How is the dramatic question of a chronologically developed sequence formulated?

The general rule for locating the dramatic question is to determine from the climax what is at stake. Even in a sequence without a propelling character there is usually a character who has something at stake. This is the character the audience is watching, no matter how much incidental detail surrounds and colors his activities – Iago, for example, in the handkerchief sequence, Romeo in the ballroom sequence, Macbeth in the sequence where Duncan's body is discovered. For each of these characters something has changed by the end of the sequence. Even in the chronological intensification the dramatic question can be precisely pointed, if the outcome is allowed to determine the formulation. *What will happen to Desdemona's handkerchief?* is better formulated as *Can Iago steal the handkerchief from Emilia? Can Benvolio prove Romeo's "swan" a "crow"?* is better as *Is it Romeo's fate to love a Capulet?* And *Will Duncan's body be discovered?* is certainly more precise as *Can the Macbeths escape detection?* The first versions put the question from the audience's perspective. But such questions cannot be played. The alternatives, because they truly describe the action, give the actors their objectives. This is not to say that Iago, Romeo, or Macbeth are propelling characters in the same way as Claudius, Celia, and Olivia are. But it does mean that even for chronologically intensified sequences some ways of formulating the dramatic question are hazy and some more exact, and that precision can be achieved only from a retrospective viewpoint.

There are thus several factors to be aware of when trying to identify the dramatic question of a sequence. One, it must be understood that the dramatic question the playwright is working with is implied by the structure but not stated in so many words: it has to be extracted and formulated. Two, because the dramatic question often becomes apparent only in retrospect, evidence culled from the climactic moment of the sequence is a more reliable indicator of the structuring question than clues pointing toward it in statements of intention. Three, if in his dramatic question Shakespeare has provided for a reversal, then a well-formulated question should reflect that reversal structure. Since the last factor is of inestimable importance in the study of sequence structure, we conclude this chapter with a few more words about Shakespeare's reversals.

II

The process of locating and formulating the dramatic question opens up a new area for critical exploration, in that it provides a means of evaluating the vast number of reversals built into Shakespeare's action at the sequence level. The reader develops, as it were, a special critical skill: the ability to detect this powerful dynamic which informs many a sequence – the 180-degree reversal. Just how important the reversal is to the study of Shakespeare's sequence structure can be seen if we consider how frequently the dramatic question is wedded to a reversal.

It is important that the reversal structure be distinguished from the intensifying structure. Both terminate in the sequence climax but they are not identical, nor is there a reversal sequence in the same sense that there is a chronological, a cumulative, or a motivated sequence. The *intensification* consists of a series of beats, each of which increases tension. The *reversal*, in contrast, is a specialized form of the dramatic question; it provides a framework that gives direction to the intensification. The reversal structure can be imposed upon any of the various types of intensification and will work with them to increase the impact. Two things locate a reversal: (1) a position statement, usually found among the sequence's introductory beats (or just before them) and marking the point of departure; and (2) the sequence's climax, in which the about-face is effected.

There is evidence of Shakespeare's conscious use of this structure (and the pleasure he took in it) in the lines he writes for Richard of Gloucester as a coda to the wooing sequence with Lady Anne, a sequence that opens with Anne's rejection of this gruesome suitor and culminates in her acceptance of his ring:

> What? I, that kill'd her husband and his father,
> To take her in her heart's extremest hate,
> With curses in her mouth, tears in her eyes,
> The bleeding witness of my hatred by,
> Having God, her conscience, and these bars against me,
> And I no friend to back my suit at all
> But the plain devil and dissembling looks?
> And yet to win her?
>
> (*Richard III* 1.2.230–7)

Shakespeare catches in these lines Richard's bemusement at the rapidity with which Lady Anne's loathing swings round to love. But he also reveals his own awareness of how a reversal action should be set up: Anne has every reason to abhor Richard, and her revulsion is concretely rendered at the beginning, even to the point of gross physical action: she spits at him. Yet as the sequence concludes, her attitude toward him approaches the opposite pole.[4] Like Richard, Shakespeare relishes the challenge of bringing a character around, against all odds, to a position that character was dead set against. To the end of his career he seemed to know that in this reversal form he had found the essence of drama.

Richard's lines call special attention to the magnitude of the reversal just effected. When Shakespeare effects a dramatic reversal he does so expansively – even when the reversal informs so basic a unit as the sequence. The turn sweeps across the whole spectrum, leaving the character not 45, not 90, but a full 180 degrees from his starting point.

Shakespeare feels it important, when dramatizing movements of the psyche, to show these movements in their fullest proportions. Heroic emotions need wide spaces, especially on the stage, where events are always moving in time and pass too quickly to be pondered. Shakespeare will pull an emotion all the way back to one extreme and then work it through until it transforms itself into its opposite. The "heart's extremest hate" turns suddenly into love, despair into hope, sorrow into joy. And, when the wind is blowing in the other direction, joy flips over into sorrow, hope becomes despair, and "sweet love, . . . changing his property, / Turns to the sourest and most deadly hate."[5] Adamant refusal turns into acquiescence, doubt into belief, fear into trust, harmony into chaos. Whether the reversal is in an emotion or an attitude or a situation, it takes the character all the way to the opposite pole.[6]

An important aspect of the reversal structure is the concrete articulation Shakespeare gives to it. Wide swings alone will not make the technique effective. Both the starting position and the altered position must be firmly established. If either pole is glossed over, whether by the playwright at the time of writing or by the actors at the time of performance, the reversal could pass unnoticed.

In Shakespeare's sequences paired statements usually identify the contrasting poles. In *I Henry IV* 2.4.113–283, Falstaff ambles on invoking "a plague of all cowards" but eventually admits that "I was a coward on instinct." In a later sequence, anticipating the glories he will acquire from the newly crowned Henry V, he boasts that "I will leer upon him as 'a comes by, and do but mark the countenance that he will give me." Too soon he is fleeing the ignominies of Hal's "I know thee not, old man, fall to thy prayers" (*II Henry IV* 5.5.1–109). In *Much Ado About Nothing* Benedick wonders how a man may "become the argument of his own scorn by falling in love." His turn at eavesdropping spins him to an antipodal point: "I will be horribly in love with her" (2.3.1–264). Romeo moves in his attitude toward Tybalt (3.1.1–136) from a "respective lenity" (I "love thee better than thou canst devise") to reckless rage ("Fire-ey'd fury be my conduct now!"). Gertrude demonstrates at the beginning of *Hamlet* 3.4.1–217 a certain ignorance of the meaning of her conduct: "What have I done, that thou dar'st wag thy tongue / In noise so rude against me?" She ends up discovering in her soul "such black and grained spots / As will not leave their tinct." Through such paired statements, and their embellishment in the surrounding action, Shakespeare articulates the poles of each reversal. Such statements naturally provide strong clues to what is "at stake" in the sequence and greatly facilitate the formulation of its dramatic question.

Of course the value of the reversal technique lies only in part in the creation of spectacular dramatic effects. Used for shock alone, the technique would hardly be worth attention. In Shakespeare, however, it is deeply rooted in human nature. Shakespeare uses the reversal to tie the structure of the action to the individual will, so that the connection between form and content becomes organic rather than arbitrary. Not only does the reversal generate excitement by giving a clever turn to the plot: it also creates an integral link between plot and character. The reversal underlying a particular sequence action becomes the means of highlighting a character's choices. As such, it is also a philosophical tool, for in calling attention to crucial choices the reversal is simultaneously emphasizing the existence of free will, the kinds of consequences that follow specific actions, and the responsibility of the individual to accept those consequences. We experience the consequences associated with certain actions and can apply the experience to our own lives.

At what points in the play does Shakespeare find it most useful to inform the dramatic question of the sequence with a reversal? The obvious answer is at the play's most powerful climaxes. The dramatic question of any sequence dealing with a major turning point in the protagonist's progress is bound to be organized around a reversal. It almost has to be, because the sequence is the means by which the reversals will be effected in the larger units of the play. This much is obvious.

But it would be a mistake to look for reversals only in sequences occurring at the ends of third and fifth acts. Shakespeare uses the reversal in almost any dramaturgical situation, sometimes in unexpected ones – for example, when exposition must be provided. Exposition is an area of drama rarely associated with dramatic reversals. But Shakespeare turns instinctively to the reversal when planning an action in his expository sequences – those involving Brabantio, for example. As we have seen, Shakespeare brings Brabantio into the first act of *Othello* to create the conflict that makes the action dramatic. A close examination of Brabantio's role in the key expository sequences of act I shows how Shakespeare builds a reversal into the dramatic question.

Giraldi Cinthio, from whom Shakespeare borrowed the play's plot, apparently felt that the story could be told without reference to the heroine's father. All that Cinthio has to say of Brabantio is that "their passion" (the Moor's love for Desdemona and hers for him) "was so successful that they were married, although their relations did all in their power to make her take another husband."[7] "Their relations." Without distorting his source Shakespeare could have imagined a whole clan. But he didn't. He gave the relative to Desdemona only and made him her father. Shakespeare requires him for only one act, then dismisses him, but it is through Brabantio that he creates the conflicts that underlie the two crucial expository sequences of that act. Brabantio lifts the play's exposition out of the realm of narrative into the realm of drama.

In sequence 1.1.1–183 Shakespeare must introduce both the situation from which the plot will develop and the persons involved in it. He casts Brabantio as a responding character who, like the audience, has no inkling that his daughter is missing, that she has eloped that very night, that she is married to Othello. Of all this he must be told. At night, and in highly inflammatory terms, Iago and the rejected suitor Roderigo rouse Brabantio with the news. But it is not Roderigo's "timorous accent" or Iago's "dire yell" alone that makes the sequence compelling; it is Brabantio's resistance. Shakespeare organizes the sequence around a dramatic question, *Can Roderigo and Iago convince Brabantio that Desdemona has eloped?* The Brabantio he introduces is committed to the idea that the informers are "full of supper and distemp'ring draughts," insane and full of malice. Brabantio takes a stand as far as possible from the point toward which he is to be worked: he doubts the veracity of the informers. And then, at the climax of the sequence, he swings round to the opposite pole: "This accident is not unlike my dream, / Belief of it oppresses me already." Doubt is replaced by conviction.

Shakespeare again uses a reversal to shape the action of the trial sequence, *Othello* 1.3.47–220. This sequence too provides exposition – not plot orientation this time but character exposition. Shakespeare needs to demonstrate to the audience that the love between Desdemona and Othello has a solid foundation in virtue and truth and in an affection that links soul to soul. To demonstrate this in dramatic rather than narrative terms, he invents a conflict between Othello and Brabantio in which the nature of that love is questioned, its origins explored, and its value asserted.

In this expository sequence Brabantio becomes the propelling rather than the responding figure. Shakespeare instills in him a strong compulsion to prove that Othello bewitched his daughter. He voices a suspicion at the close of 1.1 that there were "charms / By which the property of youth and maidhood may be abused," and by 1.2 he believes intensely that Othello had employed enchantments, charges Othello with having "practic'd on her with foul charms, / Abus'd her delicate youth with drugs or minerals," and states an intention to bring the case to trial (1.2.62–79). So he does, and all these accusations are restated before the Duke in the sequence's introductory beats. The accusations establish a dramatic question: *Can Brabantio convict Othello of bewitching*

Desdemona? With this question hovering in the air, Brabantio's response gains dramatic significance. Shakespeare could have ended the trial with a judicial decision. The Duke has been appealed to; he obviously finds Othello innocent; and he could have decided the case. But the playwright chooses a more dramatic course. At the climactic moment Brabantio reverses his stand: he drops the charge. His surrender gives this expository sequence a moving climax.

Sequences built upon reversals also give life to the expository action of both *King Lear* and *Hamlet.* In sequence 1.1.1–139 Lear takes the measure of his daughters' love. If the dramatic question is played as *How will Lear divide his kingdom?*, there will be far less drive to its enactment than if the reversal action is formulated and played in Shakespeare's way, *Will Lear reward Cordelia with the greater third of the realm?* Lear's stated intention is to "extend his largest bounty" to the daughter who loves him most. Instead, in a spectacular reversal, he takes everything from that daughter, even "her father's heart." So also in the following sequence, 1.1.139–87, where Kent's fortunes are reversed. In the opening sequence of *Hamlet* (1.1.1–125) exposition is again transformed into action through the reversal structure. The sequence asks, *Will Horatio believe in the Ghost?* Shakespeare is not twenty lines into the sequence before he sets Marcellus to recounting Horatio's doubts about the apparition: "Horatio says 'tis but our fantasy, / And will not let belief take hold of him." Horatio himself affirms this statement of his position: "Tush, tush, 'twill not appear." He soon has evidence to the contrary, and his own expression of amazement marks his reversal: "Before my God, I might not this believe / Without the sensible and true avouch / Of mine own eyes." It is the same movement from doubt to conviction that Shakespeare puts Brabantio through. The reversal shapes the exposition so as to carry the audience along with Horatio to accept the Ghost's existence.

There are other examples, of course, including the sequences from *As You Like it* and *Twelfth Night* analyzed earlier in this chapter (*Can Celia persuade Rosalind that together they can transcend adversity?, Will Olivia send Viola away?*), both of which have their expository functions and their reversals. But the examples given suffice to show that even in the earliest stages of a developing plot Shakespeare depends heavily upon the reversal structure and continually uses it to energize his sequences.

From this overview of the elements that give direction and impact to Shakespeare's sequences, we turn to particular sequence types, specifically those in which Shakespeare makes raw human energy the force that drives the action toward its conclusion.

8

Observing and meditating sequences

At the beginning of *Antony and Cleopatra* Shakespeare invites us to observe the hero and heroine of his play: "Look where they come! / Take but good note. . . Behold and see." He does this by plucking two characters out of Antony's retinue – Philo, a member of the Roman force in Alexandria who is disturbed by the transformation Cleopatra has worked upon Antony, and Demetrius, apparently a newcomer to Egypt though not to the gossip about Antony's decline. These two characters "look," "note," "behold," "see" the lovers together in that opening sequence – then judge.

> DEMETRIUS Is Caesar with Antonius priz'd so slight?
> PHILO Sir, sometimes when he is not Antony,
> He comes so short of that great property
> Which still should go with Antony.
> DEMETRIUS   I am full sorry
> That he approves the common liar, who
> Thus speaks of him at Rome; but I will hope
> Of better deeds tomorrow.
>
> (1.1.56–62)

The audience's ultimate judgment of Antony and Cleopatra may not be the same as that made by the observers, Philo and Demetrius, but the strategy is clear. Through these observers Shakespeare asks *us* to observe, and then to form a judgment.

Claudius and Polonius observe Hamlet in a similar way in the nunnery sequence (3.1.28–188) but with certain differences, for in *Antony and Cleopatra* the conversation to be observed occurs without any prompting from the observers, while in *Hamlet* the event is pre-arranged for the convenience of the two who are eavesdropping – Claudius, in one of Shakespeare's typical declarations of intention, explains the situation:

> KING Sweet Gertrude, leave us two,
> For we have closely sent for Hamlet hither,
> That he, as 'twere by accident, may here
> Affront Ophelia. Her father and myself,

We'll so bestow ourselves that, seeing unseen,
We may of their encounter frankly judge,
And gather by him, as he is behav'd,
If 't be th' affliction of his love or no
That thus he suffers for.
QUEEN   I shall obey you.
And for your part, Ophelia, I do wish
That your good beauties be the happy cause
Of Hamlet's wildness. So shall I hope your virtues
Will bring him to his wonted way again,
To both your honors.
OPHELIA   Madam, I wish it may.
                                 [*Exit Gertrude.*]
                                 (3.1.28–41)

Hamlet comes along, converses with Ophelia, then detects the spies behind the arras. Having discovered Claudius's plot, he puts on an "antic disposition" that both hides and yet exposes his incipient madness. When he leaves, each of the two observers expresses an opinion about what he has witnessed – as does Ophelia, the decoy, who has observed from a closer range. Here again Shakespeare pointedly suggests that the observing is only the prelude to judging. The King's announcement that "We'll so bestow ourselves that, seeing unseen, / We may of their encounter frankly judge" may be taken as a standard precept of the observation structure. Of course the audience, the observer of the whole, makes the final judgment.

Is there any action here? In this second half of our book we wish to delve into the dynamics of Shakespeare's motivated sequences more deeply than we did in our study of intensifying beats. We want to discover those activities he turns to when he uses the characters' motives to give direction to his sequence actions.[1] Observing seems to us a natural starting place. But where is the action in observing sequences? Can the mere activity of looking outward at the surrounding world be dramatic? What of its opposite – looking inward – can meditating give direction to a sequence? In persuading, the seeds of drama are already present, for that endeavor assumes a difference of opinion between the active and the responding character that the active one wishes to remove. But the very nature of observing implies a certain detachment of the active character from those he is watching, which increases if the observing takes the form of spying so that the observer remains hidden. And of course in meditating the active character stands in even greater solitude. Shakespeare uses both of these activities in motivated sequences. How does he make them dramatic?

The nunnery sequence in *Hamlet* has elements of both activities: after Claudius and Polonius have concealed themselves behind the arras to observe him, Hamlet delivers the most famous of his meditations, the "To be or not to be" soliloquy (3.1.55–87). Analysis of this particular combination of observing and meditating motives gives us the opportunity to clear away a possible misunderstanding about Hamlet's soliloquies – they are never sequences.

Hamlet's "To be or not to be" soliloquy is so often quoted out of context that is has come to be thought of as an independent unit and this could easily result in its being mistaken for a sequence. This soliloquy is not a sequence but a beat, imbedded in the action which Claudius and Polonius observe. Meditating drives the action only for the space of this one beat. In the succeeding beat Hamlet greets Ophelia (87–91), in the next her desire to return Hamlet's gifts becomes the propelling motive (92–101), control shifts again with Hamlet's "Are you honest?" (102–14), and so on. Hamlet's "To be or not to be" soliloquy represents only one beat in a larger whole, that larger whole being a complete action, a sequence within an observing sequence. The intricacy of the unit structure here indicates that when working up an interpretation of any unit in a Shakespearean play one must consider the exact level of magnitude of that unit, so that the part being studied is given only the emphasis due it and does not detract from the larger whole in which it is nested. The point should be obvious, but how often it is ignored in practice.

Let us pursue this line of inquiry a step further, for it throws light on one of the main questions of this chapter, can meditating give direction to a sequence?

Hamlet's "O, what a rogue and peasant slave am I" soliloquy too is treated as an isolated unit, approached as a set piece disconnected from the surrounding action by actors and discussed independently of the plot by scholars. There is more reason for mistaking this soliloquy (2.2.549–605) for a sequence. Unlike the "To be or not to be" example, which occurs in the middle of a sequence so that its function as an integral part of a sequence should not be open to question, the "rogue and peasant slave" one comes at the end of a sequence. Its position allows for the possibility of its being a separate sequence; moreover, this soliloquy is so much longer than most beats that the length itself raises questions.

Can a passage so lengthy and so well developed function as one beat? Or are there four, perhaps even five, beats here? The "What's Hecuba to him, or he to Hecuba" section of the soliloquy (2.2.550–66) resembles an introductory beat; in it Hamlet establishes the grounds for his meditation: the fact that the player, whose sorrow is but a fiction, can radiate that passion as though it touched his very soul. From there Hamlet moves (a second beat?) to a consideration of his own inactivity. His intensity deepens until he breaks out in a climax of cursing – "Bloody, bawdy villain! / Remorseless, treacherous, lecherous, kindless villain!" – in which he gives full vent to his hatred for Claudius. Then (582–7) a pause, a regrouping, a new motive that might elsewhere mark a change of beat – a revulsion against the loss of control that is embodied in that course. And finally (588–605) – with Hamlet's "About, my brains!" – a move from thought to action; Hamlet lays out his plan to trap the King in what looks strikingly like a concluding beat. Of course all of the soliloquies are remarkable for the logic of their construction: whether or not one finds Hamlet's conclusions logical, his mind reaches them through ordered steps, so much so that volumes have been filled in defense of his sanity. Hamlet's soliloquies have none of the disjointed thought that characterizes Lear's speech to Gloucester at Dover. But only here, in the "rogue and peasant slave" passages, is the soliloquy developed to a degree that makes the various phases of its thought appear like the beats of a sequence.

If the divisions indicate that the soliloquy is written as an independent action, a director would be justified in giving at least this one of Hamlet's soliloquies its independence – there would be a new start, a new build. Actually, however, one can find instances of such technically complex beats throughout the plays, and these demonstrate that when additional complexity is required Shakespeare readily constructs such a beat – extended in length, with sub-units nesting within it (the Cordelia beat analyzed in chapter 6 is another example). Such beats only appear to break down into smaller units as sequences do: they still function as beats.

Structurally, the "rogue and peasant slave" soliloquy functions as a concluding beat in a specific sequence – the one that runs from 2.2.380 to the end of the scene and brings in the players. Just as Hamlet in the "solid flesh" soliloquy (1.2.129–59) reflects upon Claudius's immediately preceding talk of "mirth in funeral, and . . . dirge in marriage" with observations that it becomes a kind of "wicked speed" to "post / With such dexterity to incestuous sheets" and as in the "How all occasions" soliloquy (4.4.32–66) he refers to the recently observed Norwegian army and makes it a spur to his dull revenge, so here (2.2.549–605) he associates an action just witnessed with his own situation and reflects upon it. Hamlet has just seen a player who is acting the role of Aeneas lament the deaths of Priam and Hecuba. Hamlet's references to Hecuba and to the play he has instructed the actors to prepare tie this concluding soliloquy in closely to the entire player sequence. Even this longest of Hamlet's soliloquies constitutes an indispensable unit of a particular action. A director who through his blocking and pacing concludes the player's sequence at line 549 (before Hamlet's soliloquy) rather than at line 605 (after it) has not understood Shakespeare's way with units.

Yet in Shakespeare's hands the seemingly static activity of meditating can indeed be the driving force of a sequence. From this point of view it is instructive to see how Shakespeare expands a soliloquy into a sequence when he wants to do so. Consider, for example, *Julius Caesar* 2.1.1–85, where Brutus is discovered in his orchard meditating upon the plot to murder Caesar just before the conspirators arrive to organize the details. This unit supplies a useful example of the *meditating sequence*.

Like Hamlet, Brutus for the most part speaks in soliloquy. He too has been called upon in the name of justice to murder a close associate in the state and now ponders the case. But in this unit an action is being developed: there is a distinct dramatic question. When the sequence opens, one of the major questions of Shakespeare's plot remains unanswered, *Will Brutus join the conspirators?* Cassius has done his best to draw Brutus in and just prior to the sequence Cassius reminds us of the pending question, when he remarks to Casca of Brutus that "three parts of him / Is ours already, and the man entire / Upon the next encounter yields him ours" (1.3.154–6). The future of the play depends on the answer to that question. But only here is it answered: this question and its resolution give form to the entire sequence. By the time the sequence ends, with Brutus about to be united in fact with the conspirators he has joined in thought, the action is ready to move forward. In Hamlet's "peasant slave" soliloquy, on the other hand, there is no propelling dramatic question, but rather a review of what has gone before, with that "hook into the future" that is so characteristic of concluding beats.

Brutus's deliberations (like Hamlet's) progress through stages, but where Hamlet's soliloquy only appeared to break down into beats, Brutus's actually does. Interruptions cause Brutus to deliver his soliloquy in four separate bursts.

In the first beat of the meditation (10–34), Brutus considers whether Caesar deserves the death Cassius proposes for him. He finds "no personal cause to spurn at him," has never known Caesar's affections to dominate his reason. Caesar's behavior so far has given Brutus no cause for alarm. But experience has shown that power corrupts. Will Caesar change? Shakespeare encompasses these thoughts in the space of one beat, introducing it with the question that most disturbs Brutus – "[Caesar] would be crown'd: / How that might change his nature, there's the question" – and concluding it with the resolution Brutus arrives at, that Caesar is best viewed as a serpent's egg, to be crushed in the shell.

As yet Brutus has made no commitment; he has merely examined the situation in the light of reason. In the second beat of the deliberation (44–58), he receives impetus from outside – a letter (composed by Cassius but seeming to Brutus an entreaty from the Roman people) urges him to "speak and strike." This seeming show of support from the populace pushes Brutus over the edge. He now commits himself: "O Rome, I make thee promise. . .thou receivest / Thy full petition at the hand of Brutus!" Because this action was prepared for in the first-act sequence between Brutus and Cassius, the development here can be brief, but it is nevertheless an action and in this beat Shakespeare effects its climax.

The two beats that end the meditation are in the decrescent: Brutus comments first upon the disordering effects of such treachery on the individual mind (61–9), then upon the monstrous nature of conspiracy (77–85), revealing in two different ways his commendable discomfort with his decision to turn against Caesar.

In the Brutus unit, Shakespeare constructs beats that are real and functional (not merely apparent, as in Hamlet's soliloquy), and this creates the sense of a larger, more developed unit. There are other mechanisms, too, that give this soliloquy the magnitude of a sequence. Hamlet's thoughts follow one another without interruption and no intervening material is allowed to detract from the intensity of his self-examination. But Shakespeare surrounds Brutus's soliloquy with resonating images of night and sleeplessness that underscore the mental and political turmoil, and contrasts Brutus throughout the sequence with the innocent boy, Lucius, whose "fault" is to "sleep so soundly" and who is awakened to light candles to dispel the darkness. Once introduced into the sequence, Lucius is kept scurrying in and out, so that his entrances punctuate the soliloquy: beats of dialogue between Brutus and the boy alternate with beats of solitary meditation. Through Lucius, Brutus's soliloquy is imbedded in a setting that lifts it out of the realm of the beat.

While Malvolio is not a character ranking with either Hamlet or Brutus, he too is the dominant character of a meditating sequence. In 2.5 of *Twelfth Night*, Malvolio, having "been yonder i' the sun practicing behavior to his own shadow this half hour," discovers a love letter designed to "make a contemplative idiot of him." Maria and her accomplices would have him deduce that the letter was written by Olivia and is intended for him. What follows is a soliloquy – when Malvolio stands alone at the front of the stage and delivers it, it should (in part) sound like this:

> To be Count Malvolio! . . . There is example for 't: the Lady of the Strachy married the yeoman of the wardrobe . . . Having been three

months married to her, sitting in my state . . . Calling my officers
about me, in my branch'd velvet gown; having come from a day-
bed, where I have left Olivia sleeping . . . And then to have the
humor of state; and after a demure travel of regard – telling them I
know my place as I would they should do theirs – to ask for my
kinsman Toby . . . Seven of my people, with an obedient start, make
out for him. I frown the while, and perchance wind up my watch, or
play with my – some rich jewel. Toby approaches; curtsies there to
me . . . I extend my hand to him thus, quenching my familiar smile
with an austere regard of control . . . Saying, "Cousin Toby, my
fortunes, having cast me on your niece, give me this prerogative of
speech . . . You must amend your drunkenness . . . Beside, you
waste the treasure of your time with a foolish knight – One Sir
Andrew" . . .

(2.5.35–80)

To make a sequence of Malvolio's meditation, Shakespeare gives
Malvolio an audience and, instead of keeping the onlookers silent, splices
their observations into the meditation. Much of the delight of the
sequence comes from the fact that Malvolio's folly is being observed by
three clowns, Sir Toby, Sir Andrew, and Fabian. In the early parts of the
sequence their comments nearly vie with Malvolio's for our attention; for
every line of soliloquy, Shakespeare interjects a line of jest, and the final
effect is the deliberate counterpoint with which we are more familiar:

MALVOLIO Seven of my people, with an obedient start, make
out for him. I frown the while, and perchance wind up my watch, or
play with my – some rich jewel. Toby approaches; curtsies there to
me –
SIR TOBY *Shall this fellow live?*
FABIAN *Though our silence be drawn from us with cars, yet peace.*
MALVOLIO I extend my hand to him thus, quenching my
familiar smile with an austere regard of control –
SIR TOBY *And does not Toby take you a blow o' the lips then?*
MALVOLIO Saying, "Cousin Toby, my fortunes, having cast me
on your niece, give me this prerogative of speech" –
SIR TOBY *What? What?. . .*

(2.5.58–72)

But counterpoint alone does not make a sequence; in fact, as the
soliloquy approaches its peak, Shakespeare will silence the jesters,
leaving Malvolio to bring the action to a climax on his own. What really
gives the soliloquy the magnitude of a sequence is that the playwright is
working with a dramatic question, *Will Malvolio believe that Olivia loves
him?* Shakespeare makes Malvolio suspect Olivia of that weakness well

before his eye falls on the forged letter, his position being pointedly established in the very first lines of the soliloquy: "I have heard herself come thus near, that should she fancy, it should be one of my complexion." In the early beats of the soliloquy Malvolio is in fact envisioning himself as Olivia's husband. Thus, here, as in the Brutus example, the meditating character has a difficulty at the beginning of the unit which must be solved by its end, so that tension builds toward his moment of decision. This action reaches its peak when Malvolio announces his intention to woo Olivia.

Though more quiescent than persuading or quarreling, meditating can indeed propel a sequence – as the Brutus and Malvolio examples show. The character's battle with his doubts as he struggles toward a choice creates enough of a conflict to make the sequence dramatic. But in the light of these sequences the dependent nature of Hamlet's "rogue and peasant slave" soliloquy becomes even more apparent. The soliloquy is drawn beyond normal length by Hamlet's exceptional intelligence and by the depth of his emotion, but it lacks the additional element that would make it a fully fledged action – a clear-cut dramatic question.

With the Malvolio sequence, this discussion has come full circle, for although Malvolio is the propelling character in a meditating sequence, his meditation unfolds within the context of an *observing sequence*. Malvolio enters twenty-three lines into the sequence, being brought onstage only after Maria has directed Sir Toby and crew to "get ye all three into the box-tree . . . and observe him," and once he exits the observers emerge to comment upon "the fruits of the sport" that will be forthcoming when Malvolio acts upon his "discovery." In this, the sequence resembles the two we looked at at the beginning of this chapter – the sequence in which Philo and Demetrius watch Cleopatra tease Antony and that in which Claudius and Polonius observe how Hamlet behaves toward Ophelia.

What then of observing? Can the activity of observing motivate a sequence? And if so how much power can Shakespeare get from it – could it ever be used, say, at the climactic moment of a play? If one considers the observing sequences we have looked at so far one might say no. In all three, the observing action forms, so to speak, a sequence-around-a-sequence. It leads us to expect, and then supplies, a judgment, but the action, per se, takes place in the sequence the observing action surrounds.

This fact itself deserves emphasis – in each instance the action being observed forms a complete action: it has its own intensifying structure. Sometimes this is quite apparent but not always. A director we very much admire insisted, for example, that since what Philo and Demetrius witness is "the mere entry (or crossing the stage) of Antony and Cleopatra" it should not be called an action. Much would be missed if the staging should be based on that premise. Philo and Demetrius observe a persuading action, in which Cleopatra repeatedly urges Antony to hear the ambassadors from Rome and he responds by ordering that Caesar's messengers "speak not to us" – exactly, the effect, by the way, that Cleopatra intends her persuasion to have. So structured, the action shows us immediately not only how much control Cleopatra has over Antony but how she achieves it.

The action in the sequence-within can take any form. Hamlet's meeting with Ophelia, where suspense is generated by a desire to know how Hamlet will respond, is the kind of situation best handled by an open-ended intensification and it is therefore constructed as a series of seemingly random episodes, with control shifting from Hamlet to Ophelia and then back to Hamlet as each reacts to the other's manner. When Duke Vincentio steps aside in *Measure for Measure* to watch Isabella inform her imprisoned brother about Angelo's proposition, the Duke observes a reporting sequence (3.1.48–173).

These observing sequences simply provide an extra set of introductory and concluding beats to the sequence-within. Let us end this chapter by looking at sequences in which the observing plays a more integrally dramatic role.

Because the action of observing presses toward a judgment, observing can indeed give direction to a sequence. As soon as Shakespeare brings the observer out of hiding and lets him interact with the other characters on stage he has ample opportunity to effect a reversal. One of the ways he creates that reversal is to have the observing character step into the action and affect the fortunes of the characters he has been watching. In *Much Ado About Nothing* 3.3.95–180 Dogberry's constables from their hiding place discover Borachio boasting to Conrade about his supposed tryst with Hero, and at the climactic moment step into the sequence to arrest him. In *Winter's Tale* 4.4.343–441 Polixenes visits the Shepherd's cottage in disguise, observes his son Florizel being contracted to Perdita and, by revealing his identity, turns Florizel's marriage proposal into a "divorce." Another way of adding a reversal is to make the events witnessed work a transformation in the observing character. In the opening sequence of *Hamlet* (1.1.1–125) the observer Horatio refuses to believe that the Ghost of the former king has been seen on the battlements. After he sees the Ghost he changes his mind, affirming its existence. This reversal of the observing character can be studied in the two sequences of *Much Ado About Nothing* where Benedick (2.3.1–264) and later Beatrice (3.1.1–116) hide and eavesdrop, believing themselves to be the plotters, with full control of the situation. Because, in both sequences, the observed event is deliberately staged by characters who mean to be overheard, the eavesdroppers are capitally deceived by those they are spying on: Benedick, observing Don Pedro, Claudio, and Leonato, is transformed from an antagonist of Beatrice into her admirer, while Beatrice's observation of Hero and Ursula effects a similar reversal in her feelings for Benedick.

As familiar as one may be with Shakespeare's plays, it is a bit of a surprise, given his propensity to use the reversal at dramatic moments, to realize that in his most powerful observing sequences Shakespeare works not with a judgment reversed (as in the previous examples) but with a judgment confirmed. But that is the structure he has given to the climactic third-act sequence in *Hamlet* – 3.2.92–295. Earlier, Shakespeare assigns Hamlet his motive (Hamlet expresses it to Horatio): to "observe my uncle" to determine whether "his occulted guilt / Do not itself unkennel." Hamlet pursues this objective throughout the sequence, which climaxes when Claudius reveals the guilt Hamlet hoped to expose. The concluding beats depict Hamlet's satisfaction that his judgment has been confirmed: he will "take the Ghost's word for a thousand pound."

Shakespeare employs the activity of observing to the same effect in another of his more dramatic sequences, *Othello* 4.1.74–213, where the Moor observes Iago's conversation with Cassio and Bianca.[2] At the beginning Iago invites Othello to "encave yourself, / And mark the fleers, the gibes, and notable scorns" that emanate from Cassio as Iago makes Cassio tell "where, how, how oft, how long ago, and when" he was intimate with Desdemona. Othello is established as an observer. Throughout the sequence Shakespeare gives Othello asides which record his reactions. Othello observes what seems to him to be damning evidence against Desdemona and Cassio. Fully deceived by Iago, he stands at the end of the sequence confirmed in his opinion that Desdemona is a whore. The whole sequence drives toward this confirmation.

The judgment section with which the sequence concludes demonstrates how delicate an instrument the observing sequence can be for probing a psyche. Shakespeare presents Othello's commentary on Cassio's performance in three beats and by doing so embodies in the judgment the tensions among the several possible viewpoints: (1) that of the satanic and pitiless Iago; (2) that of the noble Othello whose love for Desdemona was deep and holy; and (3) that of the transformed Othello, the pitiful creature which his subjection to Iago has created.

In the first of the judgment beats (170–8), Othello responds as Iago wishes: "How shall I murder him, Iago? . . . I would have him nine years a-killing." But he cannot kill his love for Desdemona as easily as he might kill Cassio. In the second of these beats (178–96), his sorrow allows him to remember only Desdemona's virtues. His "judgment" turns out to be a eulogy, which Iago must contradict:

> A fine woman! a fair woman! a sweet woman! . . . O, the world hath
> not a sweeter creature! She might lie by an emperor's side and
> command his tasks . . . So delicate with her needle! an admirable
> musician! O, she will sing the savageness out of a bear. Of so high
> and plenteous wit and invention! . . . And then of so gentle a
> condition! . . . The pity of it, Iago! O Iago, the pity of it, Iago!

Othello means to rage. He would turn his heart to stone, would "let her rot, and perish, and be damn'd." His mind, however, keeps pulling him back to dwell on images of the true and the good, on the Desdemona he believes he has lost. But the reversal that would save Othello never takes place. At Iago's insistence he shakes these sentiments off: in the third beat, his final judgment, Othello takes the stand Iago would foster:

> IAGO If you are so fond over her iniquity, give her patent to
> offend, for if it touch not you, it comes near nobody.
> OTHELLO I will chop her into messes. Cuckold me!
> IAGO O, 'tis foul in her.
> OTHELLO With mine officer!
> IAGO That's fouler.
> OTHELLO Get me some poison, Iago, this night. I'll not
> expostulate with her, lest her body and beauty unprovide my mind
> again. This night, Iago.
> IAGO Do it not with poison; strangle her in her bed, even the
> bed she hath contaminated.
> OTHELLO Good, good; the justice of it pleases; very good.
> IAGO And for Cassio, let me be his undertaker. You shall hear
> more by midnight.
> OTHELLO Excellent good.
>
> (4.1.197–213)

Ironically, Othello describes this perversion of judgment as just and good.

In rendering Othello's judgment Shakespeare moves the action toward a confirmation rather than a reversal of the observer's position. The drama results from the character's entrenchment in the position he has been tending toward all along. A judgment confirmed, insofar as it transports the observing character to greater heights – or depths – can provide a powerful sequence climax.

Obviously, then, the activity of observing can become the driving force of a sequence. When it is, the intention to "look," "note," "behold," or "see" is established at the beginning of the sequence and the action culminates in a judgment.

The ultimate observer in this multiplication of viewpoints is always the audience. Just as the observing character "beholds and sees" a sequence, so the audience beholds and sees the play. As Claudius and Polonius "frankly judge" what they observe, so we judge – more frankly, it is hoped, and with less bias. We judge not as involved characters indulging a special interest, nor as self-righteous moralists seeking a message, but as human beings learning from experience, as men and women choosing the grain and discarding the chaff, as questing individuals in search of significance. As such, let us behold and see – and frankly judge – some other sequence types that are presented to us as observers for our judgment.

9

Reporting and interrogating sequences

I

Reporting is as much the province of the playwright as of the journalist. The playwright cannot get on without reporting. He cannot even begin without reporting, for the crucial problem facing him as he raises his pen is to supply exposition. As soon as the curtain rises, somehow *someone* must report something. Nor can the dramatist continue without reporting, for any vital action that occurs offstage must be recounted to characters on it and to the audience. Reporting is an essential activity of drama.[1]

Perhaps the best of Shakespeare's expository reporting sequences is *Hamlet* 1.5.1–112, where the ghost of the dead king recounts his tale of horror to his son. In it, each of the major elements – messenger, report, and auditor – is effectively handled. There is nothing original about putting a ghost on the stage, but Shakespeare's imagination transforms the conventional ghost, as John Addington Symonds has noted, into "a spirit of like intellectual substance with the actors, a parcel of the universe in which all live and move and have their being."[2] In so doing he creates a messenger of more than ordinary interest. The Ghost's report also goes beyond the ordinary. It vilifies lust, offers exciting revelations of a murder, accuses a king. Both his call for revenge and his plea for remembrance are compelling; further, he ranges across time and into eternity, giving us glimpses of Purgatory, where spirits are "confin'd to fast in fires" of "sulph'rous and tormenting flames." Not only are the messenger and the report riveting. So also is the hearer. In this sequence the narrator speaks not to some supernumerary invented for the sole purpose of lending him an ear but to the play's protagonist, who has an intense desire to hear and understand. The response – Hamlet's famous "Remember thee!" speech – is both memorable in itself and significant in its effect, for it lays out the motives from which Hamlet will be acting during later portions of the play. In this sequence each element is developed to a degree that pushes an essentially narrative sequence form into the realm of drama.[3]

Still, expository reporting has its formal limitations. Since its object is primarily to convey information to the audience, its success depends more on the report's being absolutely clear and intelligible than on its being dramatic; consequently, it sometimes comes across as a phase of drama to be endured more than enjoyed. Anyone who has sat through Prospero's interminable expository speech in act I of *The Tempest* has probably felt that his constant admonitions to Miranda to keep awake are directed at the audience as well. And which is potentially more deadly in productions of *Henry V*: the Archbishop's 63-line report on the Salique Law or the ludicrous routines imposed on it by directors desperate to enliven the sequence? Obviously the activity of reporting in itself is hardly the most dramatic of sequence forms. Nevertheless, there are ways in which its potential for drama can be increased, and Shakespeare uses them. In his hands the reporting sequence can be remarkably effective. To go further with our study of the motivated sequence, we will concentrate here on cases in which Shakespeare dramatizes reports of events that have already taken place on the stage, so that the attention of the audience shifts from the actual report to how that report is delivered or received. Study of such sequences will bring out the main point of this chapter – that reporting very often directs or energizes sequence actions which are not at all expository – and will demonstrate how Shakespeare can give us information we have already received and still surprise us.

The reporting sequence is quickly defined. Like any other sequence it contains a complete action. The end in view is to pass information from one character to another: messages are delivered, news is relayed, secrets are revealed, events are described. Nothing could be simpler. But whatever the information, whatever its ramifications, the essential point is that the active character possesses it and his intention to report is the propelling force of the entire sequence. This basic structure, however, gives rise to two different kinds of reporting sequence, the expository and the elicitory. While *expository reporting sequences* focus on information being conveyed, usually for the benefit of the audience, *elicitory reporting sequences* (those to be examined in this chapter) have a significantly different purpose – to highlight the response of the character to whom the report is delivered. Each type solves different problems for the dramatist engaged in transforming narrative into drama.

The elicitory reporting sequence contains all the elements found in the expository type. Both sequence forms are frequently written as duets: one character reports, another listens. In both, the character who delivers the report is dominant, and the action lasts only as long as his intention remains constant. Since that intention is invariably "to report," the sequence must end as soon as the report is given. In the elicitory reporting sequence, however, the playwright is no longer hampered by the need to communicate the message detail by detail: the audience already has the information being conveyed by the messenger.

This is the first major difference between the two forms: when the event being reported in the sequence is already known to the audience, there is little need for laborious and perhaps tedious repetition of the details – better for the report to be delivered in a few well-chosen words. Thus, instead of a message of forty to one hundred lines delivered almost without interruption, as is usual in expository types, the message in the elicitory reporting sequence is condensed, often to as little as two lines:

> Tybalt is gone, and Romeo banished,
> Romeo that kill'd him, he is banished.
>
> (*Romeo and Juliet,* 3.2.69–70)

> Your castle is surpris'd; your wife, and babes,
> Savagely slaughter'd.
>
> (*Macbeth.* 4.3.204–5)

> Leonato,
> I am sorry you must hear. Upon mine honor,
> Myself, my brother, and this grieved count
> Did see her, hear her, at that hour last night
> Talk with a ruffian at her chamber-window. . .
>
> (*Much Ado,* 4.1.87–91)

The report itself is no less important than in the expository sequence; indeed, because it coincides with (or at least evokes) the sequence climax, the audience awaits it more eagerly. The intention to report remains the propelling character's objective. But because the audience is already familiar with the message, it can now be delivered succinctly and with force.

A second difference: while less space is given in the elicitory sequence to the report, more is dedicated to the response of the listener. In expository reporting the listener must not distract the audience's attention from the message. His responses usually take the form of brief ejaculations or are framed as questions, for questions (far from distracting) encourage the speaker to reveal more. In *Hamlet* 5.2.1–80, for example, Horatio listens to the Prince describing his escape from Rosencrantz and Guildenstern and their subsequent deaths, interrupting only with the briefest comments: "That is most certain"; "Is 't possible?"; "I beseech you"; "Ay, my good lord"; "How was this seal'd?" etc. In

Antony and Cleopatra 3.6.1–38, where Caesar informs Maecenas and Agrippa of Antony's conduct in Alexandria, the two Romans are equally subdued in their responses: "This in the public eye?"; "Let Rome be thus / Inform'd"; "Who does he accuse?" If the listening character in an expository reporting sequence has strong feelings, he is not allowed to express them until the bulk of the report has been delivered.

In elicitory reporting, on the other hand, the dramatist is no longer bound to subordinate the hearer: the sequence becomes more truly a dialogue. The possibility of conflict is restored, the potential for drama recovered. Now free to develop the secondary character, Shakespeare builds the action by giving him greater prominence. His desire to know, a basic attribute of the character responding to a report, can be kindled and then intensified. Though his general task is to question, he can perform this task in a range of tones, inquiring objectively, or pleading desperately for news, or even demanding to be informed. The listener may react in other ways too; he may believe or disbelieve, cooperate with or thwart the dominant figure whose task is to report. But above all he wants to know. Because of this he can be teased, harassed, pampered, threatened, or even ignored by the reporting character. In short, the secondary character's response is now a central and a characterizing element in the sequence.

A third important difference between expository and elicitory sequences is that in the elicitory type the dominant character often hesitates to deliver the report for some interesting reason. In expository reporting the narrator launches immediately into his report, which normally takes up the whole sequence. But the technique in elicitory reporting sequences, on the contrary, is to hold back the report until the final moments of the sequence. The messenger tends *to evade*. Since the question creating the tension is simply whether (or rather *when*) the message will be revealed, it is essential to the pattern that some time elapse before the report is given. This delay is so typical that the dominant character in this sequence type can usually be described as a reluctant reporter.

Of course this situation blends readily with a reversal, and Shakespeare often uses one in elicitory reporting sequences. Such a reversal has predictable effects on the sequence form. When the propelling character is reluctant to deliver the report, its ultimate revelation causes a 180-degree change. In such cases the report is positioned at the climax of the sequence, so that revelation and reversal occur simultaneously. On the other hand, Shakespeare may wish to work the reversal upon the responding character. He then places the report slightly earlier and evokes a response that supplies the climactic impact. The timing of the actual report determines which form the climax takes, but either way the result is a dramatic reversal.

The profiles of the two reporting sequence forms are thus quite different. In elicitory reporting the dominant character intends to communicate a message, known to the audience but not to his interlocutor. Shakespeare gives him subsidiary motives for withholding the message until the final moments of the sequence, when it is delivered briefly and forcefully. The message is of utmost importance to the listener, and both before and after its delivery the audience's attention is directed toward his reactions.

Let us see how Shakespeare particularizes these principles in his plays.

II

In *Romeo and Juliet* 2.5.1–78, Shakespeare is interested in the responses of Juliet to the news that Romeo has arranged their elopement. He shows us beforehand a sequence between Romeo and the Nurse, so that we hear Romeo's message firsthand; meanwhile, Juliet, who has most at stake, is left at home in impatient ignorance. Then he gives us the elicitory reporting sequence between the Nurse and Juliet.

In this sequence Shakespeare solves a challenging dramaturgical problem. As far as the audience is concerned, the message which the Nurse brings to Juliet is of minor importance: they don't need to hear it again. But Juliet has an intense desire to know Romeo's answer; moreover, Shakespeare wants to show her impatience. He obviously cannot present the report as it is transferred to Juliet in the source poem by Arthur Brooke, where the Nurse returns from Romeo "with smyling face," announces immediately that she has "good newes for thee, my girle, good tydinges,"[4] then, having satisfied Juliet, fills the episode out with some hearty moralizing. Shakespeare solves the problem of creating tension where there is none by having the Nurse withhold the message. In *Romeo and Juliet* the crusty old Nurse with her affectionate teasing functions delightfully as the reluctant reporter. The advantages of this tactic are twofold: first, the drama is intensified by keeping the audience in suspense as to when and how the Nurse will reveal the message, and second, the tensions created in the excited girl and then released make the audience share Juliet's anxiety and thus actually experience the pangs of young love.

How is this solution realized in terms of objectives? Of course the Nurse is the propelling character but what goals does Shakespeare give her in order to elicit the desired response from Juliet? One director argues that the Nurse's objective is "to tease or play with Juliet and eventually give her report." But what does this really mean? The long- and short-term goals are mixed together here.

The Nurse's ultimate goal is to report. If the dramatic question embodying this objective were to be formulated it would sound embarrassingly simple, *Will the Nurse tell Juliet that Romeo will marry her?*, yet this is undeniably the question upon which the playwright builds his structure: there would be no tension if we were not waiting with Juliet for the Nurse's revelation, and the action continues only until the report is given. The desire to report, then, is not something that develops suddenly in the climactic beat; this is the motive that brought the Nurse to Juliet in the first place.

But this sequence objective is realized through a series of shorter-term objectives, recognizable in each beat, various kinds of teasing which invest the sequence with its tone, mood, and rhythms. These beat objectives determine how the reporting is effected and intensify Juliet's desire for the information.

To begin with, Shakespeare makes the Nurse return late from her meeting with Romeo, providing the opportunity (in the introductory beat 2.5.1–17) to establish Juliet's impatience for news. The Nurse, Love's herald, should be "swift in motion as a ball" and "nimble-pinion'd"; instead, she is "unwieldy, slow, heavy, and pale as lead." This introductory beat is followed by a series of interchanges in which Juliet interrogates and the Nurse evades. The Nurse offers a battery of excuses, her beat motives: she dawdles because she is out of breath, questions Juliet's taste in lovers, talks of dinner, focuses on a headache, then an aching back, and at long last comes to "Your love says –," only to halt abruptly in mock fear that Juliet's mother is within earshot. The cumulative effect of these evasions provokes a suppliant Juliet to an outburst of impatience:

> Where is my mother! why, she is within,
> Where should she be? How oddly thou repliest!
> "Your love says, like an honest gentleman,
> 'Where is your mother?'"

$$(2.5.57–61)$$

Even yet the Nurse withholds the report, countering Juliet's tone with feigned reproaches of ingratitude which drive the intensification a stage higher. At the climactic moment of the sequence the Nurse abandons her teasing, giving the action its reversal:

JULIET Here's such a coil! Come, what says Romeo?
NURSE Have you got leave to go to shrift today?
JULIET I have.
NURSE Then hie you hence to Friar Lawrence' cell,
There stays a husband to make you a wife.

$$(2.5.65-9)$$

The report itself occupies only two lines of the sequence. "Then hie you hence to Friar Lawrence' cell, / There stays a husband to make you a wife." By withholding it, by developing the Nurse's playfulness, by dwelling on her preoccupation with her fatigue as it fires the girl's impatience, by forcing Juliet to plead for the news, Shakespeare gives the report a dramatic power it would not otherwise have. Through the report and the reporter, he elicits from Juliet the reaction that gives the scene its life and the audience its experience of the urgencies of young love.[5]

III

The strategy in *Measure for Measure* 3.1.48–173 is slightly different from the strategy in the *Romeo and Juliet* sequence. To understand the variation one must realize that the basic sequence form in each case has been combined with a reversal structure. In the simpler *Romeo and Juliet* sequence Shakespeare gives the reversal to the messenger. The Nurse at first refuses to divulge her news but eventually comes out with it. The *Measure for Measure* sequence is more complex. The reversal is given not to Isabella, the reporting figure whose motives propel the sequence, but to the recipient of her report, her brother Claudio. The delivery of the message itself is so timed as to effect Claudio's reversal.

Again in this sequence the suspense does not stem from our curiosity about Isabella's report, for everyone knows the details. Shakespeare has already shown us firsthand that Lord Angelo, "hooking both right and wrong to th' appetite" (2.4.176), has offered to free Claudio if Isabella will satisfy his lust. He has shown us Isabella's full perception of the grossness of this "foul redemption" by which her soul is made the price of Claudio's body. He has also shown that Isabella has made the moral, though very difficult, choice: "Then Isabel, live chaste, and, brother, die; / More than our brother is our chastity" (2.4.184–5). This is a powerful statement. In the current age of moral chaos her refusal to waver under temptation is held against her (people even speak as though Isabella is happy with this choice, when in fact it makes her wretched), but Isabella sees the issues clearly.[6] Shakespeare has shown us all this before Isabella arrives at Claudio's cell.

Though Isabella's need to report gives movement and direction to the sequence, her role is a catalytic one: the focus is on the auditor, Claudio. The dramatic question is, *How will Isabella's report affect Claudio?* Properly understood, the sequence is structured as a test of Claudio's courage and manly virtue. Most of what we learn about Claudio we learn from his response in this scene.

How careful Shakespeare is to establish Claudio's emotional position at the beginning of the interview. He dedicates a whole sequence entirely to this purpose, the sequence between the Duke and Claudio with which the act opens (3.1.1–47).[7] Having been persuaded by the Duke's *consolatio* that if one is absolute for death, then "either death or life / Shall thereby be the sweeter," Claudio greets Isabella already resolved to accept death: "To sue to live, I find I seek to die, / And seeking death, find life. Let it come on" (3.1.42–3).

Only after establishing Claudio's position does Shakespeare bring in Isabella. The claim is often made that she teases her brother. On the contrary, she gets the bad news out immediately:

> CLAUDIO Now, sister, what's the comfort?
> ISABELLA   Why,
> As all comforts are: most good, most good indeed.
> Lord Angelo, having affairs to heaven,
> Intends you for his swift ambassador,
> Where you shall be an everlasting leiger:
> Therefore your best appointment make with speed,
> Tomorrow you set on.
>
>   (3.1.54–60)

What Isabella hesitates to do is to communicate to Claudio the conditions proposed for the purchase of his life; here she is also a reluctant reporter, forcing the action into a characteristic pattern of the elicitory reporting sequence: the dominant character evades and the responding character interrogates. But Isabella's hesitation has a very real psychological basis. Her behavior is naturally influenced by the fact that she has come directly from Angelo and is still in a state of shock. Beyond this – and Shakespeare places the emphasis here – she fears that though Claudio can accept death when he believes there is no alternative, he might not have the same strength when he learns of the chance for a reprieve. Isabella is certain that she would give her life for him if Angelo would accept that as his price for Claudio's deliverance (she so states at 2.4.99–104 and 3.1.103–5), but she is less sure that Claudio can do the same for her, now that their positions are reversed.

Shakespeare so constructs the sequence that Claudio's initial resolution to accept death is constantly being reinforced. Isabella's hesitation in this first phase of the sequence works toward that end: Claudio is told enough about the report to warn him that Angelo's is a "devilish mercy" that would make Claudio's subsequent life one of continued self-reproach. In this knowledge Claudio chooses again, and chooses nobly: "If I must die, / I will encounter darkness as a bride, / And hug it in mine arms" (3.1.82–4).

Claudio's resolution is reinforced once more in the next beat of the sequence (3.1.86–107) where, proud of her brother's courage and convinced that he will share her sense of outrage, Isabella finally allows the horror of her recent encounter with Angelo to burst forth:

> O, 'tis the cunning livery of hell,
> The damned'st body to invest and cover
> In prenzie guards! Dost thou think, Claudio,
> If I would yield him my virginity,
> Thou mightst be freed!
>
> (3.1.94–8)

And Claudio supports her: "Thou shalt not do't" (3.1.102). Shakespeare assures Claudio of our sympathy by repeatedly showing the finer beatings of his heart.

So long withheld, so dramatically delivered, so painful to both sister and brother – Isabella's report translates into a far more gripping moment in the theater than could be obtained by expository reporting. But the sequence is not over; it has yet to climax. Shakespeare has calculated the sequence structure so that Isabella's report will effect a reversal in Claudio. Her news unsettles his resolve, and his mind clutches at the thread of hope dangling before him: if Angelo commands it, "sure it is no sin, / Or of the deadly seven it is the least" (3.1.109–10). The reversal has begun. These thoughts continue, combine with fear, and then burst out in Claudio's wrenching plea. He started the sequence "absolute for death," but now at its climax he cries, "Sweet sister, let me live."

Using this structure Shakespeare elicits emotions not only from Claudio but from Isabella. In the concluding beat (3.1.135–50), he makes Isabella turn against Claudio with all her fury, for she too is young and human. For her this is a double betrayal: Angelo, the law, would buy her; now Claudio, her own brother, would sell her. His defection is too great for her to handle rationally. Her fury, however, brings Claudio back to his senses. That his lapse is momentary, that he is subsequently ashamed of it, is obvious from the coda beat appended to the sequence (3.1.160–73). But all of this does not alter the fact that the response elicited by Isabella's report is structured as a full reversal. During the course of the sequence Claudio is moved from an acceptance of death to a grasping for life.

IV

The pattern of the elicitory reporting sequence is a common one. It is also found in *Much Ado About Nothing* when Claudio reveals to Leonato the reason he refuses to marry Hero (4.1.1–112); in *Macbeth*, when Ross reveals to Macduff the news that all his little ones have been slaughtered (4.3.159–240); in *Othello* when Othello reveals to Desdemona the news he has come to put before her, that he now looks upon her as "that cunning whore of Venice / That married with Othello" (4.2.1–109). Any of these sequences could serve as our third example, but it might be more rewarding to explore another elicitory reporting sequence from *Othello*, that in which Iago reveals to the Moor his slanderous report about Desdemona, for this sequence provides an opportunity to examine more closely the relationships between the motives of reporting and interrogating.

In our study of reporting it has been necessary from time to time to speak of the complementary activity of interrogating, reporting being the mode through which the propelling character's energies are set in motion and interrogating the mode that activates the responding character. These two modes of action are always in tension, and one must not overlook the fact that at times Shakespeare alters the relationship, casting the reporting character into the responding role in a sequence that is clearly propelled by some authority figure, an interrogator or judge. When the emphasis so shifts, we have an interrogating sequence. In other words, a sequence remains a reporting sequence only so long as the reporting character retains dominance. When power shifts to the interrogating character, a new set of relationships emerges.

Because the difference between the reporting sequence and the interrogating sequence has a bearing on the *Othello* action we are about to examine, that difference should be made clear. The interrogating sequence can be seen in *Romeo and Juliet* where, after Romeo has killed Tybalt, Shakespeare brings in the authorities to assess the situation (sequence 3.1.137–97). Benvolio's report of the events leading up to the deaths of Mercutio and Tybalt comprises the bulk of the dialogue. Yet Benvolio is hardly dominant. The active character is Escalus, Prince of Verona, whose demand for an explanation of the carnage, an "interrogation," dominates the action and drives it toward its climax – a judgment delivered by the interrogating character. The primary significance of the entire unit lies in the judgment: the Prince condemns Romeo to exile.

Othello 2.3.169–258 provides another example of the interrogating sequence. After Cassio has disgraced himself by his drunken brawling Shakespeare again brings in an authority figure, here Othello, to initiate an immediate on-the-scene trial. The pattern is the same. Iago, reporting, supplies the testimony. But Othello calls for it. And Othello passes judgment. The sentencing of Cassio – "Never more be officer of mine" – is the climax toward which the interrogating action builds. The interrogator rather than the narrator is dominant. In these interrogating sequences the reporting figure clearly occupies a secondary role. The interviewer controls the sequence: his questions determine where it will go and his judgment (an important new element) supplies the climax.

Shakespeare plays with these tensions in the sequence in which Iago initiates his temptation of Othello by reporting that Desdemona has been unfaithful. In this sequence (*Othello* 3.3.93–279) Shakespeare chooses to work with the fundamental situation of the elicitory reporting sequence: Iago, the messenger, is dominant, and his intention is to deliver a report to a secondary character, Othello. As usual, the audience is acquainted in advance with the details of the report, thus leaving Shakespeare free to concentrate on the response Iago elicits from Othello. Like Juliet's Nurse and Isabella, Iago is a reluctant reporter.

The resemblance between Iago and Shakespeare's other reluctant reporters is apparent. A practical Machiavellian whose "delay" has awed as many generations as Hamlet's, he knows it is to his advantage to postpone his revelation: the longer he refuses to speak, the more honest he will seem and the more credible will be his tale. But of course Iago's reluctance is totally feigned – a device only, to arouse the curiosity of his gullible opponent – and Iago wants nothing more than to deliver his report to Othello.

So far this summary of Iago's role makes the sequence sound like a conventional example of elicitory reporting, the only difference being that the report is a false one. But in this sequence Shakespeare adds a level of dramatic irony to the elements we have been reviewing. Othello, who, as the responding figure, would normally play a subordinate role, sees himself as the dominant one and believes he is propelling the action. To a certain extent he is. But his control is a gift from Iago. Shakespeare has the truly dominant Iago deliberately step into the subordinate role in the sequence Othello is conducting. By concealing his report Iago lets Othello force the reversal through his interrogation.

One of the interesting aspects of the sequence is the interaction Shakespeare creates between reporting and interrogating. If one attempts to discern the beat structure by analyzing Iago's motives, the effort proves frustrating – no pattern emerges. Because Iago has surrendered dominance, Othello's motives rather than Iago's supply the key to the beat structure. In 93–101, the introductory beat, Iago raises the subject he wants Othello to think about. The ruse works, and Iago gives way, leaving Othello dominant in the next few beats. Othello's task is obviously to question: he does so idly at first but with ever-increasing intensity. The interrogation begins at line 103 when he asks, "Is Cassio not honest?" Iago responds with evasions, then admits that Cassio is honest, or at least (a subtle qualification) *should be* honest: "Men should be what they seem." Othello is quick to notice Iago's hesitation and in the next beat presses the interrogation further, asking Iago to "speak to me as to thy thinkings," to "give thy worst of thoughts / The worst of words." Iago continues to evade the question, on the enticing ground that his thoughts are too vile to air. The exchanges intensify, and with them Othello's emotion. Finally all courtesy disappears – Othello *demands* to know Iago's thoughts. The entire segment moves forward as an interrogation; as Juliet to the Nurse, as Claudio to Isabella, so Othello says to Iago, "Show me thy thought." The Moor meets with a resistance so implacable that he is moved from questioning to pleading to demanding, and these beat-by-beat motives function within the overarching motive – to interrogate.

Thus, the beat structure which initially seems impenetrable is actually carefully defined as a series of questions and answers:

> (93–101) Q: Did Michael Cassio . . . know of your love?
> A: O yes, and went between us very oft.

> (102–29) Q: Discern'st thou aught in that? Is he not honest?
> A: Why then I think Cassio's an honest man.

> (130–61) Q: I prithee speak to me as to thy thinkings . . .
> A: Good my lord, pardon me . . . It were not for your
> quiet nor your good . . . To let you know my thoughts.

– and so on, up until the unit's first crux:

> (162–4) Q: I'll know thy thoughts.
> A: You cannot . . . Nor shall not.

In view of the strong climax at this point where the conflicting desires reach their peak, someone unfamiliar with sequence forms might argue that Iago's "You cannot . . . Nor shall not" at line 164 marks a sequence break. Iago's refusal is final enough, but the break is a subordinate one, a beat break. By line 164 Shakespeare has only established Iago in the position from which he is to be reversed. Since Iago has yet to deliver his report, the sequence is far from over. The next beat (3.3.165–92) confirms this. Presenting Iago's charge that Othello has rendered himself a prey to jealousy and Othello's rebuttal that neither from his wife's social virtues nor from his own weak merits will he "draw the smallest fear or doubt of her revolt," this nicely crafted beat introduces the conditions that will allow Iago to relent. Beat 165–92 proves to be a continuation, not a new beginning. In this beat Iago continues the pretense that he is acting in deference to Othello: the myth is that Othello is the victor here. This jealousy beat, in which Othello ironically assures us of his own strength against temptation, provides the transition to the sequence's second and final climax.

The apex of the sequence is reached when Iago reverses his stand. Having stated irrevocably that he would never reveal his thoughts, Iago now breaks his self-imposed silence and delivers the long-delayed report:

> IAGO I am glad of this, for now I shall have reason
> To show the love and duty that I bear you
> With franker spirit: therefore (as I am bound)
> Receive it from me. I speak not yet of proof.
> Look to your wife, observe her well with Cassio . . .
>
> (3.3.193–7)

The first climax ("You cannot . . . Nor shall not") turns out to have been only a temporary crest, a part of the intensification. The real climax of the sequence occurs at the delivery of the report, which has been Iago's goal from the start.

In the remainder of the sequence (decrescent in mood), Shakespeare gives us the response elicited from Othello by this unexpected disclosure. That response seems to be utter astonishment, to the point of speechlessness. Iago's sardonic "I see this hath a little dash'd your spirits" superbly understates Othello's deflation. Not one to let opportunity slip, Iago makes up for Othello's silence by pressing his case further, leaving Othello in utter confusion but willing to investigate the accusation. The strong statement by Othello at 278–9 marks both the end of the sequence and the position he should, would like to, and might yet choose: "If she be false, O then heaven mocks itself! / I'll not believe 't." It also marks the position from which Iago must move Othello in the concluding sequence of the temptation.

In writing this sequence, the playwright has chosen to portray two dominant characters through a sequence type calling for a dominant/

subordinate relationship. The challenge is to make the audience believe that the greater strength lies with the character who steps into the weaker role. The strategy works brilliantly: Iago's indomitable strength is rendered first by establishing his desire to report, then by having him display a rocklike resistance to the interrogation to which he submits. Othello's magnificence derives in turn from the way he assaults and overcomes this implacable resistance, the massive energies he displays in effecting the reversal in Iago that culminates in the report. But since in fact the "dominant" Othello is always doing exactly what the "responding" Iago means him to be doing, his authority is sufficiently diluted to suggest his truly subordinate role in the sequence.

Despite the structural similarities in our examples, intriguing differences occur when the basic sequence form is wedded to the reversal. The basic sequence pattern requires only that the reporter hold information back, so that the revelation occur at the end of the unit and that the reversal, if there is one, coincide with the climax. This much is standard. It is apparently not fore-ordained, however, that the dominant character must have the reversal. Either character qualifies, and the reversal comes where the drama is. If as in *Romeo and Juliet* the point of the sequence is simple – e.g., How eager is the auditor (Juliet) to hear the news? – then the drama lies in the delivery of the report and the reversal is given to the narrator (Juliet's Nurse). If as in *Measure for Measure* the question of the sequence is complex – How will the report affect the auditor (Claudio)? – the drama lies in the contrast between the auditor's before and after responses and the reversal is given to him. When the concerns of the sequence have even greater magnitude, when the opponents approach the size of Othello and Iago, energy is pulsing from both sides and a single sequence can no longer contain it. The problem in our *Othello* sequence is that the auditor Othello's desire to know is so intense and the narrator Iago's resistance so powerful that all the necessities of climax and reversal culminate naturally in the delivery of the report. Given that necessity, there is no room in the sequence for the storm that must inevitably burst from Othello when his position is reversed. Shakespeare does the only possible thing. He shows enough of Othello's shock and confusion to satisfy the demands of the current sequence but withholds the full force of his response for the companion sequence which begins at line 333, when Othello bursts upon Iago crying, "Thou hast set me on the rack." Shakespeare has it both ways. The reversal in this sequence remains with Iago the narrator. But at the end of the larger unit (the three-part temptation) follows the inevitable – and by then more powerful – reversal of Othello.

V

Since we began this chapter by examining an early attempt to solve the problems inherent in this dramatic situation, we will look now at a sequence in which Shakespeare is so much a master of the form that its outlines tend to disappear. The reluctant reporter, the delayed report, the responding auditor are all present, yet the form blurs, because the playwright is so sure of his craft that he goes well beyond it. Here content virtually obscures form.

Our choice is the closing sequence of *King Lear* where Kent attempts to make Lear comprehend the true identity of Caius (5.3.230–327). Here Shakespeare adapts a sequence form specifically designed to effect communication to an episode which demonstrates that communication is no longer possible. The marvel here is that a report which has lost all its pertinence, a report to which no one on stage can respond, becomes the vehicle through which the audience can experience the protagonist's suffering.

At first glance this hardly seems to be a reporting sequence at all. Our attention is absorbed by our fears for Lear and Cordelia, realized so immediately and so tragically in production when Lear staggers onto the stage carrying Cordelia's body. In the theater the experience of Lear's suffering is too harrowing for us to realize how essential Kent is to the structure of the sequence. This is as it should be: we are not meant to notice the structure. Yet that sequence is in fact shaped by Kent's desire to inform the King that he was Caius. Take Kent from the sequence, and you also take away the conflict of motives that makes the sequence work.

That Shakespeare thought out Kent's role in this sequence is demonstrated by Kent's hints of a plan – "my made intent" he calls it – for a formal reconciliation with Lear. He rejects Cordelia's urgings that he cast off the weeds of Caius, insisting on maintaining the disguise "till time and I think meet" (4.7.11), even when there is no longer any danger in discovery. Shakespeare uses Kent's desire to be reconciled with Lear to swing Albany's mind back to the "great thing of us forgot," the need to free Lear and Cordelia from prison. In preparation for this moment he implants in Kent a desire "to report."

Like Isabella and Juliet's Nurse, Kent does not achieve his objective immediately; however, in this case the delays that prevent the report's being heard until the end of the sequence stem from the reigning chaos: circumstances prevent Kent and Lear from meeting. Shakespeare so arranges matters that Kent must overcome several obstacles before he can report. The first is to capture Albany's full attention: Kent's arrival passes almost unnoticed, for, as Albany remarks, "The time will not allow the compliment / Which very manners urges." Albany's attention is absorbed by the deaths of the hateful sisters. Goneril has just murdered Regan, then slain herself; Edmund lies dying beside them, with only enough life left in him to gloat over his conquest of both. Compared with this, the report Kent wants to deliver seems irrelevant. Despite the confusion, Kent voices his objective: "I am come / To bid my King and Master aye good night. / Is he not here?" The request stops Albany short, reminds him that lesser concerns have distracted him from rescuing Lear and Cordelia, and redirects his attention – not, however, toward Kent but toward Edmund.

Albany's recollection of Lear only reveals another obstacle in Kent's way, one which may rob Kent of the chance to tell his tale at all: Edmund has sentenced Lear and Cordelia to death. Kent's desire to report sets in motion a flurry of activity during which Albany and Edgar draw from Edmund the whereabouts of Lear and Cordelia in a frantic effort to save them. But Kent himself stands silent – Shakespeare makes Edmund the focal point of this beat (5.3.244–57).[8] The search for Lear turns attention away for the second time from the man who, if he were to be rewarded after his own deserts, should himself be the hero of the hour.

The greatest obstacle is yet to come. In the beat at 5.3.258–79, Kent's intentions are frustrated by still another death – Cordelia's: when the King finally does arrive on stage he is carrying Cordelia's corpse and is so consumed with agony that nothing else exists for him. Kent falls on his knees in compassion beside the mourning King. The response he eventually elicits is far from what he expected – the ears of the King for whom Kent's message is intended are permanently sealed: words will no longer penetrate. Kent's reward for his devotion is, apparently, to be classed with the very enemies he has for three acts been loyally fighting against:

> KENT O my good master!
> LEAR Prithee away.
> EDGAR   'Tis noble Kent, your friend.
> LEAR A plague upon you murderers, traitors all!

$$(5.3.268-70)$$

Kent's report is not only delayed, it is delayed so long that there is hardly any point in making it. Lear is no more in a rewarding mood than he was when he banished Kent in act 1, and the long-anticipated recognition scene develops in anguish, reverberating with echoes of Lear's confused recognition of the blind Gloucester and of the "learned" Tom.

Three beats (or fifty lines) into the sequence, with Lear's "Who are you?," Kent has one last opportunity to tell his story. Hope of achieving his objective yet remains, for Lear now recognizes him ("Are you not Kent?"). This, however, is not the recognition Kent seeks. In spite of all that has passed, he still hopes to be recognized as Caius. And so, tenderly, he would inform his master:

> LEAR This is a dull sight. Are you not Kent?
> KENT   The same:
> Your servant Kent. Where is your servant Caius?
> LEAR He's a good fellow, I can tell you that;
> He'll strike, and quickly too. He's dead and rotten.
> KENT No, my good Lord, I am the very man.
> LEAR I'll see that straight.
> KENT That from your first of difference and decay,
> Have followed your sad steps.
>
> (5.3.283–90)

Thus is the report delivered. The King responds with "You are welcome hither." But Albany provides the interpretation of the King's response that Kent must finally accept: "He knows not what he says, and vain is it / That we present us to him." Edgar confirms this: "Very bootless."

To say that Shakespeare uses Kent's desire to report to elicit a response from Lear is not to say that the emotions in the sequence arise only because of Kent's role in it. Obviously much depends upon our experience of Lear's suffering. Did he not raise the mirror to see if Cordelia's breath will cloud it or did he not notice the feather stir or think he hears Cordelia speak, Kent's role would have no effect. Nor would the confrontation between Kent and Lear be so moving if one of the "mysteries" of the sequence did not revolve around the irony that the world does not necessarily reward the good. Lear has told us that if Cordelia lives "it is a chance which does redeem all sorrows." That redemption does not come. Lear's earlier actions set in motion the events that culminated in Cordelia's death, and he cannot reverse them, nor can he restore to Kent the honors he once took away. The play does not explain such mysteries, but through them the tragedy is realized.

Still, in this sequence, elicitory reporting is taken as far as it can go, for the power of the elicited response lies in the fact that the responding character's suffering is so vast that it blocks any possible comprehension of the message. To point to Kent's reporting role in the sequence is not to deny the centrality of Lear's – and our – concern with the loss of Cordelia, which is the primal source both of emotion and of meaning at this point. The aim is rather to demonstrate that Shakespeare deepens that emotion and saves it from sentimentality by introducing a counteraction which, by compelling Lear's attention, shows how his whole being has passed beyond the reach of anything mere mortals could say to him.[9]

10

Persuading sequences

I

Because Shakespeare relied so heavily on the reversal to transform narrative into action, his use of it in creating action at the sequence level can hardly be overemphasized. We have seen how effectively he combines the reversal with the cumulative intensification by varying the repeated pattern in the third episode in a way that will thwart the expectations of the presiding character and how often he uses a reversal with various forms of the motivated intensification – characters in meditating sequences are moved to new positions by the logic of their thoughts, characters in observing sequences are altered by the action they witness, characters hearing reports are changed by the information they hear. The activity of persuading of course lends itself readily to such treatment: in persuading sequences the propelling character strives to obtain the consent of the resisting character to some urgent request or proposal, and the resisting character is driven, beat by beat, toward a response to the accumulating pressure – how natural that that response be cast as a reversal. Since the general form of the persuading sequence was examined in chapter 6, with Iago persuading Roderigo to continue his pursuit of Desdemona; we can concentrate here on the various and particular ways in which Shakespeare works out the reversal in persuading actions.

Like all motivated sequences, which lack the freedom of the open-ended chronological sequence to range in any direction, the persuading sequence has its own set of constraints: an action based on persuading can obviously end in only one of two ways – the persuader can either win his opponent over or fail to influence him. This goes without saying, of course, but it has enough significance in the context of the reversal to function as the ordering principle of this chapter. Our approach here will be to examine, first, what Shakespeare does with the *successful persuasion*, where the resisting character is moved to the expected point, and, second, what he does with the *failed persuasion*, our ultimate goal being to identify the basic structures Shakespeare employs to render the motive of persuasion dramatic. Over and over again Shakespeare uses the successful persuasion. What are some of the techniques through which he achieves the variety of effect that makes us feel that he never repeats himself? And what of those cases in which the persuader is not successful? Is Robert Turner correct when he remarks that Shakespeare was particularly intrigued by the challenge of dramatizing the failed persuasion?[1] For that matter, can even Shakespeare create a reversal out of a situation in which the resisting character refuses to adopt the persuader's view? These are questions we wish to explore in this chapter.

Let us look first at what everyone will agree is the standard and most common form persuading takes in Shakespeare, the successful persuasion.

Since there is no better way to appreciate how much a reversal adds to a persuading action than to examine one that lacks it, we begin with a quick glance at an elementary form of the successful persuasion, sequence 1.1.119–85 of *The Merchant of Venice*, in which Bassanio begs Antonio to finance his expedition to Belmont. Bassanio is definitely persuading, obviously enough in doubt about the success of his plea to continue pressing for assistance in spite of Antonio's constant assurances of support. But because Bassanio has an objective that gives the sequence direction, there is more than just dialogue – there is an action – and we can formulate the dramatic question Shakespeare is working with, *Can Bassanio persuade Antonio to lend him money?* And Bassanio's persuasion is successful: Antonio agrees to stretch his credit "even to the uttermost, / To furnish thee to Belmont, to fair Portia."

But circumstances require that the sequence unfold without a reversal. No matter how compatible the activity of persuading and the reversal may be, the two will appear in conjunction only if the sequence is consciously set up to reflect an alteration, with the starting position of the character to be changed pulled back the full 180 degrees and defined in advance, sufficient opposition made evident between the two characters, and so on. Shakespeare has many reasons for not creating strong opposition in Antonio, chief among them that Antonio's generosity is being demonstrated and for him to enter antagonistically and then weaken would defeat this purpose. Here we have a persuading sequence in which Shakespeare makes the differences between the two characters as slight as possible: both desire Bassanio's good and they are separated on this particular issue only by Antonio's ignorance of the request about to be made of him. Even though Bassanio is successful in his persuasion, Shakespeare deliberately eliminates the elements that would require a reversal in Antonio. And of course the dramatic impact is (intentionally) minimal.

Nevertheless, the *Merchant of Venice* sequence does highlight an important aspect of the successful persuasion – that the responding character finishes the sequence at an expected point; his acquiescence marks the moment at which the persuader's objective is achieved and forms the climax of the sequence. Let us now examine two actions from *Coriolanus* in which the responding character also ends up exactly where the persuader wants him but only after undergoing a full reversal.

In *Coriolanus* Volumnia twice tries to influence her "too-absolute" son. In both sequences the energizing activity is persuading. In both Volumnia is the character who propels the action forward, while Coriolanus's task is to resist, and in both cases Volumnia is successful. Because the resistance is so firm, the dramatic surprise comes not so much from the position that the resisting character is moved to, for he moves to a foreseen position, as from the fact that he is moved at all: this form often highlights the power of the persuader. These two sequences may be studied as examples of the most characteristic type of reversal employed by Shakespeare when the sequence activity is grounded in persuasion. But, more important, they demonstrate that in Shakespeare standard practice does not mean insipid sameness. Using the same reversal structure Shakespeare creates two very distinct and original persuading sequences.

The earlier instance occurs at 3.2.1–145. Coriolanus's opening stance conveys the enormity of the task Shakespeare assigns to Volumnia. Coriolanus has enraged the populace with an outburst of anti-democratic and inflammatory rhetoric, for which the Tribunes have accused him of treason against the people and have even suggested throwing him from the Tarpeian rock to his death. Volumnia must persuade Coriolanus to return to the masses he despises, "bonnet in thy hand," "thy knee bussing the stones," joining with these eloquent actions words that promise to "frame / Thyself, forsooth, hereafter theirs." She asks nothing less of Coriolanus than total self-effacement. Coriolanus's opening lines point up the challenge she faces in working this reversal. He is more than adamant in his stand:

> Let them pull all about mine ears, present me
> Death on the wheel, or at wild horses' heels,
> Or pile ten hills on the Tarpeian rock,
> That the precipitation might down stretch
> Below the beam of sight, yet will I still
> Be thus to them.

(3.2.1–5)

To be otherwise, says Coriolanus, is to be "false to my nature ... I play / The man I am." He refuses to "stoop to the gods"; must he then stoop to despised plebeians? Through the powers of persuasion, Volumnia must work her son from this initial scorn for the populace to humble submission.

That Volumnia requires of Coriolanus merely feigned humility (which will carry him as safely into office as would a sincere shedding of his pride) may not be to her credit, but the more immediate point here is the effect of Volumnia's reasoning on Coriolanus. Throughout the first phase of the intensification (3.2.13–98) Volumnia presses the argument that he must dissemble: only thus will he safeguard the city, only thus satisfy all the people he holds in esteem. This, she argues, is the only course of "honor." Coriolanus eventually submits. How does Shakespeare effect the reversal?

To make us experience the force of Coriolanus's resistance, Shakespeare stretches the reversal out over thirty-eight lines (99–137), breaking down that resistance in slow stages. The turn begins when, after Cominius has joined Volumnia and the Senators in insisting that Coriolanus "frame his spirit" to fair speech, Coriolanus says, "I will do 't" (3.2.101). Subsequent lines, however, indicate that this is a false climax, for there is little conviction in the decision. Further urging evokes from Coriolanus a more determined "I must do 't" (110). This step on the path to compromise, however, arouses in his mind vivid images of what that compromise entails – the transformation of his martial voice into "a pipe small as an eunuch," "school-boy's tears" in his eyes, "my arm'd knees ... bent like his / That hath receiv'd an alms!" – and he retreats: "I will not do 't" (120). More urging (this time his mother's pointed refusal to insist further) finally swings Coriolanus to the desired point, 180 degrees from where he began and exactly where the persuader wanted to see him:

> Pray be content.
> Mother, I am going to the market-place;
> Chide me no more. I'll mountebank their loves,
> Cog their hearts from them, and come home belov'd
> Of all the trades in Rome. Look, I am going.
>
> (3.2.130–4)

In this persuasion sequence the reversal serves Shakespeare well. It is directly to his purpose to establish the strength of Coriolanus's resistance, for that character trait is crucial to the subsequent action of the play and, in addition to demonstrating that strength, he sets a precedent for Coriolanus's submission to Volumnia that lends credibility to the climactic submission of act 5. Through the opposition of Coriolanus's desires to Volumnia's, Shakespeare establishes her strength as well.

Further, because we can see that Coriolanus's submission is imposed from outside rather than stemming from a deeply rooted change of heart, we can predict that his conversion from anger to mildness will not last. But there is a danger that a sequence which vibrates with such energy as does this one at 3.2.1–145 will dwarf anything that follows (sequels rarely succeed), and Shakespeare intends to use the same structural pattern for the confrontation between Volumnia and Coriolanus at the end of the play. How does he vary the form so that the second confrontation exceeds the first in emotional power?

Though the reversals in both the first and the second persuasion sequences depict the hero making the change that the manipulator counted on (rather than jumping to some unforeseen point), there are several differences between the two sequences that lift Shakespeare's reversal structure out of the realm of formula. First, in the earlier sequence Shakespeare makes Coriolanus himself the force that Volumnia must conquer: we feel his strong will directly. In the later sequence the force of that will is established in advance. Of course in both situations we have prior knowledge of his character but in terms of structure more is involved than our prior knowledge of him: in preparation for the later persuasion, long before he brings Coriolanus and Volumnia together, Shakespeare lets us experience his protagonist's resistance through the reports of individuals who have been stunned by it. Because it distances Coriolanus further from Rome, this strategy increases his power to legendary proportions. Second, in the earlier sequence the reversal is withheld as long as possible, and even when made is recalled again; in the later one the movement toward reversal surfaces at the very beginning. A third difference: in the earlier sequence the struggle is between one psyche and another (Coriolanus against his mother). In the later sequence the struggle is primarily within the psyche of Coriolanus: the outcome depends upon whether his unnatural anger can resist the more natural impulses of love, family, and community to which Volumnia appeals. These differences illustrate not only the techniques Shakespeare uses to escalate the dramatic impact but also the psychological depths he can plumb by means of this reversal structure, "standard" though it may be in skeletal form.

The structure is worth examining closely. Volumnia's task in act 3 is difficult, but in act 5 it is impossible, for, between this and the final persuasion sequence, Coriolanus's attitude toward Rome and the Romans has been inflamed in the furnace of revenge; hatred and anger have transformed him "from man to dragon." The need now is not as before to convince him to perform a beggar's part. With his army poised to destroy Rome and having cause in Rome's ingratitude to do it, he must be swung around to a point where he will not only sacrifice his military advantage and his ego but will even put his life at risk: in fact, his capitulation will so compromise his position with the Volscians that his choosing mercy for Rome leads Aufidius to order his death.

The difficulties facing Volumnia are rendered formidable by the context in which Shakespeare sets this climactic persuading sequence. First Cominius, then Menenius, is assigned the task that will shortly fall to Volumnia, the task of deflecting Coriolanus's wrath, and both fail. Shakespeare does not show us firsthand the interview between Coriolanus and Cominius, but the latter's report (sequence 5.1.1–74) increases our sense of Coriolanus's strength and of his thirst for vengeance. Cominius tells us that Caius Martius Coriolanus had divested himself of the name with which, in the beginning of the play, Rome had honored him: that name "he would not answer to; forbade all names; / He was a kind of nothing, titleless." In the images of Cominius's report, Coriolanus becomes a Vulcan who would fire the city as the furnace for his forge. Cominius keeps the idea of imminent conflagration constantly before us, offering no hope that some drop of human feeling will cool Coriolanus's rage:

> He does sit in gold, his eye
> Red as 'twould burn Rome; and his injury
> The jailer to his pity.
> . . .
> All hope is vain.

(5.1.63–70)

Menenius, Rome's next ambassador to attempt the desired reversal (sequence 5.2.1–111), is held off and humiliated for most of the sequence by Volscian guards. That he has an audience with Coriolanus at all seems to be an accident. And though he tries with an offering of love and tears to alter the harsh judgment that has hardened Coriolanus ("O my son, my son! thou art preparing fire for us; look thee, here's water to quench it"), Coriolanus is not changed: he remains with Menenius only long enough to say "Be gone. / Mine ears against your suits are stronger than / Your gates against my force." Further attempts to penetrate his heart seem futile. The reversal Volumnia will be sent to effect is established in advance as impossible.

Shakespeare now brings Volumnia and Coriolanus together. J. L. Styan formulates the dramatic question as *Will Coriolanus reject Volumnia's pleas and save his life?*,[2] but as in the earlier sequence the action is persuading (not rejecting) and again Volumnia (not Coriolanus) is the active character; the formulation *Can Volumnia persuade Coriolanus to spare Rome?* reflects the whole situation more precisely.

Notice, however, the second difference between the two sequences – that Shakespeare achieves his effect here not so much by withholding the reversal as by introducing the potential for it immediately. In the earlier sequence Coriolanus was so entrenched in his position that he was ready to suffer "death on the wheel, or at wild horses' heels" rather than change his course: his will was firmly aligned with his anger. And this same state of affairs is suggested here in the preparatory sequences that pit Cominius and Menenius against Coriolanus. But having established the difficulties Volumnia must face, Shakespeare shifts strategies. As Volumnia, Virgilia, and the young boy arrive on the scene he focuses upon how much power the very sight of these loved ones has to weaken Coriolanus.

This fact casts into question the common assumption that Volumnia is an aggressor. An interpretation which charges that she has an "unfulfilled ambition to dominate and destroy" Coriolanus or that her persuasion consists of "over a hundred lines of emotional blackmail," with Volumnia "putting the screws on him like an enormous nut-cracker,"[3] turns the meaning of the reversal encounter on its head: Shakespeare's text does not support such an interpretation. Volumnia is dominant but as the persuader she is meant to be dominant, and the force she applies must be recognized as a positive force; otherwise, the build thus far examined goes for nought.

In act 5 at least, Shakespeare presents Volumnia as a peacemaker. He has Coriolanus remark that "all the swords / In Italy . . . could not have made this peace," shows Menenius praising her as "our patroness, the life of Rome!," and celebrates her return to the city with a pageant of triumph (sequence 5.4.1–5.5.7) wherein the clamor of shouts, drums, and trumpets that announce her arrival cancel out the frenzy that accompanied the banishment of her son. Everything about the structure tells us that Volumnia is a character who has been given the impossible task of effecting a reversal in Coriolanus and has achieved it, saving the entire city from destruction.

Shakespeare reinforces the positive aspects of Volumnia's role in this reversal in another way, by emphasizing the movement from the unnatural world order Coriolanus has created, where a general leads an enemy army against his own country and a mother kneels before her son, to a natural order where normal hierarchical relationships are restored – as nearly as they can be in a pagan society where honor is a value anchored in human reason rather than in divine love. Volumnia rightly focuses her argument on the disruption in the natural state of things when "the mother, wife, and child [must watch] / The son, the husband, and the father tearing / His country's bowels out" (5.3.100–2). Coriolanus's insistence on his own self-sufficiency and his deliberate refusal to feel pity has led him in the direction of inhumanity. Shakespeare likens him not only to a dragon, the image of wrath, but also to a senseless stone – the language constantly suggests that Coriolanus is willfully shutting his ears and closing his eyes, which to an Elizabethan represent the "gates" of the mind; consequently, softening influences, blocked at the senses, are unable to penetrate to the imagination or the heart. If Coriolanus's humanity is to be restored, hatred must give way to compassion. He must stop denying natural affections and attachments, human duties and hierarchies. To be entirely natural is to recognize his place in the whole, even though he has the power to reduce that whole to nothing.

Our focus, then, must be on the faults of Coriolanus, not Volumnia, if this reversal is to evoke in us the emotions appropriate to the climactic moments of a tragedy. Coriolanus has made choices throughout the play that have had unhappy consequences, and as a direct result of his own actions he is now clamped into a position where whatever choice he makes will be both right – and wrong. He has thrown in his lot with the Volscians and owes them loyalty. On the other hand, if he rejects the embassy from Rome he must deny both blood and affection, breaking "all bond and privilege of nature" (5.3.25). As Coriolanus recognizes, "My young boy / Hath an aspect of intercession, which / Great Nature cries, 'Deny not'" (31–3). In the very poetry of the speech in which Coriolanus perceives his position Shakespeare subtly suggests the nature of the choice Coriolanus must make. Throughout the play he has refused to recognize that there are forces in the universe beyond himself. He feels the necessity of obeying these forces at a level that he calls "instinct,"[4] and he understands their nature well enough to realize that a man is not "author of himself." To honor this natural law, the proud Coriolanus must bow. As a Roman with pragmatic values, Volumnia may not be worthy of Coriolanus's adulation. But here in act 5 Shakespeare makes her a mother who also represents patriotism and country (she does not, after all, desert Rome in its peril and flee to Coriolanus for safety). As such she symbolizes those unifying forces which hold the line against chaos. The reversal – and recognition – required of Coriolanus is that which every man must make if he is to be truly human, the recognition that he is not sufficient unto himself.

If this is the reversal Shakespeare's persuasion sequence is building toward, then it is beside the point to blame Volumnia for Coriolanus's choices. The fact is that the pressure that Volumnia creates in the final act offers Coriolanus an option that will restore his humanity.

In the introductory beat (5.3.1–19) Shakespeare unambiguously presents Coriolanus's starting position. Coriolanus takes a vow, in it reasserting to Aufidius his intention to hear no "fresh embassies and suits, / Nor from the state nor private friends, hereafter." That position is confirmed in the second beat (5.3.19–37, where Virgilia, Volumnia, Valeria, and young Martius enter), in the very speech that reveals Coriolanus's inclination to surrender. The ever-important enclosing lines give us Coriolanus's intention – "I will not . . . infringe my vow." "I'll never / Be such a gosling to obey instinct." He refuses to be tempted to hear Volumnia's plea. Yet in these lines Shakespeare reveals a psyche already moving toward submission. Everything Coriolanus says resonates with an awareness of a natural law which he is violating. To keep his vow he must stamp out affection, break "all bond and privilege of nature." He must believe that to "be obstinate" is a virtue. A man who had tried to be "of stronger earth than others" suddenly sees himself as "a molehill" before Olympus. Even Great Nature is against him. Ironically, the "temptation" which Coriolanus fights is the temptation to be human. This beat shows that the primary struggle in the sequence will be between Coriolanus and his higher instincts. Volumnia's urgings become the urgings of Great Nature herself, and to obey them Coriolanus will have to don the cloak of humility, but at this point Coriolanus asserts that "I'll never be such a gosling": he chooses to stand as firm against his loved ones as he has stood against the state (Cominius) and friendship (Menenius).

This brings us to a third difference between these two persuasions: in the earlier one the conflict is strictly between Volumnia (supported by the Patricians who share her views) and Coriolanus, who stands aloof, while in this later instance Coriolanus is also in conflict with himself.

Coriolanus cannot shut his eyes to his loved ones, and in the first phase of the intensification – the four-beat cycle of greetings (5.3.37–76) – he loses his battle to stifle affection. Virgilia's kiss is "long as my exile, sweet as my revenge!" Greeting Volumnia he is already "your corrected son." Nor can he block his ears. He tries, when Volumnia introduces her persuasion (beat 5.3.77–93) with the announcement that "even he, your wife, this lady, and myself / Are suitors to you," for he warns her that what she asks is "the thing I have forsworn to grant." Yet with Volumnia's request, "Therefore, hear us," Coriolanus, who had vowed to "hear nought from Rome," moves to the point where he will only "hear nought from Rome in private."

The beat divisions in Volumnia's long persuasion speech mark the further erosion of Coriolanus's resistance. He knows what Volumnia's arguments will be, knows she will tell him "wherein I seem unnatural" (86). This is indeed the tenor of her first thirty lines (beat 5.3.94–131), after which very little resistance survives in Coriolanus, who by then sees that his only chance of holding to his original course is to flee:

> Not of a woman's tenderness to be,
> Requires nor child nor woman's face to see.
> I have sat too long.
>
> (5.3.129–31)

Coriolanus could not block his eyes or ears but he does keep his tongue from speaking words of surrender. From here to the reversal (131–82), his response is silence. Volumnia caps her argument with the warning that infamy is the benefit Coriolanus will reap from destroying Rome, and awaits his reaction. Coriolanus says nothing; the battle goes on within him, as we see from the series of short, suspenseful beats in which Volumnia repeatedly urges him to speak.

In both sequences, while Coriolanus moves to the expected place, suspense is maintained by delaying the moment of reversal. In 3.2 Coriolanus surrenders, then retracts his decision, and after that gives in a second time. In 5.3 the delay derives from his refusal – or inability (is he choked up?) – to speak. He probably knows he has lost by the time Volumnia reminds him that his name would "remain to th' ensuing age abhorr'd" (148), and she probably guesses as much. She does her best to provoke words, even finally to the point of requesting that he at least "give us our dispatch" (180). Shakespeare holds Coriolanus in silence a few seconds more, long enough for the actors to effect the tender gesture he calls for at the end of the sequence – *Coriolanus holds her by the hand, silent.* Only then does the climactic reversal occur.

Both this sequence and the earlier one between Coriolanus and Volumnia illustrate the successful persuasion, in which the resisting character moves to the expected place. But the contrast between the two tells us much about the particular playwriting techniques through which Shakespeare can make that general pattern deliver up an action that seems totally fresh.[5]

II

Though a successful persuasion climaxes quite naturally with a reversal, the situation is otherwise with the failed persuasion, in which affairs remain as they were: no change; consequently, no reversal. Because a totally ineffective persuasion arouses disappointment but no surprise, its potential for drama may seem small. But the failed persuasion seems to have intrigued Shakespeare and in fact he finds more latitude for formal variation at the end of the failed persuasion than in the successful one. He not only creates interest in failed persuasions in which the responding character does not change at all but he also manages to do what seems highly unlikely – to conclude the failed persuasion with a reversal. This he accomplishes in two different ways, sometimes by moving the responding character to some new and unexpected position, and at other times by arranging matters so that the persuading character himself undergoes a reversal.

Let us look at one or two actions in which the persuading character fails to alter his opponent. *Richard II* 2.1.147–223 offers an excellent starting point for any study of the failed persuasion; here York attempts to persuade the King that in confiscating Gaunt's land he will be violating the laws of primogeniture through which the kingship derives its authority. "Take Hereford's rights away," argues York, "and take from Time / His charters and his customary rights." Needing Hereford's income to finance his wars in Ireland, Richard, unchanged, proceeds with his intention.

In this sequence the Duke of York speaks eloquently for honor and virtue, which require Richard II to control his destructive prodigality. But though wisdom demands a correction of Richard's behavior, the state of his soul rules out a reversal. Richard is a character who repeatedly disregards wise counsel, one whose "will doth mutiny with wit's regard," and "whose way himself will choose" (2.1.28–9). Any sign of repentance at either end of the sequence would obscure the callousness in Richard's character that Shakespeare wishes to highlight. Shakespeare in fact involves Richard in more than one refusal. In an earlier sequence he has already refused Gaunt's sound advice. This rejection of York's wisdom marks the second failure of a powerful pleader to shake Richard's complacency. In this situation, a straight failed persuasion is more appropriate than any of the reversal strategies. Because Richard ought to change, the failed persuasion emphasizes his obduracy.

Divorce between the two elements – persuasion and reversal – is the better strategy also in *Antony and Cleopatra* 1.1.1–62, where Cleopatra presses Antony to admit certain messengers from Rome and he, ignoring the messengers, lets "Rome in Tiber melt." Of course this is a mock persuasion, handled with humor, for, far from wishing to see Caesar's ambassadors admitted, Cleopatra is throwing up teasing arguments on their behalf that will make it embarrassing for Antony to take them seriously. But the sequence does develop as a failed persuasion: Antony's refusal to be persuaded, however ironic, shows us how far he is from exercising good sense. With the persuasion itself Shakespeare emphasizes Cleopatra's charm and indicates how cleverly she controls Antony; moreover, by withholding the reversal at its end, he can later surprise us by revealing the reserves of power within Antony that allow him to assert himself against Cleopatra after Fulvia's death.

Shakespeare uses the failed persuasion to suggest reserves of power in another way in the sequence introducing the ladies in Coriolanus's life (1.3.1–111). Valeria, the persuader, supported by Volumnia, tempts Virgilia to "play the idle huswife" and go visiting. Virgilia's refusal to make even charitable visits while her husband remains in danger on the battlefield demonstrates her virtue. This resistance to the combined pressures of two committed persuaders emphasizes Virgilia's inner strength.

These sequences of unsuccessful persuasion are effective and entirely appropriate to the given circumstances. Surely, however, their success stems more from certain passages of poetic power in them than from the way they build. They would never appear on anyone's list of the most dramatic persuasion sequences in Shakespeare. Take away the reversal and you take away the impact that makes an action memorable *as an action*.

When he wants to give the failed persuasion power, Shakespeare unites it with a reversal. In many cases, for example, a persuasion is attempted and it fails but, quite suddenly, the responding character shifts to some unexpected and contrary position. In persuading sequences of this type the responding character undergoes an unpredictable and aptly surprising reversal.

A typical example occurs in *Twelfth Night* 1.5.167–311, the third and last sequence of the scene in which Viola and Olivia first encounter one another. Viola – that is, Cesario – has been sent by her master Orsino, one of the many suitors Olivia has rejected, to persuade Olivia to marry Orsino. The audience already knows that Viola's chances of winning Olivia for Orsino are slim, but her appearance and her wit intrigue Olivia, as do her boldness and her arguments. Yet the persuasion falls short of its desired effect. Olivia's attitude to Orsino is unchanged:

> Your lord does know my mind, I cannot love him,
> Yet I suppose him virtuous, know him noble,
> Of great estate, of fresh and stainless youth;
> In voices well divulg'd, free, learn'd, and valiant,
> And in dimension, and the shape of nature,

> A gracious person. But yet I cannot love him.
> He might have took his answer long ago.

(1.5.257–63)

The sequence does not end here, however. This refusal effects no climax, and the intensification continues. Ultimately there is a reversal that Viola could not have anticipated. Olivia reveals the change at the climactic moment:

> Get you to your lord,
> I cannot love him; let him send no more –
> Unless (perchance) you come to me again
> To tell me how he takes it.

(1.5.279–82)

As this veiled invitation reveals, Olivia has fallen in love with the page.

The same pattern informs the persuading sequence written for Isabella's first visit to Angelo in 2.2.1–186 of *Measure for Measure*. Isabella has been sent to appeal for mercy for her brother Claudio, whom Angelo has recently sentenced to death. Angelo takes great pride in his "gravity": he has in fact been appointed to his position because of his "unsoil'd name" and "th' austereness of his life." When Isabella first approaches him, he is a pillar of virtue. Isabella's task is to persuade him to free Claudio. At first bashful, she warms to eloquence. But Claudio remains firmly under Angelo's sentence of death at the end of Isabella's attempted persuasion: she has failed to effect any change in Angelo's judgment of Claudio. Shakespeare adds a reversal that has nothing to do with Claudio: Angelo, who "scarce confesses / That his blood flows; or that his appetite / Is more to bread than stone," discovers at the close of this sequence that his "sense breeds" – he conceives a passion for Isabella. Her eloquence does effect a reversal in Angelo, but it is hardly the one she hoped for.

These unexpected reversals are worked on the responding character. In other cases, however, the persuader himself undergoes the reversal. The persuader is still the propelling character, and here again he fails to achieve his objective. But the responding character is so determined that the attempt to influence him boomerangs and alters the persuader's situation.

The failed persuasion of Menenius in *Coriolanus* 5.2.1–111 takes this form. In order to persuade Coriolanus to be merciful, Menenius travels to the Volscian camp, where Coriolanus and Aufidius are preparing to fire Rome. The tone is light, and the essence of the reversal lies in a movement from assurance to defeat.

164

The reversal in this sequence derives its impact from the pose of haughty self-confidence adopted by Menenius in the opening beat, where he is denied access to Coriolanus by the camp guards. In these passages Shakespeare establishes the positive attitude Menenius maintains in approaching his task. "The general is my lover," he boasts, expecting to be conducted immediately to Coriolanus's side, and, though he is ridiculed instead, he seems confident of success, so much so that when Coriolanus finally appears, Menenius predicts the hanging of the guards who insulted him. Still confident, he turns to Coriolanus and begins the persuasion. Coriolanus responds with a terse "Away! . . . be gone." The reality turns out to be as the watch had said, "My general cares not for you." In this sequence the responding character rejects the persuader so forcefully that the persuader himself makes the 180-degree turn. Initially so proud and at the start full of hope, Menenius ends in despair:

> I neither care for th' world nor your general; for such things as you,
> I can scarce think there's any, y' are so slight. He that hath a will to
> die by himself fears it not from another.
>
> (5.2.102–5)

Once again Shakespeare renders dramatic a situation in which the persuasion fails, this time by altering the position of the persuader.

This pattern may also be studied in *King Lear* 1.1.139–87, a persuading action in which a loyal servant becomes an exile. When Lear proclaims Cordelia "a stranger to my heart and me," Kent (the persuader) defends her, urging Lear (the responding character) to forgive Cordelia. At the beginning of this sequence, Kent is one of the nation's most loyal and secure ministers, devoted to his king. During it, he seeks only his master's good. His desire that the King's most loving daughter be treated fairly is an honorable one: Lear ought to heed Kent's advice. But Lear is not persuaded. Kent braves his wrath to no avail and, in fact, increases Lear's rage. Since Lear refuses to relent as expected, there would seem to be no reversal, yet a radical change does occur. Incensed by the pressures of Kent's persuasion, Lear banishes him.

The effect of this fourth kind of reversal is to place additional emphasis on the intractability of the persuader's opponent. Through Menenius's hurtful rejection, we experience more keenly Coriolanus's ruthless determination. Kent's fate points up the irrational fury that activates Lear. When Shakespeare wishes to stress a particular case of obstinacy as dramatically as possible, he turns to this form of the persuading sequence.

These examples demonstrate both the ubiquity of the reversal structure and the inventiveness with which it is implemented. They also show its effectiveness as a means of ensuring that characters do not merely declaim but influence and alter one another. The device is so well conceived that it can deny the expected or the predictable without evoking the improbable. Its grounding in the will gives it that psychological depth that always accompanies moral choice.

Clearly, then, the reversal structure combines effectively with the persuasion sequence, and variety is obtained by employing to the full the four possible outcomes of a persuading action: the propelling character may bring about the desired change; he may have no effect; he may cause an unexpected change; or he may himself be changed.

11

Disputing sequences

Once Lady Macbeth steels herself against remorse so that "no compunctious visitings of nature / Shake my fell purpose," she sets herself the task of persuading her husband to murder the king. It is no surprise that her fervid persuading borders at times on attack. Macbeth's resistance angers her. Shakespeare keeps the sequence (1.7.1–82) within the bounds of persuading, but it would take only a slight increase in intensity, a few subtle touches here and there, to turn it from a persuasion into a quarrel. At what point does persuading become quarreling or arguing or (to settle on the term that seems best suited here) *disputing?*[1]

The sequence-generating conflict between an active character and a resisting one is present in both the persuading and the disputing sequence, but in the disputing sequence (at least in the very dramatic form of it being examined here) the active character often exhibits a resentment against the subordinate character from the outset. He believes he has been wronged and, when he enters, is hardly in a forgiving mood. Not surprisingly, he lacks the control of the persuader; he initiates the action in a state of emotional upset. Usually his attitude arouses a corresponding anger in his opponent. The battle for dominance that is the natural basis for every motivated sequence here becomes more overt – the conflict rises to the surface.

Because the characters are often at the mercy of their emotions, beat structure becomes more chaotic. Certainly a heated argument cannot proceed with the same logic as a reasoned persuasion. Characters interrupt or badger or accuse one another. The number of aborted beats is apt to be high: subjects are begun but then abruptly cut off, left unfinished. And dominance may change several times within the sequence, as one or the other character secures the advantage.

What of the ending? Just as in other motivated sequences the sequence motive keeps the outcome of the action within certain limits (i.e., reporting sequences conclude with the delivery of a report and/or a response to it, interrogating sequences with a judgment, persuading sequences with the acceptance or rejection of the persuader's proposal), so also is the outcome closely determined in disputing sequences. Despite the chaos which a quarrel may generate, the action seems to end in one of two ways. Sometimes it progresses from conflict to reconciliation, in which case the differences will be buried in an agreement. But unresolved conflicts are equally possible and in certain situations even necessary: the victor's triumph may dramatically exacerbate the rift.[2] For convenience' sake, this chapter looks first at disputing sequences that end happily, then examines some that move in the opposite direction.

The power of the structure in which the warring opponents are brought into accord is apparent in the quarrel initiated in the final sequence of *Othello* 3.3 when Othello approaches Iago with a chilling threat: "Villain, be sure thou prove my love a whore . . . Give me the ocular proof, / Or . . . woe upon thy life!" (359–66). Persuasion is of course being effected during the sequence (Iago has not abandoned his campaign to convince Othello that Desdemona is a whore), yet the persuading is not overt, nor is it the propelling activity. The action takes its form from Othello's desire to quarrel with Iago: the protagonist launches an attack which the antagonist must counter.

Who is the dominant character here? In the preceding sequence between these two characters (3.3.93–279), when Othello forced Iago to reveal his thoughts about Desdemona's alleged affair with Cassio, Othello appeared to be dominant, but he held the dominant position only because Iago let him believe he was in control. Here (3.3.333–480), Othello commands the dominant position through the power of his own personality, at least initially. In this sequence Shakespeare demonstrates that in courage and strength Othello is a match for Iago by emphasizing the danger of the game Iago is playing – discovery could well mean Iago's death. But Othello is not dominant throughout. In a disputing sequence like this one, where the characters are evenly matched, dominance shifts back and forth, and Iago's intellectual strength eventually asserts itself.

The dramatic question of sequence 3.3.333–480 might be stated thus: *Can Othello force Iago to resolve his doubts?* Shakespeare begins with Othello's attack, the four beats of which make up the first block of the sequence. The opening beat (333–58) is largely introductory, for Othello has been offstage for some time, brooding over Iago's insinuations. The audience must be shown the transformation that has taken place within him; consequently, in this initial beat Shakespeare depicts him looking inward, occupied with his own plight. Torn by jealousy, Othello complains to Iago that "'tis better to be much abus'd / Than but to know't a little." The emphasis, in this introductory beat, is on the change Iago has wrought in Othello's life.

The second beat (359–73) intensifies the mood to violence as Othello's wrath turns outward, energized in a harsh attack upon Iago, the source of the information that caused his torment. Here Othello issues the challenge from which all else in the sequence flows:

> OTHELLO Villain, be sure thou prove my love a whore;
> Be sure of it. Give me the ocular proof,
> Or by the worth of mine eternal soul,
> Thou hadst been better have been born a dog
> Than answer my wak'd wrath!
> IAGO Is't come to this?
> OTHELLO Make me to see't; or (at the least) so prove it
> That the probation bear no hinge nor loop
> To hang a doubt on; or woe upon thy life!
> IAGO My noble lord –
> OTHELLO If thou dost slander her and torture me,
> Never pray more; abandon all remorse;
> On horror's head horrors accumulate;
> Do deeds to make heaven weep, all earth amaz'd;
> For nothing canst thou to damnation add
> Greater than that.
>
> (3.3.359–73)

With this attack Shakespeare establishes a disjunction between the two characters that sets the stage for the later reversal: in the staging it must be clear that Othello means his "or woe upon thy life!," so that the full turn from enmity to friendship will be noted. Shakespeare also establishes the position of doubt which Othello will be moved away from. Of course by asking for proof Othello puts Iago at an advantage, and he errs even more seriously in accepting fabricated proof, as he eventually does; however, his request for proof is intended as a defence. "If thou dost slander her . . ." There is still a part of him that cries out against belief in a story that has far more the ring of slander than of truth, and he desperately hopes Iago is lying. Should Iago know the story to be untrue, Othello warns, he is courting damnation. "If thou dost slander her and torture me . . ." Othello enters this sequence totally at odds with Iago.

A man less bold than Iago would cower from an attack of such ferocity, but Iago is exhilarated. Having his own intention, to turn Othello against Desdemona, he does not retreat from the accusation – he advances, meeting Othello's anger with (in beat 3) a feigned rage of his own:

> IAGO O grace! O heaven forgive me!
> Are you a man? Have you a soul? or sense?
> God buy you; take mine office. O wretched fool,

That lov'st to make thine honesty a vice!
O monstrous world! Take note, take note, O world,
To be direct and honest is not safe.
I thank you for this profit, and from hence
I'll love no friend, sith love breeds such offense.
OTHELLO Nay, stay. Thou shouldst be honest.
IAGO I should be wise – for honesty's a fool
And loses that it works for.

$$(3.3.373-83)$$

Iago's ploy works. Othello is distracted from his quest for truth by Iago's intentionally distracting cry that "to be direct and honest is not safe." Consequently, in the fourth beat (383–90), tension slackens off: Othello backs away from the charge of slander and his search for truth into his earlier mood of doubt and self-pity. ("By the world, / I think my wife be honest, and think she is not; / I think that thou art just, and think thou art not. / I'll have some proof"). Shakespeare captures Othello's sense of frustration perfectly in the line that signals both the end of this fourth beat and the end of Othello's term of dominance: "Would I were satisfied!" Iago will take advantage of his confusion to wrest control away from him.

In the next phase of this disputing sequence, the argument narrows to a discussion of the kind of evidence that will be admissible. This begins at beat 5 (391–409) when Iago seizes upon Othello's "Would I were satisfied!" to assume the role of aggressor in the dispute, with the intention of working the quarrel to a resolution – on his terms. Continuing to parry Othello's accusations with counter-accusations, he angrily resents being asked to perform the impossible and suggests that circumstantial evidence instead of "ocular proof" should suffice. This counter-challenge makes Othello tone down his demands. From "give me the ocular proof" he moves to "give me a living reason she's disloyal." His capitulation on this point allows Iago to take a second step toward resolution of the dispute: in beat 6 (410–27), Iago tells a lie, but a lie boldly calculated to increase the Moor's anger. Iago knows that the only safe course is to divert Othello's anger from himself to Cassio and Desdemona, and of course this is easily done by deepening Othello's sense of their guilt: Iago thus spins out in vivid detail his fictitious account of Cassio's lascivious dreams.[3] The disputing continues in beat 7 (427–33), but the relationship between the characters is altered, for in this beat Othello has become the hasty accuser whom "honest" Iago may chastise for judging on thin evidence. To complete his victory, Iago now needs only to submit his final bit of "imputation" (beat 8, 433–41): "Such a handkerchief / (I am sure it was your wife's) did I today / See Cassio wipe his beard with." Phase 2 of the argument – the haggling about the kind of evidence that will suffice – is thus completed: Iago has supplied the "proof" and satisfied Othello.

The sequence reaches its peak in the last phase, the macabre union of the two who had begun in deadly enmity. Shakespeare places the climax at the moment when Othello's wrath turns in full force upon the supposed lovers:

> O that the slave had forty thousand lives!
> One is too poor, too weak for my revenge.
> Now do I see 'tis true. Look here, Iago,
> All my fond love thus do I blow to heaven.
> 'Tis gone.

> (3.3.442–6)

These last lines mark the completion of Othello's movement from doubt to certainty: he now exchanges "fond love" for "tyrannous hate," this reversal of his attitude toward Desdemona marking, of course, the success of Iago's scheme.

The reversal at the end of this sequence also marks a reversal in Othello's attitude toward Iago. The initial suspicion has been dispelled, and the two who were at odds when, racked by the pain of uncertainty, Othello cried, "Villain, be sure thou prove my love a whore," are now as one: Iago's "truth" has become Othello's truth. Iago now pledges his "wit, hands, heart / To wrong'd Othello's service," and Othello greets his proffered love "with acceptance bounteous." The quarrel that generates the drama in this sequence has ended in a reconciliation.

While the patterns in the disputing sequence are simple, such sequences are often vehicles for the revelation of complex psychological relationships. In this regard it is instructive to compare Shakespeare's handling of the sequence in which Othello quarrels with Iago and that in which Cassius quarrels with Brutus. Despite the similar structure, the motivating psychologies in each case are vastly different, and by watching Shakespeare take narrative material from radically different sources and order it in a similar way, one can appreciate not only the dramatic value of the structure itself but also its abilty to reveal character.

The Cassius/Brutus quarrel of *Julius Caesar* 4.3.1–162 also moves from discord to harmony. Cassius, too, throws out an accusation, finds it challenged by his opponent, and eventually backs down, in a reversal which stands as the climax of the sequence and effects a reconciliation.

Here the dramatic question is simply, *Can Cassius settle his differences with Brutus?*

The discord erupts when Cassius meets Brutus at Sardis. The characters are well matched: both strong-willed, both at the edge of their endurance, both fitted out with plausible motives for anger. They are also nicely contrasted. Cassius is blustery and quick to take offense, but his anger is short-lived, a "hasty spark," that "straight is cold again." Brutus is slow to anger but powerful if provoked. When he becomes indignant, it is in honor's cause.[4]

The quarrel brewing between these two generals breaks out in an interlocking beat at the very end of the previous sequence, where Cassius enters Brutus's camp fired by a complaint:

> CASSIUS Most noble brother, you have done me wrong.
> BRUTUS Judge me, you gods! wrong I mine enemies?
> And if not so, how should I wrong a brother?
> CASSIUS Brutus, this sober form of yours hides wrongs,
> And when you do them –
> BRUTUS Cassius, be content,
> Speak your griefs softly; I do know you well.
> Before the eyes of both our armies here
> (Which should perceive nothing but love from us)
> Let us not wrangle. Bid them move away . . .
>
> (4.2.37–45)

With this warning, Shakespeare prepares us for the confrontation between the two friends.

Like the Iago/Othello disputing sequence, this one proceeds in phases marked by changes in dominance. In phase I (1–28), Cassius is dominant, in the sense that he takes the offensive, insisting that Brutus has wronged him by condemning Lucius Pella:

> CASSIUS That you have wrong'd me doth appear in this:
> You have condemn'd and noted Lucius Pella
> For taking bribes here of the Sardians;
> Wherein my letters, praying on his side,
> Because I knew the man, was slighted off.
> BRUTUS You wrong'd yourself to write in such a case.
> CASSIUS In such a time as this it is not meet
> That every nice offense should bear his comment.
>
> (4.3.1–8)

The challenge is pointed. Can Brutus defend himself?

Though cast in the responding role, Brutus is more than Cassius's equal: his answer is a strongly worded counter-accusation, condemning

Cassius for sullying an honorable cause with devious behavior (9–28). This response momentarily stuns Cassius, who had thought his own behavior politic and militarily correct. By line 28, where Brutus concludes his counter-attack by assuring Cassius that he "would rather be a dog, and bay the moon" than "contaminate our fingers with base bribes," the basic issue of the quarrel has been clearly stated.

What follows (phase 2) is in effect a jockeying for position. But it is consciously so only on Cassius's part: he sorely wants Brutus's respect. Brutus attempts no manipulation; his position is what it is because he is "arm'd so strong on honesty"; he need not strive for strength, for it radiates from him. In this second phase of the sequence, Cassius moves first, by taking offense at Brutus's charges. But his peevish and huffy threats merely irritate Brutus (4.3.28–38). Cassius believes in his own ferocity and throughout this phase of the action he maintains the pose, even when he senses that Brutus is not taking him seriously. The reality of the situation is of course quite different from Cassius's perception of it, for he is fooled by his own rhetoric.

Brutus's authoritative "Hear me, for I will speak" at line 38 probably signals a change of dominance as, from here on, Brutus has lost patience with his friend's posturing and turns to ridicule. His portrait of Cassius is hardly flattering:

> BRUTUS Must I give way and room to your rash choler?
> Shall I be frighted when a madman stares?
> CASSIUS O ye gods, ye gods, must I endure all this?
> BRUTUS All this? ay, more. Fret till your proud heart break;
> Go show your slaves how choleric you are,
> And make your bondmen tremble. Must I bouge?
> Must I observe you? Must I stand and crouch
> Under your testy humor? By the gods,
> You shall digest the venom of your spleen
> Though it do split you; for, from this day forth,
> I'll use you for my mirth, yea, for my laughter,
> When you are waspish.
>
> (4.3.39–50)

Cassius, cast into the responding role by the strength of Brutus's counter-offensive, keeps believing he can inspire fear and earn respect by ranting, and continues in the same vein ("When Caesar liv'd, he durst not thus have mov'd me"; "Do not presume too much upon my love, / I may do that I shall be sorry for"; etc.). This second phase of the sequence concludes when Brutus declares emphatically that respect cannot be earned in that way. "There is no terror, Cassius, in your threats . . . They pass by me as the idle wind."

In lines 69–85, Brutus makes another charge against Cassius: "I did send / To you for gold to pay my legions, / Which you denied me." This source of contention is eliminated by the end of the passage, and the way is cleared for the next phase of the intensification, in which Cassius crumbles. Cassius's submission takes place in two stages, each the focus of a beat. The submission involves as much posturing as did the ranting. When Cassius admits his "infirmities," he does so in the form of an accusation (beat 85–92); Brutus is to blame for not overlooking Cassius's faults: "A friend should bear his friend's infirmities." When this fails – for Brutus refuses to be deceived by this bid for pity – Cassius takes it even further (beat 93–107): the world – especially Brutus – has been so cruel to him that he has nothing left to live for:

> O, I could weep
> My spirit from mine eyes! There is my dagger,
> And here my naked breast; within, a heart
> Dearer than Pluto's mine, richer than gold:
> If that thou be'st a Roman, take it forth.
> I, that denied thee gold, will give my heart:
> Strike as thou didst at Caesar; for I know,
> When thou didst hate him worst, thou lovedst him better
> Than ever thou lovedst Cassius.
>
> (4.3.99–107)

Posturing it is, but the posture of a man deeply hurt and, worse, hurt by a friend. Anger turns to pathos.

By abandoning his aggressiveness, Cassius opens the way to reconciliation. The pathos of his lament, while it may not deceive Brutus, does disarm him. The appeal to friendship touches Brutus's heart; his anger vanishes too, and the quarrel issues in a new tolerance of each other's faults. The climactic reconciliation beat has a quiet beauty:

> BRUTUS   Sheathe your dagger.
> Be angry when you will, it shall have scope;
> Do what you will, dishonour shall be humor.
>   . . .
> CASSIUS   Give me your hand.
> BRUTUS And my heart too.
> CASSIUS   O Brutus!
> BRUTUS   What's the matter?
> CASSIUS Have not you love enough to bear with me,
> When that rash humour which my mother gave me
> Makes me forgetful?
> BRUTUS Yes, Cassius, and from henceforth,

When you are over-earnest with your Brutus,
He'll think your mother chides, and leave you so.

(4.3.107–23)

Technically, the action ends here, for the dramatic question has been answered, and a reversal effected: discord has turned to harmony. The succeeding beats (124–38, 143–57, 158–62) belong to the decrescent stage of the sequence. But Shakespeare brings everything together at the very end of this disputing sequence with one more emblem of unity:

> BRUTUS   Give me a bowl of wine,
> In this I bury all unkindness, Cassius.
>   CASSIUS My heart is thirsty for that noble pledge.
> Fill, Lucius, till the wine o'erswell the cup;
> I cannot drink too much of Brutus' love.
>
> (4.3.158–62)

The disputing sequence is useful to Shakespeare in *Antony and Cleopatra*, where the hero and heroine are constantly falling out. Each of the quarrels between them has a different cause as well as a different tone, but in each case Shakespeare begins the sequence with a verbal attack, which the accused deflects, and they all progress from discord to agreement. Consider 1.3.1–105, where Cleopatra anticipates Antony's impending departure for Rome and tries to detain him in Egypt. As soon as Antony appears on stage, Cleopatra accuses him ("O, never was there queen / So mightily betrayed! yet at the first / I saw the treasons planted"). Her challenge compels Antony to defend his intention to leave Egypt. They spar, Cleopatra mocking Antony, until he threatens to walk out and she realizes she cannot hold him. At the climactic moment, she reverses her stand ("Courteous lord, one word . . ."). The sequence ends with two touching beats of reconciliation (86–95, 95–105).

Another variation of the structure is found in 3.11.1–74, in which the lovers are estranged, this time because of Cleopatra's too precipitous withdrawal of her fleet from the battle of Actium, which caused Antony's shameful defeat. Antony is distraught and, at the beginning of the sequence, remains estranged from Cleopatra, blaming her for his dishonor. She begs his pardon and bears his reproaches. The sequence climaxes when Antony reverses his position, agreeing to a reconciliation: "Fall not a tear, I say, one of them rates / All that is won and lost. Give me a kiss."

In the Actium sequence, Antony's accusation of Cleopatra is understated, but in sequence 3.13.85–200, where he catches Caesar's emissary, Thidias, kissing her hand, his attack is harsh and dramatic.

Antony initiates the sequence by having Thidias taken out to be whipped, then turns on Cleopatra with twenty-five lines of savage tirade. Cleopatra waits patiently until Antony is calmer, then offers her defense (153–67). Again the quarrel ends in harmony: Antony's "I am satisfied" marks the point of his reversal, and in the concluding beats of the sequence the lovers are united.

Tone and mood differ vastly in each sequence. In 1.3.1–105 Antony has a "Roman face" upon him, Cleopatra is playful but aggressive; in 3.11.1–74 Antony is numbed with shame, Cleopatra nervous; in 3.13.85–200 Antony is wild, Cleopatra submissive and patient. But despite the variety, the sequences share a common structure – all move from quarrel to resolution – again and again the lovers are reconciled.

To these examples one might add sequence 4.5.96–220 in *Hamlet*, where Laertes accuses Claudius of murdering his father. There again one character throws out a challenge, while the other tries to deflect it. In this sequence, Laertes launches an attack on the King, far more literally so than in the previous cases, for he enters with an army at his back. By line 149, Claudius gains control of the dispute and (despite a slight setback when Ophelia bursts upon the scene) works Laertes towards a reconciliation (213).

II

Not all disputing sequences move from discord to unity; in others, the discord widens, as, for example, in those between Leontes and Hermione in *Winter's Tale* 2.1.1–125, where Leontes charges Hermione with carrying on an affair with Polixenes and finally orders her imprisoned; or between Lear and Regan in *King Lear* 2.4.127–309, where father and daughter argue over Goneril's treatment of Lear until Lear stalks out into the storm. In each case the dispute widens into a rift. We conclude this chapter by examining two disputing sequences that end in violence – first, the one in which Emilia exposes Iago and is killed by him and, second, the one in which the Tribunes quarrel with and then arrest Coriolanus.

Shakespeare uses the disputing sequence in an interesting way to effect the peripeteia at the end of *Othello* (sequence 5.2.168–251). Before analyzing the sequence itself, let us look quickly at the context in which it occurs, the play's final scene. Othello kills Desdemona in the first sequence of 5.2, and Shakespeare's next task is to make him realize the magnitude of his error. He builds this scene in four stages. The initial murder sequence (1–105) is followed by a sequence between Emilia and Othello in which Emilia discovers not only that Othello has strangled his wife but also that he did so at Iago's bidding (105–67). In the third sequence, Othello learns that Iago's story about Desdemona's affair with Cassio was untrue (168–251), and in the last sequence Othello commits suicide (252–371). How in that third sequence of this scene does Shakespeare use disputing to bring about Othello's climactic recognition that Desdemona was innocent?

The action Shakespeare invents to awaken the Moor to his errors takes the form of a quarrel – not, however, between Othello and Iago, for Othello is, in a sense, but a bystander in the sequence. Emilia is the propelling character, Iago the resisting one, and the two fall out because Emilia disputes Othello's claim that Iago knew of Desdemona's guilt. In the introductory beat, Emilia addresses herself immediately (and only) to Iago, who has come into Desdemona's chamber with various lords in response to Emilia's cries. At this point, Emilia is loyal to her husband, believes Othello has accused Iago falsely, and wants Iago to deny the charge. The sequence begins with her challenge:

> Disprove this villain, if thou be'st a man.
> He says thou toldst him that his wife was false.
> I know thou didst not; thou'rt not such a villain.
> Speak, for my heart is full.
>
> (5.2.172–5)

When Iago maintains that Desdemona *was* false, the elements fall into place for the quarrel.

In the next beat the quarrel breaks out: Iago's goal is to silence Emilia; hers to speak. Shakespeare makes the accusation she throws out at Iago the means by which the statesmen learn that Desdemona "here lies murdered in her bed," then has Emilia appeal to them as arbiters of the dispute. In this beat, Emilia makes a formal break with Iago ("'Tis proper I obey him; but not now"), and throughout it Shakespeare keeps our attention on her growing desire to expose Iago's treachery.

In beat 198–217 Emilia is given the impetus to reveal the whole truth. Here again chance seems to govern: Othello himself appeals to the arbiters, intending to justify his judgment of Desdemona and in doing so mentions how he saw Desdemona's handkerchief in Cassio's hand. Suddenly Emila understands everything, and the conflict between her desire to blurt out the truth and Iago's desire to silence her intensifies. Within the structure of this quarrel, Othello learns the truth:

> EMILIA O God! O heavenly God!
> IAGO 'Zounds, hold your peace.
> EMILIA   'Twill out, 'twill out! I peace?

No, I will speak as liberal as the north . . .
    IAGO Be wise, and get you home.
    EMILIA I will not [*Iago offers to stab Emilia.*] . . .
O thou dull Moor, that handkerchief thou speak'st of
I found by fortune, and did give my husband;
For often, with a solemn earnestness
(More than indeed belong'd to such a trifle),
He begg'd of me to steal't.
    IAGO   Villainous whore!
    EMILIA She give it Cassio? No, alas, I found it,
And I did give't my husband.

                                        (5.2.218–31)

Emilia supplies the revelation that effects a recognition in Othello; however, for her loyalty to Desdemona she pays with her life.

Othello may be a bystander in the sequence but he remains a presence in it and of course speaks its climactic line, "Are there no stones in heaven / But what serve for the thunder?" (234–5). Nevertheless, the action which gives the sequence its movement and makes the climax possible unfolds in the dispute between Emila and Iago, in her heroic defiance of Iago and her final revelation of the truth to Othello.

Another classic example of a quarrel that widens the gap between disputing opponents occurs in *Coriolanus* 3.1.1–186, where Coriolanus is being escorted by the Patricians to the Senate House to be invested with the insignia of his new office and his way is barred by the Tribunes, Sicinius and Brutus. Coriolanus is at the apex of his career at the beginning of this sequence, while his election threatens to ruin the Tribunes, whose office he wishes to abolish. Since they dare not oppose Coriolanus openly, the challenge the Tribunes make as the sequence opens has a semblance of deference; they affect friendly concern. By the end of the sequence they are demanding his death.

The disposition to quarrel – calculated on the Tribunes' part, temperamental on Coriolanus's – makes the disputing form an apt vehicle for the sequence. All sequences display a contest of wills, of course, but here, because the antagonism is right at the surface and the Tribunes' intention is to arouse their opponents animosity, the struggle for dominance is highly explosive. Moreover, Shakespeare has structured events so that the opposing forces seem evenly matched.

Coriolanus wishes to go on; the Tribunes to stop him, both literally and metaphorically. The dramatic question might even be formulated in those terms: *Can the Tribunes "stop" Coriolanus?* The last time we saw Coriolanus, the rift between him and the Tribunes had been healed; the

Tribunes had given official approval to his election (2.3.142–4). Thus Coriolanus enters the stage in full confidence. The Tribunes remain cautious. Though they issue a challenge, they do so by affecting concern: they "fear" lest the procession walk into danger (3.1.24–33). Their opening sally, "It will be dangerous to go on," is a bluff, a neutral position from which they can easily retreat. But their intention is to provoke. And their challenge, however mysterious, stops the procession.

There are two more beats in the first phase of the intensification. In beat 33–41 Coriolanus responds with curiosity: his mind attempts to grasp the reason for the interruption, and he opines (correctly) that the alleged disturbance "is a purpos'd thing, and grows by plot." In beat 41–57 he lets himself be drawn into that plot by exchanging insults with Brutus. Sicinius puts an end to their mocking but not overheated exchange by throwing out a more pointed challenge:

> You show too much of that
> For which the people stir. If you will pass
> To where you are bound, you must inquire your way,
> Which you are out of, with a gentler spirit,
> Or never be so noble as a consul,
> Nor yoke with him for tribune.
>
> (3.1.52–57)

The barrier remains: to pass it, Coriolanus must be more humble.

The action now enters its second phase. At this point (beat 57–64), the Patricians, who have been given the goal of keeping Coriolanus calm and who act as mediators throughout the sequence, interpose themselves between Coriolanus and the Tribunes. Cominius sets about to remove the barrier of hostility diplomatically. But his lead is aborted. Coriolanus has heard the word "corn," which enrages him as a red cape would a bull and starts him railing once more against the "mutable, rank-scented meiny." The Patricians' entreaties that he "be calm" cannot silence him; on the contrary: "So shall my lungs / Coin words till their decay."

Sicinius began the quarrel by ordering Coriolanus to "pass no further," immobilizing his forward progress. But Coriolanus believes he can move beyond the Tribunes through the power of his invective, and the disputing action is shaped to depict Coriolanus pushing past a series of verbal warnings. We have just seen him ignoring the first: far from assuming the "gentler spirit" Sicinius held up as the prerequisite for continuing on his way, Coriolanus heaps contempt upon the people. This abuse leads to still another warning from Brutus and Sicinius, who forcefully resent Coriolanus's addressing the people as if he were "a god, to punish; not / A man of their infirmity" and repeat their ultimatum: his "is a mind / That shall remain a poison where it is; / Not poison any further" (beat 65–88).

As the characters who initiated the quarrel, the Tribunes of course are the propelling characters in all of this, yet by the very power of his personality Coriolanus, the responding character, appears to be dominant. Certainly he seems to have control from line 88 on when, incensed by Sicinius's warning that he "shall remain . . . where he is," he focuses his contempt on that "absolute 'shall'," making it the center of an attack on the Tribunes (beat 88–112). The rift widens. At the end of this beat, Cominius tries to deflect Coriolanus with his "Well, on to th' marketplace," and Coriolanus pushes past Cominius's cautions, too. In the final stage of the intensification, Coriolanus, now at full steam, returns to the corn controversy, a subject which as usual allows him to denigrate the Plebeians:

> Thus we debase
> The nature of our seats and make the rabble
> Call our cares fears; which will in time
> Break ope the locks a' th' Senate, and bring in
> The crows to peck the eagles.
>
> (3.1.135–9)

The warning with which Shakespeare caps this diatribe is ominous, not only because this time Coriolanus's patrician friends and the enemy Tribunes speak in concert but also because the lines signal that the Tribunes have achieved their end:

> MENENIUS   Come, enough.
> BRUTUS Enough, with over-measure.
>
> (3.1.139–40)

"Enough" here means that Coriolanus has given the Tribunes sufficient evidence to unseat him. From here on, dominance rests with the Tribunes.

One of the master strokes of Shakespeare's construction is that though Tribunes, Patricians, and audience alike sense from Brutus's "Enough, with over-measure" on that Coriolanus has pushed through one barrier too many, he himself is totally unaware of how dangerous the situation has become. Everyone has said "Enough!" and reason counsels not angry words but discreet silence, yet Coriolanus responds with "No, take more!" and another twenty lines of argument. The outcome is that, as a result, he is branded a traitor:

> BRUTUS   H'as said enough.
> SICINIUS H'as spoken like a traitor, and shall answer
> As traitors do.
> $$(3.1.161-3)$$

And even this final ultimatum Coriolanus pushes past:

> CORIOLANUS Thou wretch, despite o'erwhelm thee!
> What would the people do with these bald tribunes?
> On whom depending, their obedience fails
> To th' greater bench. In a rebellion,
> When what's not meet, but what must be, was law,
> Then were they chosen; in a better hour,
> Let what is meet be said it must be meet,
> And throw their power i' th' dust.
> $$(3.1.163-70)$$

By themselves the Tribunes could not have defeated him, but Coriolanus has charged headlong onto their blades.

With this beat the sequence reaches its climax: Coriolanus crowns his diatribe not only with abuse of the Tribunes but also with his ultimate appeal, a direct attack on their office: Rome must "throw their power i' th' dust." Yet at that moment the Tribunes unseat him:

> BRUTUS Manifest treason!
> SICINIUS   This a consul? No!   (3.1.171)

The dramatic question *Can the Tribunes stop Coriolanus?* has been resolved: Sicinius and Brutus present Rome's greatest general and her newest consul as a traitor.

The initial dispute has led to a quarrel, quarrel to accusation. Shakespeare sustains the climax in this sequence at a high pitch for two more beats by widening the rift between the disputing parties still further, as accusation now leads to arrest, and arrest to riot. First, in the penultimate beat, Sicinius tries to apprehend Coriolanus personally and is repulsed (172–9). Then, in the final beat (179–86), the Aediles and the Plebeians attempt en masse to apprehend the traitor, while the Senators defend him. The Tribunes now preside over an insurrection. They have succeeded in one thing more: they have stopped Coriolanus's mouth. For the next forty-six lines he utters hardly a word.

From this point on the question is whether the Tribunes have the power to execute Coriolanus. But that question belongs to another sequence. Here we need only review the basic traits of this disputing sequence, in which Coriolanus's movement from consul-elect to traitor turns his fortunes around a full 180 degrees.

Though in the final analysis a dominant/subservient relationship becomes evident, with the Tribunes emerging as the propelling characters, that relationship is far less obvious when the sequence opens than, say, in a persuading sequence, and the two powers are much more evenly matched. Coriolanus appeared able to push through one ultimatum after another without repercussion. But what he regarded as rhetorical victories are all being used against him as evidence of his "inveterate hate" for the commoners. Far from healing the rift in the state, they exacerbate it.

Whether the disputing sequence moves from agreement to rupture, as here, or from rupture to reconciliation, as in the examples cited earlier, usually starts with some act of aggression. Othello reviles Iago for "setting him on the rack." Cassius attacks Brutus for condemning Lucius Pella. Laertes demands revenge from Claudius for the murder of his father Polonius. Cleopatra calls Antony a traitor. Leontes accuses Hermione of adultery. Emilia brands Iago a base villain. The Tribunes bar Coriolanus's progress. Often the original accusation is only a spark that ignites emotions and becomes irrelevant in the course of the dispute. Since the passions themselves are under scrutiny, the drive is toward tense emotional states, with rapid shifts of direction within the sequence resulting from the jumps that the mind takes when governed by anger. The shifts may be illogical and jerky, without the rhetorical regularity of some other sequence forms. The range of emotion can vary tremendously within the sequence. Dominance itself may change, with now one, now the other character usurping control. Though the structure of the disputing sequence is rarely chaotic, it is designed to reflect chaos.

12

Commanding sequences

The activities that give direction to a motivated sequence cover the full range of possible relationships between two characters – observing, meditating, reporting, persuading, and disputing. Commanding stands at the far end of that spectrum. Commanding resembles persuading, insofar as the active character of a commanding sequence wishes to impose his will on another character, but here of course the element of compulsion is added. If the propelling character is an authority figure commanding deference from the secondary one, the action is no longer persuading, however gently the authority is exercised. Such situations fall into the realm of commanding.

Occasionally Shakespeare bases the sequence structure on this activity. Consider *As You Like It* 1.3.1–89, where Duke Frederick banishes Rosalind. The Duke has absolute authority. His sole function here is to order the banishment, after which he exits. The protests of Rosalind and Celia are heard but make no difference and, since their responses never challenge the Duke's authority, this is not an instance of disputing; in fact, there is evidence that Shakespeare deliberately holds opposition back. Here, for example, though Rosalind and Celia are appalled by the command, their deeper reactions are withheld from this sequence (which always remains the Duke's) and dramatized in the next. Or consider *Twelfth Night* 1.4.1–42, where Orsino commissions Viola to woo Olivia for him. Though no task could be more repulsive to Viola than having to urge her rival to marry the man she herself loves, she submits to the request without complaint. Shakespeare's emphasis when constructing the action remains on the way Orsino issues the order. Consider also *Hamlet* 2.11.1–71, where Polonius sends Reynaldo to spy on Laertes. Polonius detains Reynaldo for the full length of the sequence, elaborating on the instructions he expects Reynaldo to follow. Reynaldo's boredom shows through and his surprise that Polonius would order the maligning of his own son is evident, but he offers little active resistance. His speeches serve only to punctuate Polonius's: "I will, my lord," "My lord, I did intend it," "Very good, my lord," and so on. The commanding sequence lends itself well to comedy, even to low comedy – consider the intensity with which the constable Dogberry gives instructions to his watchmen in *Much Ado About Nothing* (3.3.1–94).

One of the more dramatic commanding sequences is 1.3.1–129 of *1 Henry IV* in which the King orders the Percys – the Earls of Worcester and Northumberland and young Hotspur – to deliver up their prisoners to the Crown. King Henry is in full command here, his authority manifest as he sets "his greatness" against that of the lords who have made him so powerful. Henry wants the prisoners. First Northumberland, then Hotspur, and finally Blunt raise objections to the order, initially with reasonable courtesy. But the issue is a charged one and, as the sequence progresses, emotions intensify: Hotspur's resistance mounts; Henry grows more demanding. How easily this confrontation could have crossed the borderline between commanding and quarreling to become a dispute. Notice how Shakespeare prevents that. So long as Henry is present he retains full command. Only after the King withdraws is Hotspur's rage against Henry vented; Shakespeare focuses on Hotspur's anger in the following sequence, a reporting sequence (1.3.130–302) in which Shakespeare makes Hotspur's ranting the means of delaying Worcester's climactic report of the brewing rebellion. By carefully manipulating unit boundaries Shakespeare keeps Henry at the center of a commanding sequence and thereby suggests greater authority, an authority Hotspur never manages to wrest from him.

The commanding sequence can also demonstrate a monarch's weakness, as in 2.4.88–126 of *King Lear*. Here, though Lear is the authority or propelling figure and Gloucester is the responding one, circumstances are such that Gloucester fears to obey King Lear. The sequence opens in the middle of the conflict. Having arrived at Gloucester's castle, Lear has discovered his servant Caius in stocks and wishes to confront those responsible for the insult, his daughter Regan and her husband Cornwall. He has already (offstage) issued the order that propels the sequence – that Regan and Cornwall appear before him to answer for their actions – and Gloucester, the go-between, has informed Regan and Cornwall of the command, but they have refused to comply. In the first beat of the sequence, Lear contemplates the refusal, then reissues his command:

> Deny to speak with me? They are sick? They are weary?
> They have travell'd all the night? Mere fetches.

The images of revolt and flying off.
Fetch me a better answer.

(2.4.88–91)

Fearing Regan and Cornwall more than Lear, Gloucester balks. In beat 2 (2.4.92–104), Lear has to frame the command in stronger terms:

> LEAR Dost thou understand me, man?
> GLOUCESTER Ay, my good lord.
> LEAR The king would speak with Cornwall, the dear father
> Would with his daughter speak, commands, tends service.

(2.4.99–102)

Then Lear himself hesitates (beat 105–12): perhaps the Duke really is sick, as he claims. The sight of Kent, still in the stocks (beat 112–20), clears these doubts from Lear's mind and provokes the climax of the sequence: Lear demands for the third time that Gloucester carry out his order:

> Go tell the Duke, and 's wife, I'ld speak with them –
> Now, presently. Bid them come forth and hear me,
> Or at their chamber-door I'll beat the drum
> Till it cry sleep to death.

(2.4.116–19)

This time Gloucester apparently carries the message:

> I would have all well betwixt you.   *Exit.*

(2.4.120)

This example of action driven by the activity of commanding shows Lear losing the ability to command instant obedience. Shakespeare has given his propelling character a desire – to exert the authority that should be his – and he demonstrates that the King still has the energy to give orders. But by displaying Cornwall's disregard for Lear and Gloucester's fear of Cornwall the sequence tells us in still another way that the kingdom no longer respects the King's authority.

In the commanding sequence, then, someone in authority issues an order, which instigates action or creates suspense. Such a sequence may provide exposition, advance the plot, or introduce a new stage action. The command can also characterize the individual through the amount of authority he can muster and the way he delivers the order. As with any activity in which opportunities for resistance are limited (and they are limited indeed when someone has total authority, even temporarily), the dramatic interest of the completed sequence may also be limited. But with sufficient resistance, as in the *Henry IV* and *Lear* examples, even the commanding sequence can be compelling.

This brief review of the commanding sequence brings to an end our survey of the types of motivation Shakespeare uses to give direction to a sequence. It is our hope that by identifying the common activities – reporting, interrogating, persuading, disputing, etc. – and by demonstrating the ways in which Shakespeare renders each activity dramatic, we can be of help to those who want to analyze Shakespeare's action.

13

Sequences combined: the frame

Central to the purpose of this book is the question, how does one locate the conventional rising action that has habitually been associated with the word *scene?*, the precise identification of each successive rising action being understood here as an essential first step toward the clear articulation of the play's action in any stage production. But though we have argued that the conventional rising action occurs in the sequence and that the entire play is one long series of sequences, Shakespeare's plays are certainly far more than chains of cleverly interlocked sequences. Plays that merely string sequences together would prove both boring and exhausting – boring because of the endless repetition and exhausting because each successive repetition would be driving toward yet another climax. Obviously Shakespeare's action is neither boring nor fatiguing, even when one focuses, as one does in this study, so very precisely on the raw structure, for to get at that structure is to get at the dynamics of the drama, the relative force and intensity that activate its individual units. One is discerning the primal energies that are the source of the play's emotional rhythms.

Already evident from the preceding chapters is the remarkable variety of sequence forms – a variety that comes from the several different patterns of intensification observed in chapter 6, from the great reservoir of possible motives that Shakespeare employs to drive a sequence forward, and from the necessity of uniting these motives with new and varied situations as well as of endowing each sequence with a tone appropriate to the genre in which it appears. While all sequences are alike in that all drive toward a significant climactic moment, each sequence is nonetheless unique. As we come in this chapter to speak about sequences in their larger dramatic context, the constant vitality Shakespeare displays while writing in sequences should be even more apparent. The sequences are so combined as to create an infinite variety of rising and falling rhythms, and this interplay between repetition and variety, between form and content, adds emotional life to the action.

But to understand fully how Shakespeare combines his sequences, we must turn at this point to a unit of greater magnitude than the sequence, not only larger in size but also of greater importance because embracing more – a unit we have called the *frame*. The frame might be roughly defined as "a designed group of consecutive sequences,"[1] or as an action constructed of already complete actions. As the beat is to the sequence, so the sequence is to the frame – a frame normally consists of from two to four sequences, which tell a specific segment of the story, its boundaries being largely determined by the fact that the story it is telling has a readily detectable start and finish. By studying the frame we can discover certain principles about the way Shakespeare weights and orchestrates his sequences that help to reveal how individual sequences contribute to the developing rhythms of a finished production.

It is at the level of the frame that Shakespeare establishes the major accents of the drama, for only within this larger context can the relative weight, tempo, tone, and pitch of intensity of each sequence be experienced. Frames too are characterized by movement – movement toward greater intensity, movement away from intensity, smaller units merging into larger ones, lesser climaxes preparing us emotionally for more explosive ones. All sequences are not of equal weight, though in isolation they may seem so.

Take, for example, the *key sequence*. In every frame there is one key sequence, which dramatizes some major event in the plot, the omission of which would leave a gap in the story. The innate intensity of the key sequence derives of course from the fact that the plot's major events are inevitably its highly emotional ones. Thus, the key sequences in a frame are like the accented syllables in a word and, just as the accented syllables of each word supply the meter in a line of poetry, so the accented sequences of each frame supply the dominant climaxes in the play. Consider, for example, the key sequences in *Othello*: Iago's incitement of Brabantio against Desdemona, Brabantio's attempt to convict Othello of witchcraft, Othello's safe arrival at Cyprus, Cassio's brawl with Roderigo, Desdemona's appeal for Cassio's recall, Iago's report of Desdemona's infidelity to Othello, Othello's demand that Iago supply proof, and so on. These are the sequences in which the action of the frames will crest.

All other sequences in the frame are subordinated to the key sequence: these lead up to it or away from it, fleshing out the key incident with additional details. Such subsidiary sequences can be identified by their functions: introductory, intensifying, sustaining, or concluding; thus, the intensity of each part is determined by its function within the frame itself. The same is true here as was true of the beat within the sequence. But here we have the whole sequence, that is, completed actions, that must be subordinated to the other actions because in the larger scale of things they are less important. The way the relative importance of the various sequences is conveyed to the audience is through the play of the tone, the tempo, and the emotional intensity of the juxtaposed sequences.

Because space limitations prohibit us from covering every technique Shakespeare uses to create dynamic relationships and lively rhythms in his sequence groups, we have chosen to concentrate on an aspect that has received little attention, this relative weighting of sequences within a frame. The subject is best approached by studying the uses Shakespeare makes of the crucial key sequence – where he places it in the context of the whole and how the position it appears in affects and often changes the structure of the rising action. We will look at four different ways of handling the intensification – first, the standard intensification, then an inversion of it, third, a variation of the inverted intensification which we shall call the sustaining intensification, and finally the ABA intensification – the aim being to demonstrate that the method of unit analysis does not leave us with an endless series of interlocked sequences related to one another like beads on a chain but rather sharpens the ability of directors to orchestrate or of viewers to experience the rising and falling rhythms of the play in performance.

I

What are the characteristics of the standard frame? Although the rising action is the hallmark of the sequence, Shakespeare sometimes utilizes a similar format in constructing frames – many frames are composed of (1) an introductory sequence, followed in turn by (2) an intensifying sequence, (3) the key sequence, and (4) a concluding one. Everything in the first two sequences builds toward that key sequence, the sequence of highest intensity, which is naturally positioned as the third of these four sequences, so that the combined actions follow the conventional dramatic curve, thus creating an action at an intermediate level, between the sequence and the act. We begin our analysis of the frame structure by examining one or two frames that follow this standard pattern, first to demonstrate how the components of this structure differ from those of the sequence and second to provide a norm against which other types of frame can be considered.

In our initial example, *Coriolanus* 2.1, where the victorious general is transported from Corioli to Rome with all the appropriate honors, the boundaries of the frame are easy to discern, for they happen to coincide with those of the scene. Here Shakespeare employs the standard form of intensification. Let us look first at the focal point of this frame: it has at its heart a procession, which occupies lines 162–204, the frame's third and key sequence. Everything in the early part of the frame builds toward this sequence, in which Coriolanus proceeds in triumph through the streets of Rome to the Capitol to be honored by the Patricians. The stage directions for the procession are explicit. Trumpets announce its entrance. Coriolanus appears, crowned with an oaken garland and flanked by his fellow generals in the Volscian war, Cominius and Titus Lartius. Captains and soldiers escort the hero to the Capitol. The dialogue makes it evident that throngs witness his passage. Coriolanus's entry as victor over the Volscians is not only the technical but also the emotional focal point of an entire frame. But how, exactly, is the rising action of this frame created? How are its individual sequences weighted?

The frame's first sequence is 2.1.1–96. Notice the many ways in which the action of this sequence is introductory. For one thing, the setting has to be moved from the battlefields of Corioli back to Rome, the city the victorious hero will return to. Thus the characters are people we know as Romans – Menenius and the two Tribunes, Sicinius and Brutus. At the outset Menenius in particular is waiting for news: his first words are "We shall have news tonight." The sequence prepares us in yet another way for Coriolanus's return: it makes us aware of what Coriolanus will have to face when he gets to Rome – the enmity of the Tribunes. In the very frame that celebrates Coriolanus's triumph Shakespeare reveals the nature of his chief antagonists, for this sequence gives us the first real indication of the Tribune's importance to the play.

Notice also that even though characters are simply waiting and there is no intrinsic action, Shakespeare invents one. He engages the characters in a dispute: the Tribunes denounce Coriolanus for his pride and Menenius defends him. The strategy gives the sequence a dramatic question, *Can Menenius win this battle of wits with the Tribunes?* The charges the Tribunes lay against Coriolanus are thus boldly deflected, his faults minimized, the air cleared for a sincere welcome. But the tone is light-hearted; in fact, the sequence is a delightful plum for the actor playing Menenius, who functions like the presenter in a satire, chronicling the failings of the Tribunes. The climax this sequence builds to – a definitive put-down of the two whose "beards deserve not so honorable a grave as to stuff a botcher's cushion" (2.1.87–9) – is hardly world-shattering: though the dispute is somewhat acerbic, the sparring is jocular and leaves plenty of room for emotional expansion later in the frame.

In the second stage of Shakespeare's preparation for the victory procession, Menenius receives the news he had been hoping for (sequence 2.1.97–161). Since the action of this second sequence is focused more squarely on the returning hero, it is a sequence of intensification: in the initial sequence of this series we are told only that Rome expects word; from this intensifying sequence we learn that the hero is on his way home.

To add variety, Shakespeare constructs sequence 2 as an interrogating sequence. Messengers – Volumnia, Virgilia, and Valeria – arrive to announce that Martius approaches – "with most prosperous appro-bation." As Menenius interrogates, the ladies gladly report, until the whole story of Coriolanus's victory is revealed. Because this is less the story of a battle than a story of its general, attention is directed toward the military virtues which Rome demands of its heroes and which Coriolanus possesses: in this sequence, as the ladies say, "there's wondrous things spoke of him." Volumnia in particular praises Coriolanus effusively, thereby heightening our expectations. The climax of the sequence is not simply another climax of the same intensity. Here trumpets sound to reinforce Volumnia's enthusiasm and Coriolanus is made to seem an incarnation of Mars:

> These are the ushers of Martius: before him he carries noise; and
> behind him he leaves tears:
>> Death, that dark spirit, in 's nervy arm doth lie,
>> Which being advanc'd, declines, and then men die.
>
> (2.1.158–61)

The effect of sequence 2 should be to make us – like the "prattling nurse, " the "kitchen malkin," and the "veil'd dames" who make up the popular throngs along the parade route – all "agreeing / In earnestness to see him."

This joyous anticipation of the hero's arrival leads to the key sequence of the frame – the triumphal procession itself (2.1.162–204). This third sequence opens with a proclamation that brings Coriolanus to center stage:

> HERALD Know, Rome, that all alone Martius did fight
> Within Corioles gates; where he hath won,
> With fame, a name to Martius Caius; these
> In honor follows Coriolanus.
> Welcome to Rome, renowned Coriolanus!
>
> (2.1.162–6)

Here Martius is awarded the honorary name by which he will be known for the remainder of the play, and the Herald's final lines express the sense of triumph that characterizes this key sequence: "Welcome to Rome, renowned Coriolanus."

The cumulative pattern upon which the hero's reception is structured is well chosen to heighten emotions here at the apex of the frame. Each lady in turn welcomes Coriolanus to Rome: Volumnia receives "my good soldier . . . worthy Caius . . . by deed-achieving honor newly nam'd"; Virgilia, his wife, receives him in gracious, loving silence, her emotion beyond words; Valeria receives him by her unobtrusive but loyal presence. The intensification builds toward the point where all join together in one magnanimous and overwhelming welcome (beat 2.1.181–92):

> I know not where to turn. O, welcome home;
> And welcome general, and y' are welcome all.

> A hundred thousand welcomes! I could weep,
> And I could laugh; I am light, and heavy. Welcome!

> Yet welcome, warriors.

It is in this context of exultation that Shakespeare raises the question of whether Coriolanus can "go on." The Herald who opened the sequence now concludes it with his call to "give way there, and go on!" The essence of a procession is movement; eventually this one must continue to its destination, the Capitol. But before the characters exit Shakespeare hints at another way of going on: Volumnia here expresses her desire to see Coriolanus go on to be made consul.

Having examined only three of this frame's four sequences, we can already see significant differences between the rising action of the frame and the rising action of a sequence. Not only is the rising action at this level constructed of sequences rather than of beats but an important characteristic of that rising action is that tone and mood are varied from sequence to sequence. There is another significant distinction. The frame does not have a separate climax of its own; rather, the climax of its dominant sequence functions simultaneously as the climax of the frame. The rising action of the Coriolanus frame reaches its peak at the very moment when Coriolanus is engulfed in welcomes, the same moment at which its key sequence peaks. For the rising action of the standard frame, at least, this can be taken as a rule.

The frame has one more sequence: it ends as it began – with the two Tribunes. As the stage direction "*Brutus and Sicinius aside*" after line 96 indicates, the Tribunes have remained on stage, observing but not participating, from the entry of the ladies in the second sequence until the triumphal procession exits. They are there as "nettles" in a hayfield or "old crab-trees . . . that will not / Be grafted to your relish," with hearts "cursed at very root," hearts "not glad to see thee" (2.1.85–9). The Tribunes too perceive the direction in which Coriolanus's fortunes are heading ("On the sudden / I warrant him consul," 2.1.221–2), but the thought does not give them the same pleasure it gives Volumnia.

But the action is no longer rising. This is a concluding sequence decrescent in pitch, subdued in tone; once again the rhythm is being varied. In this fourth and final sequence (2.1.205–70), the Tribunes, now on stage alone, ruminate on the preceding action, supplying a rather jaundiced vision of the procession and of the people they represent:

> All tongues speak of him, and the bleared sights
> Are spectacled to see him. Your prattling nurse
> Into a rapture lets her baby cry
> While she chats him; the kitchen malkin pins
> Her richest lockram 'bout her reechy neck,
> Clamb'ring the walls to eye him; stalls, bulks, windows
> Are smother'd up, leads fill'd, and ridges hors'd
> With variable complexions, all agreeing
> In earnestness to see him . . .
>
> (2.1.204–13)

. . . and so on. Then, looking into the future, they focus once again on their adversary's pride, predict his further advancement in the state, perceive its effects upon their office, and determine how they can unseat him. This is the sequence in which the Tribunes state their intention to anger Coriolanus in the hope of removing from the political arena the force most likely to interfere with their burgeoning power. Looking both ways, the concluding sequence of the frame not only provides a sense of completion but also thrusts forward into a new action.

In this frame, then, the successive sequences are hardly repetitious. They are not only varied in tone and tempo but are also pitched at different intensities, each either leading up to or winding down from the frame's dominant sequence. Sequence 2.1.1–96 introduces the setting and the situation, as Menenius and the Tribunes wait for news from Corioli. Sequence 2.1.97–161 intensifies the situation, through Volumnia's excitement at the prospect of her son's return, thus raising expectations higher. So eagerly awaited, Coriolanus appears in triumph, in the frame's key sequence (2.1.162–204), bringing the intensification to its emotional peak. The tension then falls off as, in a concluding sequence (2.1.205–70), the Tribunes plot Coriolanus's downfall. Each sequence stands as an action in its own right. But, taken together, the four actions form a new action at a larger scale of magnitude.

The *Coriolanus* frame just examined is built upon the standard pattern; its action follows the traditional dramatic curve. Viewed by itself, the example might give the false impression that the frame is no more than a multipartite scene, for in this example the stage happens to be cleared at either end. But there is a significant difference between the frame and the multipartite scene. A scene can never survive the clearing of the stage that takes place when the location changes: the cleared stage invariably signals the commencement of a new scene, an event unfolding at some new place. A frame, however, can extend well beyond the confines of a single scene. Unity of place is not a consideration in the definition of a frame.

One reason for this difference is that frames often contain ancillary sequences, just as sequences contain ancillary beats. *Ancillary sequences* do everything the ancillary beats do but on a larger scale: an ancillary sequence may be inserted into a frame to create a time interval within which some offstage action can take place, to supply necessary information that the audience must have at this moment, or to unify plot segments by interlocking them to other material. Most ancillary sequences perform all of these functions at once. Because ancillary sequences are usually populated by characters from one of the play's other plots, the scene changes for the duration of that sequence (and unmitigated repetition is in still another way avoided), but the interruption does not destroy the integrity of the frame. This difference in function, as well as the need for precision in articulating the rising action, makes it advisable to distinguish ancillary sequences from *integral sequences*, those in which the action of the frame itself is unfolding. Let us look at another example of Shakespeare's rising action with this in mind. In this instance the frame spans several scenes.

Much like *Coriolanus* 2.1 in structure is the interesting frame in *Twelfth Night* that runs from 1.5.1 to 2.2.41: here Viola, dressed as Cesario, comes to woo Olivia for Orsino. The action in this frame builds toward that clash of wits which leaves Olivia infatuated with the young page Viola impersonates. Here again the sequences are ordered to create a standard rising action. The first is introductory, that between the Fool and his mistress which sets the stage (sequence 1.5.1–98). The second increases expectations, as Viola turns up at the gates demanding an audience with Olivia (sequence 1.5.99–166). Both actions build toward the third or key sequence, the apex of the frame, 1.5.167–311, in which Viola proposes on Orsino's behalf, and Olivia declines the match but falls in love with Viola (and here both sequence and frame crest). In 2.1.1–48, following Viola's exit, Shakespeare includes a sequence between Viola's brother Sebastian and his friend Antonio. Obviously an ancillary sequence, it has a neutral effect on the frame's action. Finally, in a sequence that has its introductory beat in 1.5 (beat 299–307) but is developed and completed only in 2.2, Malvolio receives orders from Olivia to deliver a ring to Viola, follows her, and forces the ring upon her. The first three sequences occur in Olivia's chambers, the next one near the sea coast, the last on the way to Orsino's court. But the action leading up to Olivia's infatuation with Viola in sequence 1.5.167–311 has such close links with the action between Malvolio and Viola in 2.2.1–41 that, despite the obvious segmentation, the whole has an integrity of its own, and the staging should be designed to preserve the essential continuity (for instance, there should never be the monumental break after Viola leaves Olivia that is suggested by the editors who insert an act division at that point). The frame takes its dramatic question from the dramatic question of the key sequence, *Can Viola persuade Olivia to marry Orsino?*, and, like the frame just examined from *Coriolanus*, traces out a conventional dramatic curve.

These two examples illustrate the standard pattern at its fullest: an introductory sequence followed by an intensifying sequence, then a key sequence (this third sequence decidedly more powerful and clearly a focal point of the plot), and, finally, a concluding sequence, decrescent in pitch, that brings the whole to a close, each of the four sequences varying in tone and tempo. Four, of course, is not an inviolable number. Shakespeare very often creates a rising action with three sequences or occasionally with only two,[2] and of course the inclusion of an ancillary sequence alters the number in still another way. But size does not change the point: though the action in the standard frame follows the traditional dramatic curve, the structure of that rising action is far different from the structure of the simple sequence: the rising action here is formed by combining a series of already complete actions to form a whole of an entirely different magnitude.

II

Let us look now at frames in which the expected pattern is inverted. What happens when the key sequence comes not in third position so that the earlier sequences build toward it but is moved up to second position, immediately following the introductory sequence? In such a case, there *is* no rising action. Even if an introductory sequence could by itself sufficiently convey an impression of development (which it cannot), the impact of the key sequence comes too rapidly for the audience to gain any impression of a building action; on the contrary, what the audience experiences is an immediate, highly emotional explosion, and then a period of readjustment in which the remaining sequences of the frame are deliberately subordinated. Yet the inverted frame is no less dramatic than the standard frame, and very often its impact is even more powerful.

Take the frame from *Julius Caesar* where Cassius and Brutus join forces at Sardis. The frame opens with a brief introductory sequence that brings Cassius to Brutus's camp (4.2.1–52). But Shakespeare lets Cassius lose his temper even before this first sequence concludes, so that the characters move rapidly into the frame's main action, the powerful quarrel in which Cassius condemns Brutus for his treatment of Lucius Pella, while Brutus accuses Cassius of accepting bribes (4.3.1–162). Since the climax of the quarrel is also the climactic point of the frame, the tensions in this inverted frame reach their height when this second sequence peaks.

Though there are two more sequences in the frame, both are designed with concluding functions in mind and neither has the emotional intensity that we find in the frame's key sequence. By the time the third sequence opens, the action is no longer rising: the characters have settled down and are engrossed in business (4.3.163–238). Brutus, having resolved his differences with Cassius, has gathered the commanders to discuss strategies for their forthcoming clash with Octavius. His proposal that the armies march together to Philippi completes the action being presented in this segment of the plot – the various armies have come together in sequence 1, have reached an accord in sequence 2, and, finally, here in sequence 3, have decided how to proceed against the enemy. True, in the climactic beat of this third sequence Brutus and Cassius again disagree (196–225), Cassius protesting that "'tis better that the enemy seek us; / So shall he waste his means, weary his soldiers," and Brutus insisting upon the march to Philippi; however, this time Shakespeare does not elevate the level of emotion: Cassius bends easily to Brutus's will and the sequence ends with the commanders retiring peacefully to their separate tents amidst references to deep night and the need for rest. In the fourth and last sequence, 4.3.239–308, the tranquil atmosphere created in the third is maintained. Brutus, now alone but for two faithful captains and his young servant, prepares for sleep. He calls for music and, when the boy nods off over his lute, opens a book. Even the startling appearance of the ghost of Caesar remains in keeping with this sense of a lull in the play's action. The ghost's emergence reveals that the tranquility exists more on the surface of Brutus's mind than in its depths and serves to effect a transition from deep night to dawn when the camp must arise, yet the climax here is low-keyed and affects the sequence only, not the whole frame. Shakespeare deliberately keeps these two last sequences at a subdued pitch.

This grouping of four sequences exhibits nicely the nature of the inverted frame, in which the action peaks early because the dominant sequence has been pushed forward.

The action in frame 3.4.1–201 of *Othello* also takes this inverted form: here in fact the key sequence is advanced not just to second place but all the way to the beginning (3.4.1–106); no introductory sequence precedes it. This sequence is an important one, the first in which Othello confronts Desdemona after receiving from Iago the information he takes as proof of her infidelity – that she has given to Cassio the treasured handkerchief, symbol of their love. To endow the sequence with emotional power Shakespeare casts it in the form of a dispute: Othello presses Desdemona to produce the handkerchief and Desdemona, having lost it, counters his attack by attempting to change the subject, unwittingly choosing the worst possible alternative, to plead for Cassio's reinstatement. Because Othello never says directly what he is driving at or why her defense of Cassio angers him, Desdemona is unable to allay his suspicions and the sequence climaxes with Othello stalking out in a rage:

> DESDEMONA Pray you let Cassio be receiv'd again.
> OTHELLO Fetch me the handkerchief, my mind misgives.
> DESDEMONA Come, come;
> You'll never meet a more sufficient man.
> OTHELLO The handkerchief! . . .
> DESDEMONA   A man that all his time
> Hath founded his good fortunes on your love,
> Shar'd dangers with you –
> OTHELLO The handkerchief!
> DESDEMONA I' faith, you are to blame.
> OTHELLO 'Zounds!   *Exit Othello.*
> (3.4.88–98)

Here too Shakespeare makes the climactic moments of the sequence the climactic moments of the frame.

In the two sequences that follow tension is no longer rising but winding down. After Othello goes out, Cassio and Iago join Desdemona (sequence 3.4.106–68) and the characters puzzle over the meaning of Othello's behavior. Eventually (sequence 3.4.169–201), Cassio is left on stage alone and, meeting Bianca, gives her the handkerchief Iago has by now dropped in his quarters, begging her to copy the work before it is claimed by its owner. Both sequences are minor ones, the penultimate sequence exploring reactions to the key sequence and the last one putting the fatal handkerchief into Bianca's hands in preparation for the time when Othello will see her return it to Cassio. In this frame too Shakespeare chooses not to organize the sequences in the standard way: the emotional impact of the frame occurs in the very first of its three sequences, while the concluding section (rather than occupying a single sequence as in the standard version) is now stretched out over two.

Shakespeare often places the key sequence early in the frame. When Isabella visits Claudio's cell in *Measure for Measure*, when Falstaff arrives at the tavern to be proved a coward in *I Henry IV*, some introductory action has already occurred but it is effectively subordinated. The action peaks quickly and the sequences which follow are concluding rather than intensifying sequences. Even more sudden are the instances in which the key sequence stands as the opening sequence, as with Claudio's refusal at the altar to wed Hero in *Much Ado*, with Cornwall's blinding of Gloucester in *King Lear*, or with Macbeth's massacre of Lady Macduff and her children. In all of these instances the dominant sequence no longer occupies its conventional place close to the end of a rising action; the sequence order has been inverted.

Why this inversion? Not simply to avoid the monotony that would deaden the play were the sequences of every frame to follow the same regular and expected order, though of course the variations are designed to energize the rhythms of the play. Shakespeare finds the inversion useful at those major climactic moments in the middle of the play where there is reason to move quickly to the high ground of the climactic sequence and where it is possible to do so because earlier frames have already prepared us for the play's climactic one. The groundwork Shakespeare lays in the robbery sequences in 2.1 and 2.2 of *I Henry IV*, for instance, allows him to foreshorten the build of the frame he constructs in 2.4, where Falstaff is exposed as a coward at the very beginning of the frame action, and of course he can begin a frame with the dramatic scene in which Isabella informs Claudio of Angelo's treachery only because he has already prepared the way for it in the previous act with the frame which throws Isabella and Angelo together. The preparation normally provided in a frame's introductory and intensifying sequences is already in place: earlier frames have established the required tensions, which are ready now to crest. The frame itself is going to contain that sequence which effects the catastrophe of the entire play. To delay the key sequence until late in this climactic frame would be to dull expectations rather than satisfy them; consequently, the inversion is imperative.

But the inverted frame is also valuable to Shakespeare when he wishes to draw the viewers rapidly into some new situation. By involving us in the quarrel between Cassius and Brutus, for example, he transports us quickly from the Rome of the play's first three acts to the battlefield that will decide the fates of the conspirators. And by letting us witness the dramatic slaying of Lady Macduff and her children, he aligns our emotions with those of Macduff, at the point at which Macduff is about to become the major antagonist of *Macbeth*. In all of these cases, extended development would have been inappropriate, and Shakespeare aptly chose to *start* with the key sequence.

Notice, however, that even though the key sequence appears in a new place, there is nevertheless still a key sequence: the key sequence is what makes the unit a frame, and once that sequence is located the relationship between the sequences around it can be easily discerned.

III

In both the standard intensification and the inverted variant of it, the climax of the frame coincides with the climax of the key sequence. It could therefore be assumed that by definition the climax of any frame always occurs in its key sequence. But there is an important exception to this rule, for in certain frames Shakespeare obtains further rhythmic variety by sustaining the climax beyond the key sequence. In this form, the key sequence is still placed at the beginning of the frame, but that key sequence becomes a launching pad for the sequence that follows, which then lifts the tension a stage higher. Thus, there is once again a rising action, but it is essentially different in structure from the standard one, in that here the rising action is not moving toward the key sequence but sustaining or even increasing its impact (see diagram).

A good place to observe this sustaining technique is in the opening frame of *King Lear* (1.1.1–308). The first of this frame's three sequences is between Lear and his daughters, the second between Lear and Kent, and the third between Lear, France, and Burgundy. The introductory sequence in which Lear tests his daughters' love is undeniably the key sequence: it plunges us immediately into the major subject of the play (Lear's conflict with his daughters), records the event that all of the subsequent action flows from (Lear's division of his kingdom), and reveals the character flaws Lear will have to overcome. Certainly Shakespeare musters all of his dramatic powers to make us experience

Analyzing Shakespeare's Action

Four-sequence frames

STANDARD FRAME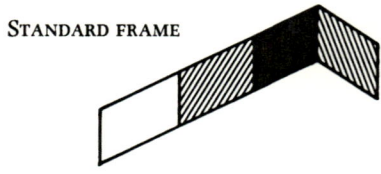

INVERTED FRAME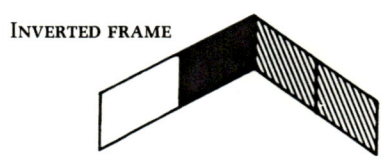

SUSTAINING FRAME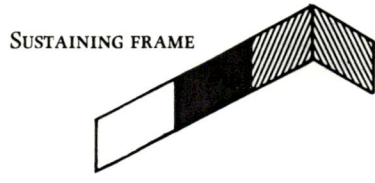

ABA FRAME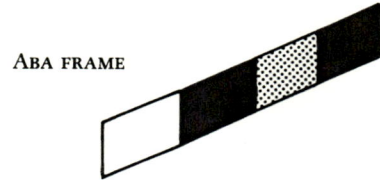

☐ Introductory sequence

▨ Intensifying sequence

■ Key sequence

▧ Decrescent or concluding sequence

▦ Ancillary sequence

the enormity of Lear's rage when Cordelia refuses to flatter him as her sisters do. By contrast the Kent sequence that follows is less important. Concerned as it is with a secondary character and a secondary aspect of the plot, Kent's "disgrace," it cannot possibly be regarded as the frame's key sequence. Yet Kent's insistence that Lear is misjudging Cordelia clearly carries the tension of the frame a stage higher: the interference from Kent increases Lear's anger, and, having just disowned his best-loved daughter, he goes on to banish his most loyal retainer. The banishment of Kent thus becomes the climactic point of the frame.

What happens in this sustained intensification is that, powerful as the key sequence is, Shakespeare effects the climax of the frame through some dramatic reaction to it in the following sequence. The result is that (1) the climax of the frame is now separated from the climax of the key sequence and (2) that climax occurs, ironically, in a sequence which is less significant in its own right, less indispensable to the plot, than the key sequence. It is only because the key sequence has been situated so far forward and provides so high a springboard that the succeeding sequence can lift the action of the frame a step higher. It helps to be aware of Shakespeare's use of this sustained intensification for, in some situations, the power of the frame's key sequence seems so much greater than that of the subsidiary but climactic sequence that the climactic function of the latter may be missed. It is vital that in the staging this seemingly subsidiary sequence be given due weight.

A case where this weighting is crucial but especially apt to be overlooked occurs in *Coriolanus* 3.1, in which Coriolanus is accused of treason by Sicinius and Brutus. The frame often seems tedious in production because faulty sequence articulation muddies the pertinent dramatic questions. The problem is compounded by the fact that divisions between the frame's three sequences are not immediately obvious. For all of these reasons, *Coriolanus* 3.1 is worth looking at in detail as our second example of an intensification in which the dramatic power is carried over from the key sequence into the sequence following it.

The first sequence has the dramatic question *Can the Tribunes stop Coriolanus?* (3.1.1–186). At its beginning Coriolanus is about to be confirmed as consul. But during the sequence the initially cautious Tribunes move from fear that their office will be abolished under Coriolanus's consulship to a position of command, while Coriolanus's fortunes fall. By manipulating his uncontrollable passions Sicinius and Brutus are able to halt his election and even accuse him of treason. The sequence reaches its peak when the Tribunes indict Coriolanus "as a traitorous innovator, / A foe to the public weal." This of course is the frame's key sequence.

The second sequence has nothing of the power of the first. But it does contain an action (3.1.187–262). Opening amidst chaos, it addresses the question of whether – or how – peace can be restored. The Tribunes are threatening to cast Coriolanus to his death from the Tarpeian rock, while Coriolanus prefers to die fighting there in the streets. Menenius, the propelling character, wants to quell the riot. The sequence receives its focus from his goal: *Can Menenius restore order?* The reasonable course of action, Menenius assumes, is to stop the riot quickly, but to his dismay the Tribunes use the opportunity to inflame the people further and end by sentencing Coriolanus to death. Not until the sequence's climax when the Tribunes, the Aediles, and the people have been beaten off the stage, does any kind of calm ensue. At this point Coriolanus withdraws.

This and the final sequence of the frame divide at line 262, where the Tribunes return, bringing their animosity with them. Shakespeare shapes the frame's third sequence as a persuading sequence, giving Menenius the task of convincing Sicinius and Brutus to "proceed by process." In their initial position statement the Tribunes revive their demand that Coriolanus "shall be thrown down the Tarpeian rock / With rigorous hands . . . Law shall scorn him further trial." They are adamant in this position, and Menenius must turn them away from it. He pleads eloquently against this demand over several beats and wins a concession from Brutus and Sicinius, who ultimately agree to let Coriolanus "answer by a lawful form, / In peace." This concession gives the sequence its reversal.

The frame's key sequence is unquestionably sequence 1. The effectiveness with which Coriolanus has been lured into a trap becomes apparent the moment the Tribunes arrest him, their sinister purpose made clear by Sicinius, when he personally attempts to seize Coriolanus in his grip. Though Shakespeare allows himself another 150 lines to "complete" this action, spinning it out into a frame, the subsequent sequences are reactive; they merely make concrete the implications of the climax of sequence 1 – that Coriolanus has given the Tribunes a degree of power they did not before possess, thereby creating a situation from which he can extricate himself only with immense difficulty.

It seems unlikely at first that the second sequence could take the tension higher. Nothing that happens after the cry of treason rivals it in shock value, and is not meant to: it remains only for the Tribunes to take Coriolanus into custody. If Shakespeare had been using the inverted intensification, the remaining sequences would both have been cast in the decrescent. But Shakespeare wants to carry the tension higher here. Having left room for further intensification, he now brings to the fore those aspects of the situation that are latent in it – first, that Coriolanus denies the Tribunes' authority to arrest him; second, that Coriolanus has the support of the Patricians against the Tribunes; and third, that the Tribunes and the Aediles lack the physical strength to apprehend Coriolanus. Their attempt to do more than accuse him carries the action to a new crest. "Let us stand to our authority, / Or let us lose it," they say, prepared to push the matter to its breaking point: "Bear him to th' rock Tarpeian, and from thence / Into destruction cast him." This, too, is an intensification – a far more dangerous threat than the "seize him" of the previous sequence. Above all, the methods of self-defense have been accelerated to new levels: whereas earlier Coriolanus had merely brushed the Tribunes aside, now he must use his sword. The second mutiny, obviously, should be given a stronger accent than the first, and this means that the stage fight cannot degenerate into a mêlée. Again in *Coriolanus* 3.1, then, the frame opens with the most explosive sequence, which contains a key point of the story, while the point of highest intensity in the frame's action is reached in a reactive sequence that follows the key episode. Only in the third sequence does the tension slacken off.

Thus, two different effects can be achieved by placing the key sequence at the beginning of the frame. Either (as in the inverted frame analyzed previously) the climax coincides with the climax of the key sequence, in which case the frame will peak early, with its later sequences pitched in the decrescent. Or (as in the form being examined here) the power generated in the key sequence may be used to push the crescendo a step higher in a subsequent sequence, so that the impact of the frame is sustained and even intensified.

IV

We shall discuss just one more example of the way Shakespeare structures the action of a frame – it can be described as an ABA structure, and we find it in *Measure for Measure* in the two scenes in which Isabella attempts to persuade Angelo to free her brother, as well as in the paired scenes in *Hamlet* where Claudius tries to calm the raging Laertes. This fourth way of handling intensification in a frame involves the combination of two very powerful sequences, separated by a brief and usually ancillary episode that allows time for emotions aroused in the opening sequence to change before the characters are seen again. Because the ancillary sequence in the middle has a different setting, the frame normally spans several scenes. This frame structure always has a rising action, the third and last sequence being naturally more powerful than the first. But the first and third sequences unfold as a pair, in the sense that they are populated by the same characters and the situation in the third sequence is a continuation of the first.

Let us look more closely at the frame in which Isabella approaches Angelo. The frame contains three sequences – 2.2.1–186, 2.3.1–42, and 2.4.1–187. The first is a persuading sequence, in which Isabella begs Angelo to spare the life of her brother Claudio. Angelo refuses, but at the end of the sequence, he finds himself desiring "to hear her speak again / And feast upon her eyes." After Isabella's departure, Shakespeare inserts an ancillary sequence, in which Duke Vincentio, disguised as a friar, interviews Claudio's imprisoned fiancée Juliet (2.3.1–42): in this sequence we meet Juliet, see her repentence, and see it "tried" by the Duke (who will later also test Claudio, Isabella, and Angelo). Angelo now reappears on stage awaiting Isabella's return. During the intervening time provided by the change of scene, his desire for her has increased substantially, and he will now be the propelling character in another persuading sequence (2.4.1–187), wherein he urges Isabella to "redeem thy brother / By yielding up thy body to my will." The earlier situation is repeated in the later sequence, in that Isabella comes a second time to inquire whether Angelo will release Claudio, but the later sequence acquires greater force from Angelo's new proposition. *Both* sequences are typical key sequences: they dramatize significant moments in the play's plot, they are pitched at a high intensity, and they stand out from the minor sequences adjacent to them. This is still another way in which Shakespeare creates dramatic power in the frame: he doubles the number of key sequences in the frame's action.

The sequences between Claudius and Laertes in act 4 of *Hamlet* also illustrate this kind of frame. Taken in its entirety the frame concerns the effects of Polonius's death upon his children; consequently, it opens with the poignant mad scene of Ophelia (4.5.1–96), which forms an introductory sequence to this frame: Gertrude and Claudius observe Ophelia's "meditation" and then comment upon it. Ophelia's exit is followed by her brother's entrance: Laertes storms the palace seeking revenge for the dead Polonius, initiating the first of the frame's key sequences (4.5.96–220). Claudius counters Laertes' verbal attack with the defense that Hamlet, not he, is guilty of the murder, and the action of the sequence builds toward the moment at which Laertres submits to arbitration. The sequence is fairly powerful, for in it rebellion threatens to break out in the kingdom and Claudius's life is in danger; moreover, its crucial role in the plot makes it more than a simple intensifying sequence – this sequence certainly has all the properties of a key sequence.

Next comes the ancillary sequence (4.6.1–34). Laertes has exited with Claudius and the adjudicators, leaving pending the question of whether Claudius can calm his rage. At this point Horatio is discovered, in another location, conversing with the sailors who brings news of Hamlet. This sequence prepares us for news that Claudius will receive when he and Laertes return to the stage – that Hamlet is back in England. Laertes and Claudius now re-enter, with Laertes in a calmer, more receptive mood. The stage is set for the dramatic persuasion sequence in which Claudius makes an ally of Laertes (4.7.1–194). This second of the paired sequences carries the tension higher, for in it Claudius draws Laertes into a plot to murder Hamlet.

This pairing of key sequences is especially useful in actions which must telescope the rapid growth of some emotion. Angelo's lust would seem unreal if he were transformed in a single episode from a man who "scarce confesses that his blood flows" to one who is overwhelmed by passion. But with the sequence in which Angelo is first infected by Isabella's beauty separated from that in which he undertakes to seduce her, we unconsciously accept the fact that his passion has been elevated during the intervening period of time. So with Laertes – because he spends time at an offstage meeting with Claudius, we can believe that his emotions have had time (and reason) to cool.

Shakespeare uses the same technique to suggest the growth of Othello's jealousy in the frame that dramatizes the famous temptation. Iago reports his suspicions of Desdemona's supposed infidelity to Othello in sequence 1 (3.3.93–279). Then, in sequence 2, Emilia and Iago are occupied with the handkerchief Iago has asked Emilia to steal (3.3.279–333). Othello is offstage during this sequence, which leaves time for his emotions to begin seething. When he returns for sequence 3 (3.3.333–480) consumed by thoughts of his wife's "stol'n hours of lust," we are inclined to accept the transformation.

Though there are two key sequences and though we have used the lettering ABA to describe them, the important factor in this type of frame is that there is a rising action – not of course the rising action of the standard frame where everything builds toward one key sequence but a rising action in which Shakespeare tops one key sequence with another. The danger to be avoided in staging this kind of a frame is that of treating the ABA configuration as a triptych, with two side panels flanking a centerpiece. There are two problems with this approach, which has a wide following.[3] First, by *centerpiece* one ought to mean the largest or longest or most significant unit in the group, but here the central unit is the *least* significant. Whether it is a full sequence or merely a beat, the central unit is invariably ancillary to the rising action and could be eliminated without causing confusion, except that the time gap it covers is essential to the structure. The elements that hold it in place are poetic and thematic; from the standpoint of the action, the central unit *could* have come elsewhere. In fact (another reason why the word *centerpiece* is misleading), the interpolated sequence generally has dramatic affinities with some forthcoming action, which it presages. Horatio's meeting with the sailors while Claudius and Laertes confer offstage, for example, looks forward to the graveyard frame in which Hamlet's promise to return is fulfilled. This brief "centerpiece" containing the sailors' report is more ancillary than central to the Claudius/Laertes sequences which surround it.

Beyond this quibble about the doubtful centrality of B in this ABA configuration is a more crucial fact regarding the true relationship between the A panels. To view them as *equal entities* is to deny the elements of movement and direction that are present. Energies are building up. The "side panels" of the temptation frame in *Othello* hardly stand side by side on a horizontal baseline. Every unit in each sequence stands higher along a line that slants steadily upward, and the force with which Othello attacks Iago in the second sequence (A^2) is many times greater than that with which he questioned his Ancient in the first (A^1). Provided these qualifications are understood, the graphic ABA formula might serve as a handy term of reference for this type of frame.

To sum up, then. The frame is a plot unit, but one with a dual nature: the frame is *also* a unit of action. If the build of that action is neglected, the stage production will be dull, no matter how engaging its plot. The performance must reflect the accents Shakespeare uses when he turns narrative into drama. Because frames are made up of sequences, each of which has its own climax, the basic accents in any frame coincide with the climactic moment in each sequence, the climax of the key sequence being of course especially prominent. Second, since sequences are conceived to form frames, these climactic accents are distributed in various ways. The positioning of the key sequence becomes an important element in the structure of the frame, as well as the factor that determines where the crescendos develop in the overall rhythmic structure of the play. The key sequence may come toward the end of the frame (the standard situation) or at the beginning (the inverted type). In either case, because by definition the key sequence is pitched at a higher intensity than other sequences, it normally effects the frame's climax. But when the key sequence is brought forward, it may be used as a springboard, infusing sufficient force into the following sequence to turn that subsequent sequence into the frame's climactic one: tension is sustained for the space of a full sequence before it is dispersed. Finally, in some frames, the impact is achieved by dividing an action into two stages, separated by an intervening but subordinate action, with each of the two main sequences pitched as a key sequence. Since the intervening action allows time for tensions to increase, the second of the key sequences will naturally surpass the first in power, and the overall build, with its two intense sequences, is an effective means of creating an overwhelming impact.

It strikes one as more than a coincidence that the era which freed itself from the Shakespearean stage practices of the nineteenth century was also the era which first began to see in the plays units intermediate between the scene and the act – scene groups, so to speak. The scenery that the nineteenth century luxuriated in cluttered the stage and thereby impeded the flow of the action. With the scenery gone, the delays involved in changing that scenery went too, and the inherent flow of the action from scene to scene became more apparent; consequently, people both in and out of the theater began searching for the nature of supra-scenic structures that they now sensed were present in the texts. However, what remained behind of the nineteenth-century tradition has proved as crippling as what was disposed of. We freed ourselves from their approach to scenery but not from idolatry of the scene. The encumbered stage which was frequently accented by the raising and lowering of the curtain fixed the scene as Shakespeare's primary dramatic unit in the minds of generations of his admirers.

This mindset has a distorting effect not only in modern-day attempts to define the structure of individual actions: it virtually negates any attempt to systematize current intuitions that Shakespeare has clustered his basic units into larger blocks of action. The intuition is there, not just in scholars but in theater people as well: many in both fields have labored to bracket units into larger groups. But their basic building block is invariably the scene, and consequently their analysis, which started with a valid insight, is predictably distorted by the necessity to structure it on a false foundation. The results have invariably been confusion, caused by the imposition of structures alien to the real structure of Shakespeare's plays.

To understand the nature of these larger units one must begin with an understanding of the parts of which the whole play consists. Essentially, therefore, this is a book about the sequence. We have tried to demonstrate that the sequence exists as a unit, is indeed Shakespeare's most essential unit of action: one might almost say Shakespeare actually "thinks" in sequences. We have shown, too, that sequences are constructed of units of motivation, or beats, examining both the nature of beats by themselves and the way they function within the sequence. And we have indicated how sequences are combined into frame units. If this study provides the groundwork for deeper penetration into the process through which Shakespeare shapes and combines his units of action, it will have achieved one of its purposes. It will have achieved another if it persuades actors and directors to look for and use the units Shakespeare was working with when he constructed his action. But if it does nothing else than to stimulate even one playwright to produce action that comes as alive as Shakespeare's does, that alone will have justified its existence.

Notes

1 Scene versus sequence

1 Mark Rose, *Shakespearean Design* (Cambridge, Mass.: Harvard University Press, 1972), pp. viii and 23. Similar definitions are offered by Jackson Barry and Kathleen George, with an even stronger emphasis on location as the factor which determines scene boundaries. See Jackson C. Barry, *Dramatic Structure: The Shaping of an Experience* (Los Angeles: University of California Press, 1970), pp. 88–9; Kathleen George, *Rhythm in Drama* (Pittsburgh: University of Pittsburgh Press, 1980), p. 106.

2 Rose, pp. 44–9. James Hirsh, *The Structure of Shakespearean Scenes* (New Haven: Yale University Press, 1981), pp. 117–207.

3 Derek Traversi, *An Approach to Shakespeare*, 3rd edn. (Garden City, N.Y.: Anchor Books, 1969), I, 215.

4 Waldo McNeir, "Structure and Theme in the First Tavern Scene (II.iv) of *I Henry IV*," in *Pacific Coast Studies in Shakespeare*, ed. Waldo F. McNeir and Thelma N. Greenfield (Eugene, Ore., 1966), p. 90. McNeir's line numbering is that of the Cambridge edition of W. G. Clarke and W. A. Wright (1863–6).

5 Emrys Jones, *Scenic Form in Shakespeare* (Oxford: Clarendon Press, 1971), p. 30.

6 For easy reference we have used the scene designations employed in *The Riverside Shakespeare* – that is, 5.6, 5.7, and 5.8. These traditional designations have been disputed. For example, James Hirsh argues quite rightly that a consistent editor, discerning that the stage is emptied after 5.7.13 and again after 5.7.23, should reflect in his printed text the new scenes initiated by the playwright at these points. See *The Structure of Shakespearean Scenes*, pp. 45, 187, 220. This scoring would bring the total number of scenes in this action to five rather than three. Our point remains valid whichever way time resolves the dispute.

7 Directors tend to use the same word for different kinds of units (basically they have one term, *unit*, synonyms for which are *subscene, motivational unit, beat*), and the term itself gives no clue as to the size or function of the particular unit being isolated.

8 For example, in *Theatrical Direction: The Basic Techniques* (Boston: Allyn & Bacon, 1971), David Welker advocates that "different directors might be expected to draw the dividing lines at different points, adjusted to their tastes and habits of thinking" (pp. 49–50).

9 Rose, p. 25.
10 Robert Hapgood, "The transcendent bard in transition," *TLS* (August 25–31, 1989), p. 928.

2 The beat defined

1 According to American theatrical tradition, this term *beat* originated as a corruption of the word *bit*, used to describe any small but unified segment of an action. We have drawn upon theater usage for this and another indispensable term, *build*, because we have not found formal substitutes. For actors who follow Stanislavski, however, the word *beat* has a slightly different meaning, since for them the beat is not inherent in the text but comes into being during their personal analysis of the role (two actors playing opposite one another in the same scene would not necessarily be using the same beats). We argue that in Shakespeare such divisions are objective, not subjective.
2 Shakespeare had introduced Edward's intention as early as 1.3.36–9, where we are told that "he desires to make atonement/Between the Duke of Gloucester and your brothers,/And between them and my Lord Chamberlain,/And sent to warn them to his royal presence."
3 See, for example, John Fletcher, *The Pilgrim*, act 4, scene 3, in *The Works of Beaumont and Fletcher*, ed. Alexander Dyce (London, 1845), 8:74–5.
4 Militating against a too-heavy reliance on exits and entrances as indicators of beat boundaries is the fact that characters occasionally enter or leave in the middle of a beat. The introductory beat of the ballroom scene gives a warning of this: the Second Servant leaves the stage; Antony and Potpan rush on. Here a clear beat function overrides the normally divisive quality of character regrouping to unify these comings and goings.
5 Benvolio's "Away, be gone, the sport is at the best" initiates the first of a series of exit beats that remove the guests from the stage at the end of the sequence. The beats in this concluding section are brief, for motivation necessarily shifts quickly as Shakespeare gives various groups of characters separate excuses to depart (see, for example, 1.5.119–24, 125–7, 143–4). Exit beats are discussed in a later chapter.
6 June Schlueter and James Lusardi study the kinds and degrees of originality different actors have brought to the same role through creative interpretations of line and speech motives. See *Reading Shakespeare in Performance: "King Lear"* (Madison, N. J.: Fairleigh Dickinson University Press, 1990).

3 Ancillary beats

1 The reader can explore the difference between ancillary and sequential beats for himself by comparing two beats from *Julius Caesar*, both of which record the fate of Portia – the ancillary beat 4.3.143–58, where Brutus informs Cassius of Portia's death as a postscript to their quarrel (sequence 4.3.1–162) and the

sequential beat 4.3.180–95, where Messala's report to Brutus of Portia's death serves an integral function in the building action (sequence 4.3.163–238).

2 When enormous gaps of time are to be traversed, some stronger device than the interval beat will, of course, be called into play – a Chorus to make apologies for the inadequacies of the stage or perhaps the insertion of a full sequence rather than a mere beat between the "earlier" exit and "later" entrance.

3 For additional interval beats see *As You Like It* 2.7.173–90; *Richard II* 4.1.158–61; II *Henry IV* 4.1.6–18, 4.1.181–222; *Julius Caesar* 2.1.101–11; *Othello* 2.1.60–5; *Hamlet* 2.2.54–8, 4.5.17–20; *Antony and Cleopatra* 3.13.41–6.

4 Emrys Jones, *Scenic Form in Shakespeare* (Oxford: Clarendon Press, 1971), p. 31. Jones's line numbers are to Peter Alexander's single-volume edition (1964 reprint).

5 Mark Rose, *Shakespearean Design* (Cambridge, Mass.: Harvard University Press, 1972), p. 75.

6 For an interesting analysis of the relationships between these two sequences and the Lady Macduff scene which precedes them, see Jones, *Scenic Form*, pp. 220–1. For beats interpolated in clusters, see *Hamlet* 3.3.1–26, 27–35; *Julius Caesar* 1.2.1–11, 12–24; *King Lear* 5.3.176–200, 200–22. For interpolated beats between sequences that have been given separate scene designations (and, incidentally, also fill intervals), see *King Lear* 2.3.1–21 and *Julius Caesar* 3.3.1–38. See also *As You Like It* 3.4.33–9, *Richard III* 1.1.121–44, *Julius Caesar* 3.1.276–97, *Macbeth* 4.1.139–56.

7 James Hirsh, *The Structure of Shakespearean Scenes* (New Haven: Yale University Press, 1981).

4 The introductory beat

1 Edmund's "Thou, Nature, art my goddess" soliloquy (*King Lear* 1.2.1–22) comes too early in the play to involve expository updating, but it "makes subsequent actions plausible" and should be studied in this context. This introductory beat points to Edmund's spiritual bastardy. The beat is not an isolated entity but an essential part of the sequence it leads into. Were this introductory beat placed later in the play, the audience would have a difficult time following the action of the sequence.

2 See J. L. Styan, *Shakespeare's Stagecraft* (Cambridge: Cambridge University Press, 1967), p. 204: "Although printed as if it starts another scene, the speech properly marks the climax of what went before." Bernard Beckerman ignores the soliloquy altogether when analyzing Lady Macbeth's persuasion. Since he refers to that persuasion as "the second half of Act I, scene vii," presumably he considers the soliloquy (the implied "first half") an independent entity. "Explorations in Shakespeare's Drama," *Shakespeare Quarterly* 29 (1978), 142.

5 The concluding beat

1 *Coriolanus* 2.1 contains four sequences: 2.1.1–96, where Menenius disputes with the Tribunes; 2.1.97–161, where Volumnia announces her son's return; 2.1.162–204, the celebratory procession (the scene's key sequence); and 2.1.205–70, where Brutus and Sicinius determine to thwart Coriolanus. See chapter 13, section 1, for a fuller analysis.

2 James L. Calderwood's assumption is typical: Hamlet's soliloquies, "though not narrative, are a kind of Inset . . . the soliloquies are independent of the plot line." *To Be and Not to Be: Negation and Metadrama in "Hamlet"* (New York: Columbia University Press, 1983), p. 154.

6 The intensifying beat

1 *Romeo and Juliet* 1.5.1–144. See chapter 2, section II, for an analysis of its beat structure.

2 The *Coriolanus* scene breaks down into three sequences: 4.5.1–49; 4.5.50–147; 4.5.148–235.

3 Ralph Berry, *Shakespearean Structures* (Totowa, N.J.: Barnes & Noble Books, 1981), p. 69.

4 Much more can be said about the psychology and character of Richard as revealed in this sequence. For a fuller discussion, see A. P. Rossiter, *Angel with Horns* (New York: Theatre Arts Books, 1961), pp. 13–22; Bernard Spivack, *Shakespeare and the Allegory of Evil* (New York: Columbia University Press, 1958), pp. 386–407.

5 Bernard Beckerman analyzes *Macbeth* 1.7 as a classic instance of persuasion in "Explorations in Shakespeare's Drama," *Shakespeare Quarterly* 29 (1978), 142–5.

6 Matthew Black, *Poetic Drama as Mirror of the Will* (New York: Barnes & Noble Books, 1977), p. 41.

7 These echoing lines occur in Q1. In the Folio version, Roderigo's confirming statement has been altered to "I'll sell all my land."

8 Spivack, p. 424.

9 The scene's introductory sequence, 2.2.1 to 2.3.63, builds to line 47, where Cassio agrees to join Iago's party of gallants, and concludes with Iago's soliloquy.

7 The dramatic question

1 See Mark Rose, *Shakespearean Design* (Cambridge: Harvard University Press, 1972), p. 26. See also pp. 8–9: "By modern standards, however, Shakespeare's techniques for the portrayal of response are notably static. The plays tend to show us discrete moments of intense emotion, 'speaking pictures' of characters fearful, despairing, in love, jealous, raging, or rejoicing. Normally the reactive moment is dwelt upon for a full realization of the emotion: . . . Often these

moments become little tableaus . . . What I am suggesting is that the presentation of character in Shakespeare is perhaps less like a modern film in which the figures are in constant motion than an album of snapshot stills to be contemplated in sequence."

2 We quote Bernard Beckerman's definition of the segment from his *Dynamics of Drama: Theory and Method of Analysis* (New York: Columbia University Press, 1970), pp. 89–90. Though Beckerman employs the term *segment* in a work that focuses upon modern drama, his *segment* has many features in common with our *sequence*, in particular the notion that a segment of a scene can encompass a complete action. His term gives the impression of a static unit, however. *Sequence* captures the dynamic element we wish to stress.

3 Michael Goldman makes an interesting distinction between the action of the characters, the audience, and the actors, which he dubs *praxis, theoria,* and *poiesis:* "It seems fair to say that when we use the word 'action' in its normal critical sense to describe the experience of a play, we are in fact referring to three distinct types of action, all of which influence us, and which combine and complement each other at every moment, often in the most subtle ways. For this reason, they are ordinarily confused. Certainly, many difficulties of criticism arise from not distinguishing them. They are: the actions the characters perform; the action of the audience's mind in responding to and trying to possess the events it watches; and finally the actions by which the actors create and sustain their roles. Most discussions of drama run the first two together and ignore the third." *Acting and Action in Shakespearean Tragedy* (Princeton: Princeton University Press, 1985), pp. 11–12. This distinction is useful but it is not exactly the distinction we are making here. We argue that there is *one* action, which Shakespeare constructs when writing the play and that that action is understood from three different perspectives: the *characters* of course know less than the *audience*, the audience less than the *actors*, who, sharing the perspective of the playwright, know in advance how an action will end and can supply adequate pointing as it unfolds.

4 A problem arises for Anthony Brennan in *Shakespeare's Dramatic Structures* (London: Routledge & Kegan Paul, 1986), pp. 26–32, when he compares Richard's wooing of Anne with his wooing, through the deposed Queen, of a second wife, the young Elizabeth. The first of these sequences runs concurrently with a scene and so presents Brennan with no problems, but the second sequence occurs in a scene that contains four sequences. Because Brennan believes that the *scene* is Shakespeare's dramatic unit and feels it necessary to compare *complete* scenes, he is unwittingly comparing one action with four actions and cannot escape the awkwardness. The like units, both persuading sequences, are 1.2 (all of it) and 4.4.199–431 (4.4's third sequence). This is a telling example of the way that the current lack of terminology obscures what should be obvious, even for commentators like Brennan, whose intuitions are correct and whose examination of the two actions is sensitive. Scholars studying Shakespeare's units so often confuse grapes with grapefruit.

5 This comment by Sir Stephen Scroop on his sovereign's lack of constancy (*Richard II* 3.2.135–6) is further evidence of the consciousness with which Shakespeare works with the reversal.

6 This observation has been made often enough about Shakespeare's larger units. Emrys Jones mentions it briefly, for example, in *Scenic Form in Shakespeare* (Oxford: Clarendon Press, 1971), pp. 14–15. But there and elsewhere the issue is generally raised in connection with scenes or plays – never with regard to sequences.

7 From Giraldi Cinthio, *Hecatommithi*, Decad. III, Nov. 7, trans. W. Parr in *Shakespeare's Library: A Collection of the Ancient Novels, Romances, Legends, Poems, and Histories, Used by Shakespeare as the Foundation of His Dramas ...,"* Vol II, ed. J. Payne Collier. (London: Thomas Rodd, 1850).

8 Observing and meditating sequences

1 We are not the first to perceive the similarities among seemingly distinct actions which render them instructive examples of a particular kind of unit. Bernard Beckerman argues that when constructing actions all dramatists depend heavily on certain activities, and he lists four or five important ones: "Just as there are character types which recur in play after play, so there are segmental types which run throughout dramatic history. Our example dramatizes a farewell. There are also persuasion, confessional, messenger, and many other segmental types." *Dynamics of Drama: Theory and Method of Analysis* (New York: Alfred A. Knopf, 1970), p. 69. But the haphazard nature of this list indicates an intuition that has not yet been seriously thought out. Our hope is to bring more order to the discussion of this subject.

2 Powerful as this action is, it occupies only one-third of a scene. *Othello* 4.1 breaks down into three sequences: 4.1.1–74, where Iago reports to Othello that Cassio has been "blabbing" of his conquest, 4.1.74–213, where at Iago's urging Othello stands aside to observe Cassio mock his mistress, and 4.1.213–82, where Lodovico brings Othello the unwelcome news that Cassio is to have his place.

9 Reporting and interrogating sequences

1 Commentators have in fact extracted a vast array of episodes involving messengers – "anonymous, characterless bearers of news," be they servants, heralds, ambassadors, courtiers, or noblemen – which illustrate Shakespeare's versatility in manipulating the report. But people analyzing reporting in Shakespeare tend to focus on reports delivered by bona fide messengers, bit-part players who appear once and are never seen again and who have little identity apart from their message; there has been little study of reports delivered by Shakespeare's *major* characters. Further, the reports studied vary in length from one line to a hundred, and no discrimination is made between the types of unit within which such reports occur. See Wolfgang Clemen,

"Shakespeare's Use of the Messenger's Report," pp. 96–123 in *Shakespeare's Dramatic Art: Collected Essays* (London: Methuen & Co., Ltd., 1972); Gary J. Scrimgeour, "The Messenger as a Dramatic Device in Shakespeare," *Shakespeare Quarterly*, 19 (1968), 41–54. See also J. C. McCloskey, "Plot Device of the False Report," *Shakespeare Association Bulletin*, 21 (1926), 147–58; Marion Perret, "Shakespeare's Use of Messengers in *Antony and Cleopatra*," *Drama Survey*, 5 (1966), 67–72; Ray L. Heffner, Jr., "The Messengers in Shakespeare's *Antony and Cleopatra*," *ELH*, 43 (1976), 154–62. Also note Francis Berry, *The Shakespeare Inset: Word and Picture*, 1965 (Arcturus edition, Carbondale: Southern Illinois University Press, 1971), an interesting study of material that is reported rather than dramatized.

2 John Addington Symonds, *Shakespeare's Predecessors in the English Drama*, 1884. (New edn. London: Smith, Elder & Co., 1900), p. 193.

3 For further analysis of this scene from a dramaturgical point of view, see Bernard Beckerman, "Some Problems in Teaching Shakespeare's Plays as Works of Drama," *Teaching Shakespeare*, ed. Walter Edens *et al.* (Princeton: Princeton University Press, 1977), pp. 305–16.

4 Arthur Brooke, "The Tragical History of Romeus and Juliet" in *Shakespeare's Library: A Collection of the Ancient Novels, Romances, Legends, Poems, and Histories Used by Shakespeare as the Foundation of His Dramas* (London: Thomas Rodd, 1850), II, 25–6.

5 Juliet's joy will of course be short-lived, and it is fascinating to see how Shakespeare uses the Nurse's report in 3.2 to elicit the contrary emotion of grief. For a comparison of these two sequences from the point of view of design, see James Hirsh, *The Structure of Shakespearean Scenes* (New Haven: Yale University Press, 1981), pp. 151–4. In Hirsh's system both sequences are classified as two-part scenes, because the Nurse does not enter until after Juliet's opening soliloquy. As we have tried to demonstrate, however, changes in character groupings are not reliable indicators of unit divisions. In both sequences Juliet's soliloquy supplies the introductory beat and should not be regarded as independent of the other beats in the sequence.

6 Remember that Shakespeare makes it part of Angelo's temptation to accuse Isabella of cruelty in refusing to save her brother (see 2.4.109).

7 The Isabella/Claudio action is generally assumed to fill the whole scene, but in fact it occupies only 127 of the scene's 269 lines. There are two other sequences in the scene – 3.1.1–47, in which Duke Vincentio persuades Claudio to "be absolute for death," and 3.1.174–269, wherein the Duke enlists Isabella's support for Mariana's cause.

8 Ironically, because Edmund twice expresses an intention "to do some good" and eventually does it, critical custom awards him full credit for turning the action back to this center. Moreover, having made Edmund responsible for the release of the King, commentators invent elaborate theories to account for his repentance. According to one version, he bestirs himself to save Lear and Cordelia because the deaths of Goneril and Regan on his account persuade him he was loved (J. Stampfer, "The Catharsis of *King Lear*," *Shakespeare Survey*, 13

[1960], 1–10). Too much emphasis on "the new Edmund" can be distorting. Certainly Edmund's cooperation allows for greater realism. Lear's entrance is more plausible because he has been sent for, because the persons dispatched to find him have Edmund's orders for his release, and because the flurry of action allows for a time interval that suggests a real search for the King. Nonetheless Edmund's proves to be a secondary intervention. Long before Edmund acts on his better instincts Kent has initiated the search for Lear.

9 Shakespeare's use of Kent in 5.3 is also noted by Michael Goldman: Kent "wants to reveal himself to his master as part of the grand finale . . . [but] the tragedy has outstripped Kent's scenario. He really can't accompany Lear here, no matter how he tries. The end he has promised us has to be scrapped. It is all yet another device . . . for giving us a sense of having gone further than we could have expected, and, consequently, as far as we can go." *Shakespeare and the Energies of Drama* (Princeton: Princeton University Press, 1972), pp. 102–5. William Matchett offers a perceptive line-by-line reading of this sequence in "Some Dramatic Techniques in *King Lear*," *Shakespeare: The Theatrical Dimension*, ed. Philip McGuire and David A. Samuelson, AMS Studies in the Renaissance No. 3 (New York: AMS Press, Inc., 1979), pp. 196–208.

10 Persuading sequences

1 Robert Y. Turner, *Shakespeare's Apprenticeship*, (Chicago: University of Chicago Press, 1974), pp. 82 ff.

2 J. L. Styan, *Shakespeare's Stagecraft* (Cambridge: Cambridge University Press, 1967), p. 205.

3 Brian Vickers, "Teaching *Coriolanus*: The Importance of Perspective," in *Teaching Shakespeare*, ed. Walter Edens *et al.* (Princeton: Princeton University Press, 1977), pp. 257–9.

4 Note that in this context *instinct* lacks the modern connotations. To obey natural instinct here means to follow one's highest instincts, not to allow the passions full sway (*that* is exactly what landed Coriolanus in this predicament).

5 For other examples of successful persuasions in Shakespeare, see *Othello* 1.1.1–183 (*Can Roderigo persuade Brabantio that his daughter has eloped?*); 1.3.301–404 (*Can Iago persuade Roderigo to follow Desdemona to Cyprus?*); 3.3.41–92 (*Can Desdemona persuade Othello to recall Cassio?*); *Hamlet* 4.7.1–194 (*Can Claudius persuade Laertes to join his cause?*); 3.4.1–217 (*Can Hamlet persuade Gertrude to acknowledge her sins?*); *Julius Caesar* 3.2.62–271 (*Can Antony persuade the mob to desert Brutus?*); *Macbeth* 1.7.1–82 (*Can Lady Macbeth persuade her husband to murder Duncan?*). Lady Macbeth is not the only character who successfully persuades another to commit murder. Macbeth himself persuades two malcontents to kill Banquo: initially reluctant, they agree under Macbeth's appeal to their manhood to "perform what you command us" (3.1.71–141). In *The Tempest*, Antonio convinces Sebastian to take Alonzo's life (2.1.191–327). Cassius persuades first Brutus (1.2.1–177), then Casca (1.3.1–164), to assassinate Julius Caesar. Menenius, in contrast,

persuades the Tribunes to spare Coriolanus's life (3.1.262–334), just as these Tribunes, later, persuade Menenius to beg Coriolanus to spare theirs (5.1.1– 74). In *Measure for Measure* Lucio begs Isabella to seek a reprieve for Claudio (1.4.1–90). Successful persuasions all, each ends with the resisting character succumbing to the persuader's arguments.

11 Disputing sequences

1 As the pressure on the responding character increases, so does his resistance. Consequently, as Bernard Beckerman points out, when the playwright works in the persuading mode, he must find ways to subordinate the opposition, powerful as it may be, so that emphasis remains on the objectives of the persuader. Usually, writes Beckerman, "the playwright avoids too explicit an articulation of the opposition, its basis being hinted at rather than fully explored. In the *Macbeth* segment, Macbeth says much less than Lady Macbeth. He communicates his resistance more through silence than through anything said. Shaw uses a contrasting method in *Saint Joan*. When Joan tries to persuade Charles to be crowned at Rheims (scene ii), Charles's resistance, instead of taking the form of silence, assumes the form of unconventional responses." Bernard Beckerman, "Explorations in Shakespeare's Drama," *Shakespeare Quarterly* 29 (1978), 143. The resisting character may argue, but he has less chance of usurping the dominant position than he would have in an out-and-out quarrel. The persuader manages to retain control, at least up until the climax. If from the very beginning the resisting character mounts implacable opposition, it makes more sense to speak of disputing.

2 These are not the only forms of the disputing sequence. Shakespeare creates battles of wit, for example, where the characters merely banter, as with Touchstone and Corin in *As You Like It* (3.2.11–85) or in the dispute between Jaques and Orlando in that same play (3.2.251–94), where Shakespeare treats us to a bout of "flyting." But the more important, more essentially dramatic examples of disputing seem to us the ones most worth exploring here.

3 Iago is a master of the technique of deflecting accusations. He will use it again on Roderigo in another of the play's disputing sequences (4.2.172–245). When Roderigo charges that Iago "every day daff'st me with some device" so that "I have wasted myself out of my means," Iago mends the rift by employing Roderigo to murder Cassio. That sequence ends with the two opponents exiting arm in arm, Roderigo content to "hear further reason for this" and Iago promising he "shall be satisfied." The diversion allows for a reconciliation.

4 Richard David's *Shakespeare in the Theatre* (Cambridge: Cambridge University Press, 1978), p. 19, stresses the importance of this contrast between Brutus and Cassius: "As John Wood, who acted Brutus, later told me, he had come to feel that in the great quarrel scene with Cassius it is Brutus who of the two is the more deeply and bitterly angry. The idea is reasonable enough, but its realisation in practical terms is not easy and at Stratford [in 1972] totally misfired. In place of the original Brutus, a still though quiveringly intense pole

round which the volatile Cassius, simultaneously in violent opposition and held by an inescapable attraction, unceasingly rampaged, we had a second rampager; and a scene, the mainspring of whose effect had been the tension of the contrast, became an indistinguishable mêlée of sound and fury."

13 The frame

1 The phrase "designed group of sequences" seems to us more meaningful than Mark Rose's "designed group of scenes." Many scholars now focus upon the *scene group*, a term used by Rose and Jean Howard but hard to define adequately. What constitutes a scene group? What are the criteria that determine where it begins or terminates? What is its normal length? Mark Rose says only that "the block of related scenes, conceived and designed as a group, is an important structural unit in Shakespeare, an intermediate unit between the scene and the play as a whole." Generally, "the group will correspond in some manner to a complete phase in the action or conception of the play." Sometimes the group will be "designed on exactly the same principles as the scene;" at other times, "a group is formed by an alternating pattern superimposed upon the individual designs of the scenes, as in the opening series of four scenes in *Hamlet*." *Shakespearean Design* (Cambridge, Mass.: Harvard University Press, 1972), pp. 81–94. Is the scene group, then, a unit of action? Jean Howard applies the term to "larger theatrical sequences consisting of several adjoining scenes orchestrated as a single unit and designed to be experienced as such by the viewer." The scenes being joined "seem narratively, thematically, tonally, and visually discrete" but are "orchestrated to evoke from the audience a sustained and, ultimately, unified response," certain aural, visual, or kinetic devices creating the structural links between them. *Shakespeare's Art of Orchestration: Stage Technique and Audience Response* (Urbana: University of Illinois Press, 1984), pp. 136, 147. But the orchestration being examined in the scene group has little to do with the real structural mechanisms through which Shakespeare transforms the narrative into action. What fascinates both Rose and Howard are Shakespeare's unifying techniques. Neither comes to grips with action; in fact, both fail to distinguish action from narrative. Beyond that, the study of scene groups involves a method of analysis shaped by the contemporary reverence for the scene as "the most important unit of construction in Shakespeare's plays." Even though Howard urges scholars to avoid focusing too narrowly upon the scene, the scene remains for her the very unit out of which she builds her groups. The inevitable danger of any approach to units that has the scene as its basis is that the commentator rarely realizes that scenes come in sizes and habitually lumps units of unlike size into a single category – among Howard's scene groups, for example, the unit *King Lear* 2.2–2.4 is of greater magnitude than the unit *Romeo and Juliet* 2.1–2.2. Meaningful statements about Shakespeare's units can be made only by comparing comparable units. Given these problems, we prefer to work instead with *sequence* groups.

2 The rising action occupies only three sequences in 5.1 of *Hamlet*, for example, where Shakespeare establishes the setting with an introductory sequence between two gravediggers (1–60), develops the situation further by bringing Hamlet into the picture to muse upon the impermanence of life (61–216), and climaxes it with Hamlet's discovery that the grave is Ophelia's and his dramatic interruption of her funeral (217–99); so also in *King Lear* 2.4 where Kent's report to Lear of how he came to be in the stocks supplies the introduction (2.4.1–87), Lear's attempt to obtain an explanation of the insult from Regan and Cornwall increases the tension (88–126), and Regan's rejection of his appeal for hospitality for himself and his fifty knights effects the climax (127–309).

3 The "triptych" approach originates with Mark Rose. See, for example, his discussion in *Shakespearean Design* of *Othello* 3.3, pp. 154–7, and of the Claudius/Laertes scenes, pp. 119–20.

Glossary

ABORTED BEAT: Occurs when a character introduces a subject but is abruptly cut off; the beat remains incomplete.

ACTION: Here understood as a unit of a certain magnitude, propelled in a discernible direction by the desires, goals, and objectives of its characters, which advances toward a climax, then enters a stage of decrescence that brings it rapidly to a conclusion. It has as its foundation a single dramatic question and therefore communicates a sense of completeness. The most "pure" unit of action is the sequence; the beat, though a unit of action, is only a component of an action, while the frame, also a unit of action, is derived by combining already completed actions.

ACTION VERSUS NARRATIVE: *Narrative* in this book usually refers to what the story is (that aspect of the plot that can be paraphrased); *action*, how that story is structured.

ANCILLARY BEAT: *See* BEAT, INTERPOLATED BEAT, INTERVAL BEAT, LINKING BEAT.

ANCILLARY SEQUENCE: *See* INTEGRAL VERSUS ANCILLARY SEQUENCE.

BEAT: A group of lines joined together by a common purpose (generally to introduce, intensify, or conclude an action) and thereby distinguishable from other beats with which it is grouped. In each beat a single character is usually given the active or propelling role, this, of course, being differentiated from the secondary or responding role. The structure of the beat derives from the motive of that propelling character. This dominant motive, the *beat motive*, provides momentum and direction, linking the beat to adjacent actions. Additional motives may abound in any beat, but these always operate to support (not challenge) the motive that unifies the beat. Linguistic devices such as the threading of a key word through the beat or the mirroring of an opening line in some closing line are frequently added to give further coherence to the beat unit. *Sequential beats* are those which advance the action of a given sequence or otherwise contribute directly to its development. Among them are *introductory beats, intensifying beats, climactic beats, sustaining beats,* and *concluding beats. Ancillary beats* play no integral part in the build of a given sequence but are inserted to solve other dramaturgical problems. Three types of ancillary beat are distinguished – the *interval beat,* the *interpolated beat,* and the *linking beat.*

CLIMACTIC BEAT: The word *climax* is used here to denote that moment at which the action peaks. Shakespeare may effect the climax abruptly, in one dramatic line, or even in some unspoken reaction between the lines that must be conveyed through the actor's skill. Some sequence climaxes, however, are maintained for a full beat, thus the term *climactic beat.*

CONCLUDING BEAT: A beat which gives a sense of closure to the end of a sequence, summing up the action, removing characters from the stage, or foreshadowing future events. The exit beat and the concluding soliloquy, which often forms a coda at the end of a sequence, are types of concluding beat. Not to be confused with the climax, concluding beats are always decrescent in tone.

DESIGNATED SCENE: A scene labeled as such in the modern printed text.

DRAMATIC QUESTION: The vector of a sequence. The sequence structure usually has two dynamic elements: a propelling force, or intention, and a goal, or climax – the intention provides the question, the goal its answer. The dramatic question, thus defined, offers a concise statement of the action the playwright is working with and therefore that which the actors must articulate. The arc of a motivated sequence, properly formulated, will identify four things: (1) the active or propelling character; (2) that character's objective, toward the fulfillment or failure of which the entire sequence is moving; (3) the means he has chosen to pursue that objective; and (4) the character he is acting upon.

ENCLOSING: The practice of inserting lines near the beginning of a beat which are then echoed toward the end of that beat and which thus identify the unit as an entity. The technique is also employed in the sequence.

ENTRANCE AND EXIT BEATS: One form of the concluding beat; beats designed to bring characters on stage or to effect their departure from it.

FRAME: That unit into which Shakespeare groups his sequences. Frames are actions constructed of complete actions. Every frame contains one key sequence. Other sequences in the frame lead up to it or away from it, fleshing out the key incident with additional details (such subsidiary sequences being identified by their functions – introductory, intensifying, sustaining, or concluding). As a unit of plot, the frame has two complementary functions, a story-telling function and a dramatic function (*see* ACTION VERSUS NARRATIVE).

INTEGRAL VERSUS ANCILLARY SEQUENCE: An integral sequence advances the plot of the frame in which it appears. An ancillary sequence is inserted into the frame for other purposes, usually creating a time interval within which some offstage action can take place, supplying necessary information that the audience must have at the moment, and unifying plot segments by interlocking them to other material.

INTENSIFICATION, IN THE FRAME: The *standard intensification* of a frame is constructed as a conventional rising action composed of (1) an introductory sequence, followed in turn by (2) an intensifying sequence, (3) the key sequence, and (4) a concluding sequence. The climax of the frame coincides with the key sequence. In the *inverted intensification*, the key sequence is moved up to second position immediately following the introductory sequence, so that the audience experiences not a rising action but an immediate explosion and then a period of readjustment in which the remaining sequences of the frame are deliberately subordinated. Tension *decreases*. The climax of the frame again coincides with the key sequence. In the *sustaining intensification*, the key sequence is moved forward, as in the inverted intensification, but it becomes a launching pad for the sequence that follows, which lifts the tension a stage higher, so that here the climax of the frame is separated from the key sequence. *The ABA intensification.* In frames of this type there is again a rising action, but it is essentially different in structure from the standard one in that here the climax is sustained beyond the key sequence by the addition of a second key sequence. This type of frame intensification involves the combination of two powerful sequences, separated by a brief and usually ancillary episode that allows time for emotions aroused in the opening sequence to change before the characters are seen again (because the ancillary sequence has a different setting, the ABA frame normally spans several scenes). This frame structure always has a rising action, the third and last sequence being naturally more powerful than the first. But the first and third sequences unfold as a pair, in the sense that they are populated by the same characters and the situation in the third sequence is a continuation of the first.

INTENSIFICATION, IN THE SEQUENCE: Shakespeare employs several different but oft-repeated patterns in building the rising action of a sequence. The *chronological or narrative intensification* relies heavily upon the story itself to build the action: incidents are recorded as they occur, usually in chronological order, one incident per beat, with a different mix of characters for each incident. These episodes or vignettes that make up the narrative usually abound in realistic detail (see the Gadshill robbery sequence, *I Henry IV* 2.2.1–111). The *cumulative intensification* is achieved through repetition, the same situation being repeated with variations in each successive beat, the last version being the most intense. Often there is a presiding figure whose expectations are thwarted in the final beat of the series (see *King Lear* 1.1.1–139). In the *motivated intensification*, usually between two characters in close-up, tension is created by pitting an active or propelling character against a secondary or resisting one. Movement and direction derive from the fact that the propelling character pursues his specific objective to some climactic point. The propelling forces most commonly discovered in Shakespeare's motivated intensifications are meditating, observing, reporting, interrogating, persuading, disputing, and commanding, any of which has the potential to create the necessary tensions (see *Measure for Measure* 3.1.48–173).

INTENSIFYING BEATS: Beats which increase the tension in a sequence, building the action toward some precise climactic moment.

INTERLOCKING: The process of linking two independent units by inserting parts of one into the other. *Fused-beat interlocking* is Shakespeare's method of linking two beats: lines from one beat are interspersed with lines from an adjacent beat, as in *Othello* 5.2.84–105. *Alternate-beat interlocking*, a common method of masking the juncture between two sequences, occurs when the final beat of one sequence is placed after the opening beat of the following sequence.

INTERPOLATED BEAT: An ancillary beat that supplies information not important enough to require development in a full sequence, yet necessary to prepare the audience for some impending action.

INTERVAL BEAT: A beat not necessarily directly related to the sequential action but inserted to create the illusion that an interval of time has elapsed.

INTRODUCTORY BEAT: A sequential beat that provides orientation at the beginning of a sequence, setting the scene, providing for entrances, identifying new situations or characters, establishing known characters in new attitudes, etc.

KEY SEQUENCE: The main sequence of a frame; the sequence which dramatizes the major event of that plot segment, the omission of which would leave a gap in the story. The key sequence is usually (but not necessarily) also the frame's climactic sequence, so that the emotional power of the frame reaches its peak in that sequence.

LINKING BEAT: A beat which has sequential functions in one sequence (the parent sequence) but which also becomes an ancillary beat because it has been lifted out of its expected location and set down into an adjacent sequence (the host sequence). As an ancillary beat, its function is to lock the host sequence tightly to the parent sequence so that action flows smoothly over the point of juncture.

NARRATIVE: *See* ACTION VERSUS NARRATIVE.

NESTING: Because larger units of action are built up from smaller units of action, these smaller units may be said to nest within the larger ones. Beats nest within sequences, sequences within frames. Within beats or sequences Shakespeare occasionally introduces additional levels of nesting.

POSITION STATEMENT: A declaration made by a character to clarify and emphasize the position he is about to be moved away from.

PRESIDING CHARACTER: In a cumulative intensification, the character (usually an authority figure) whose interest in the outcome of these events gives unity to the sequence. The third of the repeated episodes may thwart the expectations of this presiding figure, as Cordelia's response shocks her father in *King Lear* 1.1.1–139, causing the sequence to end in a reversal.

PROPELLING MOTIVE: The principal motive of the propelling character, the force which gives movement and direction to the action. The propelling motive delimits, orients, and unifies the unit, and all other motives in that unit are subordinated to it. A structural principle of the beat and also of the motivated sequence.

PROPELLING OR ACTIVE CHARACTER: The character whose motive is controlling the action for the duration of a beat and who is therefore the dominant character at that moment. In motivated sequences, the character whose motive controls and gives direction to the entire sequence.

RESPONDING CHARACTER: In a beat or sequence, the character whom the propelling character is trying to influence; the secondary or resisting character.

REVERSAL: A specialized form of the dramatic question, in which a character is moved a full 180 degrees from his starting point. Shakespeare will pull an emotion all the way back to one extreme and then work it through until it transforms itself into its opposite – despair into hope, sorrow into joy, etc. Two things characterize a reversal: (1) a statement in which the character clearly reveals his opening position and (2) the climax in which the about-face is effected. The reversal is a common structuring device in the sequence.

SCENE: A unit isolated from other units by a cleared stage indicating a change of place or lapse of time. The unifying principle is the single location within which the action of this unit unfolds. *Extended or multipartite scene*. A unit of place formed of two or more sequences.

SEQUENCE: A unit of action in which Shakespeare raises a single dramatic question and answers it. Direction in the sequence comes from the thrust toward some climactic resolution of the pending question, and the action moves consecutively through stages of exposition and complication toward that climax, following which Shakespeare normally provides a brief summary or conclusion. *For integral and ancillary sequences, see* FRAME. *For chronological, cumulative, and motivated sequences, see* INTENSIFICATION, IN THE SEQUENCE.

SEQUENTIAL BEAT: *See* BEAT.

SUSTAINING BEAT: A beat that extends or maintains the impact of the climax, so that the sequence does not immediately pass into its decrescent phase.

VIGNETTE: A short, descriptive, and self-contained "slice of life," deliberately realistic in detail, characteristic of the beats in a chronological intensification.

Index of sequences analyzed

General index

ABA intensification, in frame, 203
aborted beat, 95, 167, 220
action, relationship to scene, 1–2; versus
  narrative, 220
active character, 223; *see also* propelling
  character
Albany, 149–51
alternate-beat interlocking, 47–8
ancillary beat, 33–48, 210 n.1; defined,
  33, 220
ancillary sequence, 194–5, 204, 205,
  221
Angelo, 141–4, 164, 204, 205
Anne of Warwick, 18, 213 n.4
Antony, 34, 123, 131, 162–3, 175–6

Barry, Jackson, 209 n.1
Bassanio, 153
beat, 11–31; as unit of motivation, 11–
  12; defined, 31, 220; functions of, 11,
  12–17; motivation in, 18–28;
  overriding boundaries of, 29, 107–8,
  180–1; question/answer/reaction
  format, 23; running concurrently with
  scene, 6–7, or with frame, 194;
  sequential versus ancillary beat, 33,
  210–11 n.1; and Stanislavski, 210 n.1;
  unity in, 28–31; *see also* climactic beat,
  concluding beat, entrance beat, exit
  beat, intensifying beat, interlocking,
  introductory beat, sustaining beat
beat motive, 11–12, 18–28, 31, 100–1,
  101–2, 140; versus line motive, 26–8,
  71–5, 84, 85; versus sequence motive,
  90
beats, fused, 47–8
Beatrice, 132
Beckerman, Bernard, 109, 211 n.2, 212
  n.5, 213 n.2, 214 ch.8 n.1, 215 n.3,
  217 n.1
Benedick, 59, 132
Benvolio, 144, 210 n.5

Berry, Francis, 215 n.1
Berry, Ralph, 94
Black, Matthew, 99
Brabantio, 35, 94–5, 106, 120–1, 121–2
Bracy, Sir John, 36, 63–4, 66
Brennan, Anthony, 213 n.4
Brooke, Arthur, 139
Brutus, 42–6, 127–8, 171–5, 196–7,
  217 n.4
build, 210 ch.2 n.1

Calderwood, James L., 212 n.2
Capulet, 22–3, 26
Cassio, 38, 46, 105–6, 145
Cassius, 171–5, 196–7, 217 n.4
Celia, 72–3, 113–14, 183
centerpiece, 206
character positioning, 53, 57–61, 63, 78,
  147, 169, 211 n.1
chronological intensification, 82, 83–9,
  116–17, 131
Cinthio, Giraldi, 120, 214 n.7
Claudio (in *Measure for Measure*), 141–4
Claudius, 23–6, 30, 35–6, 42, 112–13,
  176, 204–5; as observer, 123–5
Clemen, Wolfgang, 215 n.1
Cleopatra, 123, 131, 162–3, 175–6
climactic beat, 15, 103–8, 174, 220
climax, 103–8, 147, 155, 164, 171,
  175–6, 178, 181; and dramatic
  question, 116–17; in observing
  sequence, 132; in reporting sequence,
  137, 138, 143; of frame, 192, 196,
  201, 206–7
commanding sequence, 183–6
compression, in concluding beats, 71–5;
  in introductory beats, 54–7, 67
concluding beat, 15–17, 43–5, 45–6, 68–
  79, 221; definition, 70–1
concluding soliloquy, 77–8, 125–7
controlling character, *see* propelling
  character

227

Printed in the United Kingdom
by Lightning Source UK Ltd.
123285UK00001BA/5/A